REA

whither marxism?

global crises in
international perspective

edited and
with an introduction by
Bernd Magnus and
Stephen Cullenberg

Routledge > New York and London

Published in 1995 by

Routledge
29 West 35 Street
New York, NY 10001

Published in Great Britain by

Routledge
11 New Fetter Lane
London EC4P 4EE

Library or Congress Cataloging in Publication Data

Whither Marxism?: global crises in international perspective / edited and with an
    introduction by Bernd Magnus and Stephen Cullenberg.
        p.   cm.
    Includes bibliographical references.
    ISBN O–415–91042–0 ISBN 0–415–91043–9 (pbk.)
I. Magnus, Bernd. II. Cullenberg, Stephen.
HX39.5.W49   1994
321.9'2—dc20   94–21674
                                                                    CIP

British Library Cataloguing in Publication Data also is available.

contents

editors' introduction

In the wake of the orgy of self-congratulations which followed the 1989 crumbling of the Berlin Wall, the subsequent dissolution of the Soviet Union, and a series of confrontations perhaps forever to be captured best in Tiananmen Square in the image of a single individual blocking the path of an onrushing military tank, a wave of optimism engulfed the Western democratic States. This contagious optimism was best exemplified by the confidence and popularity of Francis Fukuyama's claim that the end of history was at hand, that the future—if that word could still be said to have the same meaning—was to become the global triumph of free market economies.

At the same time many of us felt a vague sense of foreboding, a haunted sense that international changes of such magnitude were as likely to result, at least initially, and perhaps for a long time to come, in transformations as malign as they are benign. Some of us grew tired more quickly than others of the many hasty postmortems of Marxism, as if the virtually global collapse of communism and Marxism referred to the very same thing, especially in different times and places as well as to different thinkers.

And yet, it seemed to many that the collapse of communism in Eastern Europe and the Soviet Union, as well as democratic insurgencies in China, had created a new world order. Politicians from George Bush to Václav Havel had proclaimed that the ideological and political alliances which structured the global community prior to 1989 must now be rethought and restructured. Less dramatically, but just as significantly, the economic integration of Europe beginning in 1992, and the continued economic growth of Japan and the emergence of South Korea, Taiwan, and Singapore as economic forces have all profoundly changed the international economic, social, and political land-scapes. The meaning and consequences of these changes are of vital importance to us all; no discipline or sector of culture has a monopoly on potential analyses, much less a monopoly on answers.

In response to the changing social, political, philosophical, and economic dimensions of the global community, scholars and intellectuals throughout the world are rethinking the meaning of past verities and developing new the-oretical approaches. Among the central contested issues: What remains of the socialist vision(s) after the "collapse" in 1989? Has the collapse of commu-nism also spelled the death of Marxism, and of Marx as an important philosopher and political thinker? Have we indeed reached "the end of his-tory" as Fukuyama has argued, where pluralistic democracies and capitalist economies reign supreme? Is the future now to be simply a choice between Scandinavian-style social democracy on the one hand, and unrestrained free market capitalism on the other? Given the difficulties some democratic, free market economies are experiencing—including the plight of the homeless, the lack of adequate health care, environmental degradation, and enormous national debt burdens—what sort of model for the future do we have? And what is one to make of the destructive, even violent "nationalisms" which have followed in the wake of the collapse of communism, not to mention virulent forms of ethnocentrism and xenophobia perhaps not seen since Hitler's Germany? What does this imply, then, about the future structure and func-tioning of the global economy and life throughout our shared world? What

new international tensions will emerge and what will be the nature of theoretical and political discourse as we approach the twenty-first century? Who
must ask such questions and to whom must they be addressed?

In particular, how will intellectuals in the Marxist tradition respond, theoretically and politically, to the global transformations now occurring? How
has the crisis in Eastern Europe and the former Soviet Union affected the way
intellectuals, scholars, and government officials in those countries and around
the world reconceive their intellectual and political projects? What is to be
the status of Marxist social goals that informed so many Marxist thinkers and
social revolutionaries throughout the world—the egalitarian distribution of
income, increased workplace democracy, the end of economic exploitation
and the eradication of class differences—given the current rush to various
forms of capitalism in Eastern Europe, Russia, and China? Does the "end of
history" also portend the end of Marxist theory? What is living and what is
dead in Marxism?

In October 1991, in an environment charged by such questions, several of us
began a conversation at the University of California, at Riverside's Center for
Ideas and Society about what it might be like to have a conference which
would *not* consist of yet another autopsy administered mostly by Anglophone
economists and policy analysts who typically were and are very far from the
sites of struggle and transformation. We wondered how our colleagues on
location, so to speak, understand their circumstances, both historically and
philosophically.

We decided to convene a multinational, multidisciplinary conference—
"Whither Marxism? Global Crises in International Perspective"—which
would include distinguished thinkers and participants from China, Russia,
Armenia, Poland, Romania, Mexico, Germany, France, the United States and
elsewhere. Equally important, it seemed to us significant to provide a forum
within which one of the most famous and influential contemporary philosophers—Jacques Derrida—could reflect on the conference's topic, something
he had not yet been able to do in a sustained and systematic way in print. We
thought that such a sustained reflection on Marx by Derrida would be of
intrinsic as well as historical importance.

The conference itself was organized and managed by the Center for Ideas
and Society at the University of California, Riverside. It began on Thursday,
April 22, 1993 with Jacques Derrida's plenary address and ended on Saturday,

April 24, 1993. His plenary address was delivered in two parts, on the evening of April 22nd and 23rd. That lecture, "Specters of Marx: The State of the Debt, the Work of Mourning, and the New International," is the basis of a companion text which continues to bear the same name; and this longer version—"augmented, clarified…" as Derrida says—is no less marked by that occasion, setting, and interlocutors than is the original plenary address.

It would be inappropriate, indeed, impossible, to convey in summary the many specters that haunt the texts of Marx, and, through him, of Derrida. Here we would merely wish to note that in this text Derrida takes his position for a certain spirit of Marxism, that "deconstruction," if there is such a thing, always already moves within a certain spirit of Marx. It should also be noted that, for Derrida, in speaking of a certain spirit of Marx

> it is not in the first place in order to propose a scholarly, philosophical discourse. It is first of all so as not to flee from a responsibility. More precisely, it is in order to submit for your discussion several hypotheses on the nature of such a responsibility. What is ours? In what way is it historical? And what does it have to do with so many specters?

Jacques Derrida's *Specters of Marx: The State of the Debt, the Work of Mourning, and the New International* is intended to be in conversation with and supplemented by its companion volume of conference essays, *Whither Marxism? Global Crises in International Perspective.* This second volume contains selected conference essays by Ashot K. Galoian, Keith Griffin and Azizur Rahman Khan, Abdul JanMohamed, Douglas Kellner, Andrei Marga, Stephen Resnick and Richard Wolff, Gayatri Chakravorty Spivak, Su Shaozhi, Carlos Vilas, and Zhang Longxi.

While some of the essays are in direct conversation with the text of Derrida others illustrate the force of his argument, whether they intend to do so or not. Specifically and telegraphically, at least four points of contact emerge from Derrida's *Specters of Marx* and its companion volume *Whither Marxism?* (1) The proper names "Marx" and/or Marxism have always already been plural nouns, despite their grammatical form, and despite the fact that they have been understood as if they were rigid designators; (2) "communism" (in its own pluralities) is not the same as "Marxism"; (3) both communism and Marxism are historically sited, situated, inflected, mediated by particular traditions and histories; (4) the proper name "Marx" is—in a certain sense—

entirely uncircumventable.

The purpose of these two volumes, *Specters of Marx* and *Whither Marxism?* is to begin to address questions about the connection between the death of communism and the fate of Marxism. The volumes raise these questions in an international and interdisciplinary context. Their goal is not simply to produce another postmortem on Marxism, nor is it simply to defend Marxism against its critics. Rather, these volumes, each in its own way, explore the effects that the global crises engendered by the collapse of communism has had on avant-garde scholars, many of whom have lived through and often participated in these transitions themselves.

The papers published in *Whither Marxism?* represent a selection of the papers presented at the April 1993 conference. They range in style and length and reflect the diversity of the conference and the many different viewpoints, disciplines and national backgrounds of the authors. Some attempt to recast and push forward Marxian theory in light of the transitions begun in 1989. Others offer analyses and policy prescriptions for the countries or regions undergoing these transitions. And some read as passionate political polemics, clearly inflected by the dramatic lived experiences and geographic traditions from which they emerged. Thus, *Whither Marxism?* offers a bouquet of papers, all of which offer important insights into this critical period in world history.

Douglas Kellner's essay questions the now commonly heard refrain that Marxism is obsolete. This is perhaps an inappropriate question given the celebration of the end of Marxism and of history *tout court* by the popular press, neoliberal pundits, and many postmodern theorists. This is too glib and shortsighted a response for Kellner. Kellner certainly admits that Marxism is in crisis, but, as with capitalism—Marxism's object and "other"—crisis in one form or another has always characterized its history. Each crisis has lead to a transformed capitalism and Marxism as new theoretical insights and survival strategies have emerged.

Kellner further argues that there are important discontinuities between the ideas of Marx/Lenin/Stalin and recent Soviet leadership, and therefore a critique of the Soviet leadership, past and present, is not fundamentally a critique of Marx. This "guilt by association" critique of Marx and Marxism fails to recognize that there has never been a unitary Marxian theory. For Kellner, even the bonding between Leninism and Marxism is nothing more than a historical accident. In particular, Marx always linked socialism and democracy and would have been appalled by the developments in the Soviet Union. For Kellner, to equate Soviet communism with Marxism is intellectually dishonest and historically false.

As Kellner points out, Marxism has been traditionally a theory of class, and for him is one which defines the concept of class based on different power groupings. The fact that the Soviet Union collapsed can ultimately be traced to the corruption and bureaucratization of its ruling class. The Soviet Union never overcame the problem of "alienated labor," and even though Soviet industries were nationalized, they were never socialized into the hands of the immediate producers. Though contrary to its ideology, the Soviet Union never ended the oppression of its workers. For Kellner, the collapse of the Soviet Union does not imply that socialism cannot work, but rather implies that only a truly democratic worker's socialism can succeed.

The collapse of communism in the Soviet Union and the epochal transformations taking place around the world do portend changes in Marxian theory. For Kellner, one type of Marxian theory, orthodox Marxism, is now at its end. This Marxism, with its totalizing theory of history and the inevitability of socialism, has fallen into an irrevocable crisis. This crisis, however, has created space for a renewed, critical Marxism, one which is open and non-dogmatic, and is more modest in its political prognoses. Kellner argues that this new Marxism is fundamentally a theory and critique of capitalism. As the capitalist economy changes Marxian theory must adjust. One road not to take, according to Kellner, is to reject systemic, macro theories, as various postmodern theorists encourage. As the world is entering into a period of increasingly global economic and ecological crises, a critical Marxian theory is needed to act as a counterweight.

Marxian politics have perhaps been dealt the severest blow by the collapse of global communism. For Kellner, this raises the question of whether the very discourse of revolution and socialism should be abandoned. He argues that a form of Marxian politics that needs to come to an end is that which focuses on the industrial working class and proletarian revolution. A radical politics today should be multicultural, and more race and gender focused, than traditional working-class politics. Economic democracy should be the focus of an alternative Marxian vision. Finally, for Kellner, Marxism should be reconstructed, in theory and practice, out of loyalty to those who have given their lives to struggle for progressive hopes and dreams. Rather than cast Marxism aside completely, loyalty to the radical tradition suggests building on its insights, while leaving behind its failures.

Abdul JanMohamed's essay is concerned with the "withering" of contemporary Marxian thought, not as a consequence of the debacle of the former communist countries, but rather within the context of the Western analytic tradition, understood not so much as a geographical but as a cultural and epistemic space. JanMohamed uses Foucault's unacknowledged appropriation of Marxian ideas as a vehicle for assessing the theoretical status of Marxism today. In particular, he develops a "cross-reading" of Marx's labor theory of value and Foucault's exchange theory of power.

JanMohamed argues that Marx's "micro-physical" analysis of political economy, his value theory, is precisely analogous to Foucault's empirical analysis of the micro-physics of synchronous discursive practices and disciplinary formations. As a result of this homology, Foucault grounds his theory of power in "activity," just as Marx grounds his theory of value in "labor." JanMohamed locates Foucault's disavowal of Marx in Marx's focus on the commodity as the basic indicator of wealth in capitalist society. Foucault critiques liberals who conceive of power as something which can or cannot be possessed, and therefore view power as a commodity. Foucault, as is well known, understands power to be constituted only in the web of processes of social "exchange." Power is thus fundamentally a social concept, not something which can simply be possessed. JanMohamed points out that for Marx value and its form is also fundamentally a social process, constituted only through the process of production and exchange. Insofar as a commodity only comes to life as a bearer of value and form of value, commodity is not a naturalistic concept, but a fundamentally social one.

The isomorphism between theories of value and power suggest that suturing the two would provide a theory more productive than either one as it functions alone. JanMohamed begins such a synthesis by supplementing Foucault's suture of power/knowledge with a more complex Marxian/Foucaultian suture of value/power/knowledge, where power would be overdetermined by value on the one hand, and knowledge on the other. One can then pose the following types of questions: what are the possible homologies between the production of "surplus value" and "surplus power;" through what mechanisms do we allow particular discursive formations to see the individual simultaneously as object and subject; and, what are the effectivities that link the emer-

gence of capital with that of the disciplinary mode of power within a structural totality?

Why did Foucault fail to acknowledge and elaborate the conjunction and
structural relations between value and power? JanMohamed refuses a romantic, Oedipal struggle between Freud and Marx as explanation. Rather, he reads
Foucault's disavowal of Marx as a signifier of the "culturalist" tendency within progressive Western thinking. Foucault's distance from Marx is both a result
and a cause of this culturalism, which recognizes the force of political economy, but at the same time consigns it to a category "determinant (only) in the
last instance." In the end, Foucault's unconscious acceptance of Marx's work is
ultimately masked by a conscious denial, which explicitly prevents him from
linking power and value. As a result, JanMohamed concludes, Foucault has a
rather impoverished notion of power which overlooks the "ultimate nightmare of history," the continued backbreaking and needless labor of millions of
people.

The title of Zhang Longxi's essay, "Marxism: From Scientific to Utopian," is
a transposition and reversal of Engels's famous book, *Die Entwicklung des
Sozialismus von der Utopie zur Wissenschaft*, or in its English translation, *Socialism:
Utopian and Scientific*. Zhang points out that missing from the English translation of Engels's book is the word "Entwicklung" (development), and therefore
the eschatological sense of progress in time. For him, the scientific and teleological aspects of Marxism are critical for an understanding of the collapse of
communism everywhere, especially in China. In contrast, it is the utopian
aspects of Marx's work, primarily, but not exclusively, in Marx's early works
that animates a vital Marxian vision today.

Marx and Engels's "scientific method," according to Zhang, provides a
metanarrative for historical evolution. The development of the productive
forces is identified as the revolutionary drive for progress. Modes of production persist insofar as they sustain the development of the productive forces,
but as soon as a mode of production fetters the further development of the
productive forces, a new mode will develop and transcend the old one.
According to this logic, the socialist revolution is inevitable, not because of
an appeal to justice or truth, but rather as part of the objective, teleological
development of history. The proletarian revolution is not a matter of theory or
philosophy but is a necessary outgrowth of historical development.

Zhang points out that the impersonal tone of Engels's book is typical of the scientism of his and Marx's time. This scientism has come under withering attack in recent years since much of it now seems unwarranted. It was in the East, especially in Russia and in China, where this scientism had a powerful influence; belief in it did much to damage the Marxian project, and turned Marx's vision into a nightmare. If history is thought to develop according to objective laws, then it is but a short step to see how these laws can be manipulated by a party or its leaders, and Zhang claims that this is exactly what happened in the Soviet Union and China. The cult of the individual, as developed in Stalin's Russia and Mao's China, was a direct outgrowth of the orthodoxy and scientism of the Marxism practiced there.

For Zhang, communism is dead, not the communism in Marx's theory and vision, but communism as actually practiced. Communism is dead not because those in the capitalist West say so, but because those who have lived under and through it have rejected it. Have we reached the end of history? Does the future only hold liberal-democratic capitalism as the only viable alternative? Though communism is dead and along with it one type of Marxism, for Zhang, socialism as a vision, and Marxism as a theory and *Weltanschauung* is very much alive. As long as corporate capitalism dominates the world's economies, Marxism as an oppositional force and vision will play an invigorating role in political and academic life. It is the visionary power of Marx, especially with reference to the end of alienated labor, which will sustain the quest for alternatives to capitalism, not the putatively inexorable laws of capitalist development, the belief in which has caused so much havoc and misery in the erstwhile communist countries.

The collapse of actually existing socialism at the end of the 1980s in Eastern Europe brought with it the end of official, public discourse about Marxism. However, as Andrei Marga's essay points out, no theory which has had such a profound impact on history can disappear from the scene so quickly. Indeed, Marxism still survives in the everyday discourse of many in Eastern Europe and motivates important decisions. Given this persistent, yet repressed, presence, Marga critically analyzes Eastern Marxism and traces its lineage back to Marx.

In Eastern Europe and in Romania in particular, the former communist regimes often took the form of family dictatorships. As a result, the debate concerning the "guilt" of Marxism has often degenerated into superficial recriminations rather than providing analytical arguments for and against

Marxism. In order to understand the present situation in Eastern Europe, Marxism must be analyzed theoretically, examining its theories of history, society and humanity. Marga locates the fundamental problems of Eastern Marxism in the tension between an overly flexible and contingent empiricism and a formal rationalism. The actual experience of 'man' could not be grasped by this Marxism, because the reality of human experience and praxis was forced into preformed Marxian theoretical categories, while the contingent empiricism allowed the real lived experience of those under communist regimes to be ignored.

Marga argues that this failing of Eastern Marxism is not peculiar to it as such, but is endemic in the theoretical structure of Marxism itself. For him, the frequency of communism's failure points to a deep-seated problem in Marxism, and, ultimately, communism's failure is intellectual and not political. Marxism's flaw lies in its inability to incorporate the actual lived experience of the individual. For Marga, Marxism needs a new philosophical anthropology, whose focus is broader than that of work, and which also includes the concepts of human needs and the capacity to choose. A reconstructed Marxism would incorporate these new anthropological concepts and a rejection of monism. For Marga, this new Marxism would be only a distant follower of Marx, and would no longer warrant the name "Marxism." Thus, the necessary transformation of Marxism to correct the errors of Marx, and the horrors of Eastern European communism, must in the end lead to the dissolution of the Marxian project as it is historically understood.

Gayatri Chakravorty Spivak seeks to supplement Marxism. For her, supplementing does not simply mean the addition of new theoretical and political concerns, but rather is a supplementing which is transformative, creating risks as it opens new incalculable territory. Spivak argues that Marx uses the concept of the 'social' in two senses. In one sense, he uses it as a rationalization of the merely individual. The bourgeois subject, however, is displaced by the proletarian subject whose rationalization is projected in its class consciousness. Alternatively, Marx uses the notion of the social in the Enlightenment sense of the public use of reason, relying on an untheorized, humanist notion of the social. Systemic Marxisms which carve out a space in the pores of these two concepts of the social always run the risk of failure for Spivak.

The critique of the reification of labor provides, for Spivak, the strongest humanist support of Marxism. This critique of reification derives from Marx's use of reason as class consciousness in a socialized society, where only the agents of production can become the agents of the social. Spivak argues that this humanist critique of reification can be extended to recode global capitalism as democracy. Breaking from the economism of the class subject and its teleological end gives rise to a different critique of capitalism, one which perceives socialism as capitalism's other, and communism as a figuration of the impossible. Communism is about justice, not primarily about development, and justice is incalculable, which, following Derrida, is the spectrality of communism.

What does the critique of the rationality of the subject imply for various political struggles occurring around the globe today? Spivak first considers the role of the new immigrant to the United States, a self-reflexive reference to her own group, those professional migrants who have left post-colonial problems, hoping for a new life and justice under capitalism. Spivak sees this group as embracing an unexamined culturalism which allows the recoding of capitalism as democracy. By raising this issue, Spivak hopes to raise the issue of responsibility that comes with the decentering of the subject. In a broader political context, the diversified struggles of feminism, anti-racism and anti-colonialism are exploding the traditional Marxian idea of crisis. These movements should swallow and digest Marx's nascent ideas about crisis rather than simply adapt to pregiven Marxian discourse.

Finally, the role of the state has to be de-emphasized given the "great globe-girdling" movements of resistance to capitalist development. These non-Eurocentric movements, such as the ecological and reproductive rights movements, are globe-girdling in two senses: one, because they transcend the nation-state, and two, because they take seriously subalternity and woman-space. These movements are not interested in state power as were older Eurocentric opposition groups, but are concerned with creating new and incalculable political spaces. Supplementing Marxism, whether theoretically or politically, is not about filling holes, but is about creating these new theoretical and political possibilities.

Latin America has been the site of some of the most turbulent political struggles during the last twenty years. Carlos Vilas examines the most recent articulation of politics and economics taking place in Latin America by looking at capitalist strategies for economic restructuring, the role of the state, and working-class politics. Vilas argues that the economic transformations taking place today are creating a Latin American version of post-Fordism. Full-employment and growth in mass consumption are no longer collective goals, and distinction between domestic and international markets is losing heuristic value as Latin American economies are becoming increasingly part of the global economy.

Vilas points out that another critical transformation in Latin America is the receding importance of state intervention in the economy, once considered vital to the economic development of Latin America, even under repressive military regimes. According to Vilas, massive privatization of state-owned enterprises, ports and other public facilities, have lead to "a neoliberal, post-Marxist withering away of the state." The change in state/market relations is not merely a zero-sum game, where market relations replace erstwhile state ownership. Rather, a new articulation is being forged between the state, the market, and specific social classes with diverse economic interests. Vilas argues that this articulation produces a new political economy in Latin America where some fractions of the capitalist class "win," large segments of the middle class are downgraded economically, and conditions fall into place for a renewed marginalization of the working population.

The working class in Latin America has been especially affected by these new economic transformations. The wage share in national income has fallen precipitously, and inequality, as well as poverty, have increased dramatically. Vilas links this to the attempt of capitalists to increase their profit rates. The sociodemographic dimensions of the working class have also been redefined. The formal wage labor market has suffered a relative decline and there has been a large increase in the urban informal sector. On a political level, the inability of unions to incorporate gender and ethnic issues into their programs has led to increased labor market fragmentation. In turn, this fragmentation has caused class identity to become feebler and has progressively diluted the organizational dimensions of working-class identity. All hope is not lost, however, according to Vilas. Freed from the Manichean dialectics of the Cold War, new progressive political and social alternatives can be developed. Vilas calls for a strategic articulation of the social movements working at the grass roots level with unions and political parties which are working "from above," at the national level. For Vilas, the romantic notion of the autonomy and purity of social movements relative to the authoritarianism of parties and unions leads only to the political fragmentation of popular struggles. Thus, a new dialectical articulation of social movements with unions and parties will have to provide the way forward.

Keith Griffin and Azizur Rahman Khan look to the transition to market socialism which began in China in 1978 for lessons for the current transition to market-guided economies in Russia and Eastern Europe. The transition from a quantitatively planned economy to a market one had never been fully accomplished before 1978, although the reconversion of Western Europe after World War II and the experience of some developing countries provided some useful, albeit partial case studies. Griffin and Khan argue, however, that it is China's transition experience which can best serve as a guiding light for Russia and Eastern Europe. Of course China is not a perfect model; in no small part because China is still committed to a socialist economy whereas Russia and the Eastern European economies are not.

Griffin and Khan focus on four critical issues in the Chinese transition experience. These are: (1) macroeconomic financial stability during the reform process, (2) the pace of growth and the level of investment, (3) property relations and the reform of state economic enterprises, and (4) changes in the distribution of income that have accompanied reforms. Chinese reforms have not been implemented from the commanding heights of the economy according to a predetermined grand scheme. On the contrary, they have been highly pragmatic and experimental. At times, reversals in policy have occurred. In agriculture, where the reforms began, the reform process was characterized by an experimental approach to policy making, a tolerance for diversity, a willingness of policymakers at the center to learn from experience at the grass roots, and a tendency for reforms to be concentrated where substantial gains could be made. This approach to reform, with its lack of uniformity—anathema to western economists—accounts in large part for the success of the Chinese reforms, according to Griffin and Khan.

A feature of the Chinese reform process which is often criticized is that economic liberalization is not matched by political liberalization. While the former Soviet Union under Gorbachev attempted economic restructuring (perestroika) along with a political opening up (glasnost), China has yet to fundamentally alter its political structure. Griffin and Khan see the Chinese approach as perhaps a necessary sequencing of economic and political reforms. The "Russian model" has been a huge failure, according to them, in both economic and political terms. The enormous and wrenching changes that must be made during the transition to market-guided economies, suggest that maintaining political stability during this period has distinct advantages.

One of the major issues of transition economies is which change to implement first: privatization of state-owned firms or price reform. Griffin and Khan see privatization as clearly being a second-order priority. Premature privatization will slow down reform, reduce government tax revenues, increase pressure for government expenditures, and thereby slow down investment, causing the rate of growth to fall. This will likely result in greater inequality of wealth and income. Rather than forcing the issue of privatization, it is better to release obstacles to the formation of private enterprises so that the private sector may expand spontaneously. As they see it, an important lesson for all the transition economies is that there is no need to destroy the state sector in order to create a dynamic private sector alongside it.

The basic message of Griffin and Khan for the Russian and Eastern European economies runs directly counter to the "shock-therapy" that has been advocated by some Western economists. Of fundamental importance is the recognition that each transition is both a political and an economic one. Each transition is also historically specific, and while there are certain well-established pitfalls to avoid, each country must find its own way to a market-guided economy. Although China's experience provides some lessons for a successful transition, these lessons must be tempered by the particular political and economic experiences of each country finding its way out of the economic chaos confronting it today.

The break-up of the Soviet Union has brought with it the emergence of new nation-states and wrenching ethnic strife. For Ashot Galoian this is not surprising, because the "nationality" question is the political issue which has had the most sustained and enduring impact on the Soviet Union throughout the twentieth century.

Both Tsarist Russia and the communist Soviet Union were comprised of an uneasy alliance between Russian and non-Russian peoples. By the 1930s, as Galoian points out, there was tremendous indigenous pressure for the formation of separate non-Russian countries. However, the early communist leaders of the Soviet Union, following the internationalism expressed by Marx and Engels in the *Communist Manifesto*, insisted that class strife transcended national borders. They fully expected that nationalism would not survive the end of capitalism, and would cease to be an issue with the advent of socialism.

Galoian makes clear that Lenin and Stalin had in fact very different positions with regard to the nationality question. Lenin understood the need for national autonomy, especially towards the end of his life. Stalin, in contrast, insisted on the predominance of the Russian state, language and culture in order to build socialism and internationalism. As a result of Stalin's ideology, repression, and terror, one of the most complex political units in the world was established. Organized on the basis of nationality, it was not without severe internal strain.

The nationality question persisted through the Kruschev, Brezhnev and Andropov eras. The issue of nationality came to a head under Gorbachev, perestroika being a perfect vehicle for awakening national consciousness. In February 1988 when the Nagorno-Karebakh issue exploded, perestroika and glasnost were directly threatened, according to Galoian. National unrest in other areas of the former Soviet Union led to its eventual breakup. For Galoian, while perestroika and glasnost failed to accomplish their stated goals, they succeeded in (re)awakening national consciousness and allowed dormant national states to reemerge. Galoian's message for Marxism, then, is that it ignores the nationality question at great risk.

Stephen Resnick and Richard Wolff also see Marxism as the dialectical "other" of capitalism. Marxism at times stands in the shadows, only challenging capitalism at a distance, and at times fully emerges, throwing into question the very existence of a continued capitalism. Resnick and Wolff are quick to point out, however, that capitalism does not manifest itself as a singular, uniform economic system. Capitalism has taken and continues to take on many forms, oscillating between private and state capitalisms. Marxism, in a related fashion, has many different theoretical tendencies, and, in particular, employs differing theories of class analysis. Indeed, Marxian class analysis, if built on concepts of power, property or surplus labor, will give rise to different readings of what the collapse of the Soviet Union means for Marxian theory and the socialist project.

Resnick and Wolff employ the surplus labor definition of class and ask the provocative question: what was the class structure of the Soviet Union? They argue that after the Bolshevik revolution in 1917, those who controlled property relations as well as those who wielded political power changed dramatically, but that the basic form of economic exploitation remained fundamentally the same. According to their argument, the Soviet Union had been mainly characterized throughout its history by a form of capitalism; namely state capitalism. Just as in the West, and especially in Europe, there has been an oscillation between private and state capitalism, so too has the Soviet Union oscillated between forms of private and state capitalisms. The NEP during the 1920s, they argue, was an experiment in private capitalism. Since the collapse of the Soviet Union, private capitalism has again emerged, this time in Russia and the other former Soviet Republics. After this period, until recently, the Soviet Union's history was characterized by a form of state capitalism.

Why do Resnick and Wolff define the economic system in the former Soviet Union as state capitalist? In contrast to power and property theories of class which focus on ownership patterns (collective versus private) and market allocation of resources (command versus market), they are concerned with the different question of who performs and who appropriates the surplus labor. On the basis of their reading of the history of Soviet economy, surplus labor is largely performed by a class of workers who do not also directly appropriate it. Instead, a state bureaucratic organ, the Council of Ministers, appropriates the surplus labor and then decides how to distribute the product the surplus labor is embodied in. Analogous to private capitalism, where surplus labor takes on a value form, surplus labor in the Soviet Union—Resnick and Wolff argue—acquires a form of value which they call the "administered value."

On the basis of this distinctive type of class analysis, Resnick and Wolff pose the question "what failed?" in the recent collapse of the Soviet Union. The commonplace image of the Soviet Union as a socialist country has meant that its collapse has been understood as proof of the failure of the socialist or communist model. In their view, however, what collapsed in the Soviet Union is one form of capitalism, state capitalism, which is now being replaced by a private capitalism. For them, the critical question is when will the oscillations between private and state capitalism result in not one or the other, but rather in a true revolution to communism.

Su Shaozhi's essay provides an evaluation of the development of China's political economy according to Marx's materialist theory of history. Rather than seeing the recent reforms in China as vitiating Marxian theory, Shaozhi argues instead that Marx's materialist theory has been vindicated. Critical to Marx's theory, as Shaozhi understands it, is the relationship between the forces of production and the relations of production. A society cannot develop its relations of production beyond what the forces will sustain, and according to Shaozhi, this is exactly what happened in China, before the reforms of 1978.

The early years of China's revolution were largely successful. Land reform was accomplished and the economic recovery of the war-time economy occurred in three years. This success created an arrogance in China's leaders who pressed for a premature transition to socialism, premature because the forces of production were still very backward. The Cultural Revolution, and the displacement of the prioritizing of economics with that of politics, class struggle and morals, lead to a voluntarism which brought China to the brink of absolute disaster. The cause of the crisis, according to Shaozhi, can be located in the attempt to circumvent Marx's materialist theory.

The economic reforms in China, with their foundation in the market economy, are a return to Marx's materialism, which reestablish a correspondence between the forces and the relations of production. In order for China's economy to develop, economic incentives are required, different forms of ownership need to be encouraged, and techniques of business administration, advanced science and technology, and financial systems need to be learned from capitalist countries. In short, China must undergo a capitalist transition in order to develop its productive forces. Just as the former socialist countries must undergo market reforms in order to develop materially and eventually back towards socialism, Marxian theory should be reformed in light of current conditions and modern science.

These papers, then, despite their diverse origins, their grounding in different disciplines and their various conclusions, all attest to the fact that Marxism (if not communism) seems to persist as an important intellectual force, in large part because many avant garde Marxists have incorporated or appropriated insights from theoretical work developed by non-Marxist discourses. Their reflections on the structure of such discourses, on the interaction between Marxist and non-Marxist forms of discourse, on cultural, economic and political forms of subjectivity, and on the relationship between theoretical and political practice are constantly redefining the universe of Marxist and post-Marxist theory. The political crises of our times gives special meaning to this theoretical work.

—Bernd Magnus & Stephen Cullenberg

PART ONE

marxism's future?

DOUGLAS KELLNER

the obsolescence of marxism?

Crises of Marxism have erupted regularly throughout the twentieth century. The concept of crisis within Marxian theory has its origins in theories of the "crisis of capitalism," which were linked to notions of the collapse of capitalism and triumph of socialism. The term "crisis" itself is a medical metaphor that suggests the possibility of breakdown, collapse, or a terminal illness that could bring death to its patient, in this case, Marxism.[1] The term "crisis" was applied to Marxism by Georges Sorel, Karl Korsch, and others earlier in the century (see Gouldner 1980). In recent years, there have been many claims that with the collapse of the Soviet Union, the era of Marxism is over and the theory is now obsolete. Consequently, it is claimed that the crisis of Marxism has terminated in collapse, that the patient has died, that Marxism is no longer a viable theory or politics for the present age.[2]

The discourse of the crisis of Marxism has had a long history. During World War I, the failure of the Second International and Marxist parties and individuals to stop the war put in question the political efficacy of Marxism as an organized movement. The failure to carry through European revolutions after the war produced new crises of Marxism, and the triumph of fascism threatened to eliminate Marxist governments, parties, and militants. After World War II, the integration of the working class and stabilization of capitalism in the so-called democratic capitalist countries seemed to portend the obsolescence of Marxism.[3] Thus Marxism, like capitalism, its object and other, has been in crisis throughout the century.

However, just as capitalism has survived many crises, so has Marxism. And just as Marxist critics too quickly proclaimed the demise of capitalism, so too have critics of Marxism too glibly forecast its death. Moreover, just as various crises of capitalism have elicited new survival strategies that in certain ways have strengthened the capitalist system (i.e., imperialism, organized capitalism, state capitalism, the welfare state, the consumer society, transnational capitalism, technocapitalism, and so on), so too crises of Marxism have periodically led to the development and improvement of Marxian theory. Indeed, Marx's historical materialism is intrinsically a historical theory, and its categories demand revision and development as new historical conditions and situations emerge. Revision is the very life of the Marxian dialectic, and the theory demands development, reconstruction, and even abandonment of obsolete or inadequate features as conditions emerge that put tenets of the original theory in question.

Marxism has, of course, been regularly denounced and declared over, especially by its one-time adherents. During the Cold War era, a whole generation of former Marxists denounced the "God that failed," and Sidney Hook and others declared the movement dead by the 1940s. As Derrida reminds us (1993), during the 1950s intellectuals in France proclaimed the end of history and the obsolescence of Marxism; similar "end of ideology" discourses and "postindustrial society" theories emerged in the United States in that decade to proclaim the end of Marxism. In post-1960s renunciations of earlier utopian hopes, many previous adherents turned on Marxism. In *The Postmodern Condition* (1984 [1979]), one-time Marxian radical Jean-François Lyotard argued that the era of totalizing theories of history and grand narratives of emancipation was over. Earlier, former Marxist theorist Jean Baudrillard declared in *The Mirror of Production* (1974) that Marxism merely mirrored capitalist development and ideology and was inadequate as a radical theory of emancipation. In his next book (still untranslated), *L'échange symbolique et la mort* (1976), Baudrillard declared the end of political economy and the end of Marxism in the emergence of a postmodern society of media, simulations, and hyperreality.[4] Indeed, the success of post modern theory is largely parasitical because it rests on its proponents' claims concerning the obsolescence of Marxism, which positions postmodernists as the most advanced radical social theorists.

In recent years, many books and articles have argued that the collapse of Soviet communism definitively signifies the end of Marxism. Francis Fukuyama's celebrated book *The End of History* (1992), in fact, argues for the end of Marxism. And, of course, there have been a wealth of articles in the mainstream press and opinion journals, too numerous to mention, that have declared the obsolescence of Marxism. Against these positions, my argument will be that the collapse of Soviet communism does not constitute a refutation of Marxism or signify its demise. I will argue, first, that there are important discontinuities between Marx/Lenin/Stalin and the later Soviet leaders, so one cannot blame the collapse of communism on Marx himself or the doctrine associated with his name. Secondly, I will argue that Rousseau, Hegel, and the Right Hegelians and not Marx are more appropriately read as the spiritual ancestors of Soviet totalitarianism and the modern totalitarian state *tout court*. Further, I will argue that Marx's concept of socialism and democracy is dramatically at odds with Soviet communism, Leninism, Stalinism, or whatever one wants to call the system of bureaucratic collectivism that collapsed in the Soviet Union and its satellites. I will also suggest that the overthrow of Stalinism was consistent with, or justified by, Marx's principles and that Marxian theory provides an illuminating analysis and critique of Soviet communism and its empire, providing important theoretical resources to explain the collapse of Soviet communism and to make sense of contemporary historical reality. Finally, I argue that Marxism continues to possess resources to theorize and criticize the present age and that Marxian politics remains at least a part of a progressive or radical politics in the current era.

DISCONTINUITIES WITHIN THE MARXIAN TRADITION

For decades, Marxism has been blamed for the historical catastrophes of the era. In *The Open Society and Its Enemies* (1963 [1945]), philosopher of science Karl Popper argued that the totalitarian state has its origins in the political philosophies of Plato, Hegel, and Marx. This refrain was repeated in the 1970s by former Maoist André Glucksmann, one of the darlings of the French "new philosophers," who claimed that "master thinkers," such as Marx, were responsible for the evils of communism and other totalitarian societies. And, of course, throughout the Cold War, anticommunists have tried to pin all of the problems of the era on the philosophy of Karl Marx and his followers.

Such polemics are, of course, hopelessly idealist and greatly exaggerate the roles of ideas in history. Blaming the evils of the modern world, and especially the trajectory of Soviet communism, on Marx covers the significant differences between Marx, Lenin, Stalin, and the later Soviet leadership as well as the material and social conditions that inhibited the development of the sort of socialism envisaged by Marx—and even Lenin—in the Soviet Union. Accordingly, I shall first provide some reasons why it is a mistake to blame the catastrophe of Soviet communism on Marx and then will provide a sketch of a Marxian analysis of why Soviet Communism failed.

To begin, there has never been a unitary Marxian theory that has been the basis for socialist development. Marxism has always had a divided legacy between those following socialist as opposed to communist parties, institutionalized in the divisions between the Second International and the Third International. Both the democratic-reformist and insurrectionist-revolutionary strategies for constructing socialism could appeal to Marx's texts and practice for legitimation of their own theory and politics, but as it turned out the Social Democrats of the Second International, beginning already with Eduard Bernstein in the 1890s, distanced themselves from Marxism, while the Leninists of the Third International proclaimed themselves loyal Marxists and the authentic heirs of classical Marxism.

Vladimir Lenin and the Bolsheviks actually carried through a revolution in 1917 in the name of Marxism and made Marxism the official state ideology. However, this historically accidental bonding between Marxism and Leninism should not obscure the profound differences between Marx and Lenin. Lenin advocated the formation of a conspiratorial party of professional revolutionaries and privileged violent insurrection and a vanguard party as the instruments of revolution. Marx, by contrast, was committed to people's democracy and the tenet that the liberation of the working class could only be achieved by the activity of the working class itself. Marx and Friedrich Engels published the "Communist Manifesto" to openly proclaim the ideas and goals of the communist movement, and both pointed to the Paris Commune, marked by popular sovereignty of the people, as the model of what they meant by socialism. In contrast, once Lenin and the Bolshevik party achieved power, the Central Committee of the Communist party became the self-proclaimed vanguard of the revolution, and power and sovereignty were in effect concentrated in the party's hands.

Indeed, on many occasions, Marx proclaimed a democratic road to socialism and always equated socialism and democracy. His early 1843 commentary on Hegel's *Philosophy of Right* championed democracy as the highest form of government and contained a powerful critique of the absolutist state and bureaucratic government. During the 1848 revolution, Marx allied himself with the bourgeois-democratic movement and with progressive elements of the bourgeoisie in a two-stage road to socialism. In his address to the First International Workingmen's Association, Marx proclaimed the winning of legislation to shorten the working day and the worker's co-op movement as the two great victories for the political economy of the working class. In his 1871 address on the Paris Commune, Marx championed the popular sovereignty exercised by the citizens of the Paris Commune as "the finally discovered form for the liberation of the working class." And in his 1872 Hague address to the International, Marx also proclaimed that a democratic road to socialism was viable in many developed countries.

Of course, Marx always had a contextual political theory and thus in certain contexts supported revolutionary class war and insurrection, while in other contexts he defended a more democratic and reformist route to socialism. Hence, one can find support for various theories of the construction of socialism in Marx's own writings. Yet, in his key texts, Marx was a consistent democrat, supporting workers' self-activity as the locus of popular sovereignty. Marx never advocated a party state, never defended a communist bureaucracy, and would no doubt have been appalled by the deformation of his ideas in the Soviet Union, so to pin the failures of Soviet communism on Marx is absurd.

Indeed, there are important differences between Lenin and Joseph Stalin as well, with Stalin eliminating the democratic centralism of the party for one-man rule and literally exterminating all political enemies and opposition.[5] While Lenin championed a vanguard party to make the revolution and then to run the state, he allowed factions, practiced democracy within the party, was sometimes outvoted, and practiced what he and the Bolsheviks called "democratic centralism." An early Leninist text, *State and Revolution*, was even quite populist, following Marx's text on the Paris Commune as the model of socialism and celebrating the Soviets, or workers' councils, of 1905 and 1917 as the authentic organs of socialist construction. To be sure, Lenin established a revolutionary bureaucracy that could be manipulated by a Stalin, but Stalinism had nothing to do with any sort of democratic socialism, centralist or not. Such a regime was a throwback to a feudalistic Czarism and had little to do with Marx's vision of socialism. The later collective bureaucratic Soviet leadership was also at odds with Marxism, which was always strongly antibureaucratic.

Although this point is somewhat tangential to my argument, I believe that the later Soviet leadership primarily continued Stalinism, despite the critiques of Stalin at the 20th Party Congress. Perhaps one of the few moments for genuine reform appeared during the Khrushchev era, when another sort of socialism, one closer to Marx's vision, was possible. Such a socialism was grounded in the workers' revolts in East Germany in 1953, in Hungary and Poland in 1956, in the denunciations of Stalin in the Soviet Union in 1956 and 1958, in the reform movement throughout the communist world, and in the movement for "socialism with a human face" during the "Prague Spring" of 1967–1968. The post-Khrushchev leadership, however, until the emergence of Mikhail Gorbachev, crushed dreams for reform and the creation of a genuinely democratic socialism and reinforced the repressive Stalinist bureaucratic form of state socialism, which caused deep alienation from the system, corruption, economic inefficiency and stagnation, and the eventual collapse of Soviet communism. By the time Gorbachev arrived it was too late to reform this system, and his removal pointed to the demise of the previous form of Soviet communism.[6]

In any case, it is hard to see why the Marxian theory should be blamed for the debacle of bureaucratic communism in the Soviet Union. The polemic that blames the evils of Soviet communism on Marx also fails to notice that there are many distinct traditions and political tendencies within Marxism.

Rosa Luxemburg, for instance, associated socialism intimately with democracy, arguing that one could not exist without the other. She was an early critic of what she saw as the deformations of socialism in the Soviet Union. Likewise, the council communists of the post-World War I revolutionary movement consistently supported a view of socialism as a workers' democracy and advocated a libertarian concept of socialism, as did Herbert Marcuse and his comrades in the Frankfurt School, Korsch (for much of his life), and many other so-called Western Marxists. These theorists were often critical of the deformation of socialism in the Soviet Union and usually supported a democratic version of socialism. Thus, to equate Marxism with the bureaucratic collectivism of the Soviet Union is simply historically false and intellectually dishonest.

SPIRITUAL ANCESTORS OF THE MODERN TOTALITARIAN STATE

In this section, I wish to suggest that it is Jean-Jacques Rousseau and the Right Hegelians who provide legitimating ideologies for the modern totalitarian state and not Karl Marx. While many readings of Rousseau are possible,[7] including those that claim him for radical democratic theory, there are passages in his writings that clearly qualify him for the title of father of the modern totalitarian state. There are absolutely shocking passages in Rousseau that legitimate the most oppressive practices of the totalitarian state, providing a legitimation in advance of the worst excesses of Soviet communism. In *The Social Contract* (1987 [1762]), for instance, there are a large number of provocative statements, such as the idea that individuals "must be forced to be free," or the paradox that the overcoming of alienation requires total submission to the community, whereby individuals gain their liberty—propositions taken up later by Hegel and Stalin.

Rousseau also champions the indivisibility of sovereign power, in opposition to Montesquieu's doctrine of the division of powers. Although Rousseau's anchoring of the indivisibility of sovereign power in the people appears highly democratic, it is in fact a dangerous idea, especially when he defends and legitimates censorship and a unitary civil religion to which all must subscribe. There is no concept of freedom of the press and nothing regarding a bill of rights in Rousseau's theory. Indeed, there are really no individual rights and liberties at all in Rousseau's collectivist conception.

Marx, in contrast, was a newspaper editor and journalist who wrote some of the most brilliant defenses of the freedom of the press that we possess. In a series of newspaper articles written in 1842, Marx attacked the Prussian state's "censorship instruction" and spiritedly defended the freedom of the press. Freedom of the press, Marx wrote, "is itself an embodiment of the idea . . . of freedom, a positive good, whereas censorship is an embodiment of unfreedom" (Marx and Engels 1975, 154). Further, the "essence of the free press is the characterful, rational moral essence of freedom. The character of a censored press is the characterless monster of unfreedom; it is a civilised monster, a perfumed abortion" (Marx and Engels 1975, 158). Finally—and I know of no more eloquent defense of freedom of the press—he wrote:

> The free press is the ubiquitous vigilant eye of a people's soul, the embodiment of a people's faith in itself, the eloquent link that connects the individual with the state and the world, the embodied culture that transforms material struggles into intellectual struggles and idealizes their crude material form. It is a people's frank confession to itself, and the redeeming power of confession is well known. It is the spiritual mirror in which a people can see itself, and self-examination is the first condition of wisdom. It is the spirit of the state, which can be delivered into every cottage, cheaper than coal gas. It is all-sided, ubiquitous, omniscient. It is the ideal world which always wells up out of the real world and flows back into it with ever greater spiritual riches and renews its soul (Marx and Engels 1975, 164–165).[8]

It is thus a historical anomaly and a perversion of Marx's philosophy that Soviet communism did not allow the freedom of the press. There is nothing in Marx's writing to legitimate censorship, while Rousseau provides arguments for a censor! Worst of all is Rousseau's defense of the imposition of civil religion on the people, as when he writes in *The Social Contract*:

> While not having the ability to obligate anyone who does not believe, the sovereign can banish from the state anyone who does not believe them. It can banish him not for being impious but for being unsociable, for being incapable of sincerely loving the laws and justice, and of sacrificing his life, if necessary, for his duty. If, after having publicly acknowledged these same dogmas, a person acts as if he does not believe them, he should be put to death; he has committed the greatest of crimes: he has lied before the laws. (1987 [1762], 102)

There is, of course, nothing like this idea in Marx, so Rousseau's views go much further in legitimating later forms of societal repression than Marx's more genuinely democratic theory. Moreover, throughout his work Marx championed the development of free individuality and argued for the superiority of socialism over capitalism on the grounds, beside other arguments, that socialism would more fully develop and realize individuality. Furthermore, Rousseau's attack on luxury and his celebration of simplicity and frugality provide a good legitimation for communism's repressive egalitarianism and remind one of the "crude Communism" that Marx himself attacked in the *Economic and Philosophical Manuscripts* and elsewhere.

Thus, it is Rousseau and not Marx who provides a legitimating ideology for communist totalitarian societies. Furthermore, Hegel and the Right Hegelians follow Rousseau in providing legitimation for modern totalitarian states. For Hegel, the state was the incarnation of reason and freedom, and it was the citizens' duty to recognize this and to submit to the dictates of the state. The Right Hegelians followed the master in arguing for the necessity of submission to state authority, while Marx and other Left Hegelians polemicized against this position, calling for democracy and attacking the authoritarian states of their day, which Hegel and his followers defended. The Right Hegelians claimed that democracy would produce chaos and that only a strong state, sanctioned by religion, could preserve order and stability. Thus, from the perspective of political theory, it is dishonest and misleading to blame Marx for the horrors of Soviet communism and other authoritarian communist regimes when the ideas of other thinkers are more closely connected with modern totalitarian theory and practice.

And yet, as I suggested earlier, it is unfair to blame historical disasters on any specific theory because political philosophies at most provide legitimation for political actions and regimes and do not usually "cause" events to happen. Major political events are overdetermined and are rarely, if ever, the product of ideas alone. Certainly, the Bolshevik revolution was made in the name of Marxism, but this could simply be a historical anomaly rooted in the important role of Lenin and the fact that Lenin and other key Bolsheviks were highly committed Marxists, with, however, their own version of Marxism. Later communist revolutions influenced by Marx, Lenin, and other Marxists took up Marxism as a legitimating ideology—though different versions of Marxism were developed in most of the countries that adopted it. However, Marxism itself did not provide legitimation for the forms of oppression that developed in these societies, for Marx never advocated the development of a party state and in fact urged construction of the precise opposite: a free society in which individuals exercised popular sovereignty.

TOWARD A CRITIQUE OF SOVIET COMMUNISM

Far from being implicated in legitimating Soviet communism, I believe that the Marxian theory and tradition provide some of the most powerful critiques of the deformation of socialism in the Soviet Union. Historically, it was Marxian theorists who produced the first and most powerful critiques of the Soviet system and its divergences from classical Marxism. These critics include Luxemburg, Korsch, Trotsky, the Frankfurt school, and later Trotskyist and Maoist-inspired critics as well as critiques ranging from the French *Arguments* group to Italian "autonomous" Marxists to one-time East German theorist Rudolf Bahro (1978). Moreover, I believe that the Marxian theory continues to provide the resources for analysis of the collapse of Soviet communism and for providing an account of why bureaucratic communism doesn't work.[9]

Marxian theory has traditionally been a class theory, which analyzes the role of social classes in history. From this perspective, one can argue that one of the reasons that communism collapsed in the Soviet Union concerns the corruption of its ruling class. The privileges of the Soviet bureaucracy inspired critiques of the "new class" that ruled the society. After the excesses of the Brezhnev era, which saw rampant corruption, nepotism on a grand scale, and the alienation of the ruling elite from the masses of the people, it was clear that the system of Soviet communism was a system of bureaucratic collectivism ruled by a corrupt party elite.[10] The system was also highly inefficient, ruled by rigid, centralized plans, arbitrary deals cut between central planners and managers; and resistance to work by the oppressed working class. The form of oppression in the Soviet Union and its satellites produced growing bitterness and alienation that terminated in intensifying unrest and struggle.

In the classical Marxian conception, socialism was supposed to overcome alienated labor, but in the Soviet system it provided new forms of the alienation of workers, leading eventually to mass resistance and struggle and finally to the collapse of communism. As Marcuse argued in *Soviet Marxism* (1985 [1958]), the means of production were nationalized but not socialized, not put into the control of the "immediate producers."[11] The reality of workers' oppression and struggle provided a refutation of the communist ideology that the Soviet system was a workers' state, and the struggle of the workers against this system dramatically confirmed the salient power of the Marxian theory of class struggle.

Boris Kagarlitsky, a Russian democratic socialist critic of the Soviet system, argued that "the cultural level of the masses became on average somewhat higher during the 1970s than the cultural level of the ruling elite" (1990, 292). On this account, rising levels of education and consumption produced rising expectations that the system could not fulfill. Marcuse (1985 [1958]) had earlier argued that the need to incorporate technological rationality in the system would help produce critical consciousness, and Bahro (1978) contributed the concept of surplus consciousness to describe the growing subjective need for a better life that could fuel social dissent. Although both Left and Right critics of communism pessimistically argued that decades of Stalinism in the former Soviet Union and its East European empire had blunted the potential for social change, this diagnosis turned out to be incorrect and to signal the continuing validity of the classical Marxian concept of mass politics and the importance of the activity of the masses in promoting social change.

There were other reasons why Soviet communism collapsed that can also be described by the Marxian theory. Marcuse (1985 [1958]) distinguished between a ruling class that owned the means of production and one that controlled them, and following this distinction, one could argue that the fact that the Soviet elite did not own the means of production made its members more susceptible to abandoning the Soviet system, with the hopes that they could actually come to own or profit from the means of production in a new system. The ideology that the goal of socialism was to develop productive forces also might have contributed to the rapidity of the transition from a bureaucratic collectivist to a market system. For if the Soviet system proved inefficient, then the ideology of the primacy of the importance of developing the forces of production might have led some one-time Soviet communists to conclude that perhaps capitalism was a better system to develop the forces of production after all.

There were, of course, many economic, political, and ideological reasons why the Soviet system failed, too complicated to go into here in any detail. Military competition with the West during the Cold War overburdened the Soviet system, and the rise of a transnational capitalism cut the Soviet bloc out of world trade and weakened the Soviet bloc in relation to the system of global capitalism. Furthermore, the Soviet economy was too highly central-ized and not responsive to consumer demand or local conditions; the system failed to incorporate important new technologies (blocking, for instance, such things as photocopiers and computers); the Soviet educational system and health system were inefficient; apathy and corruption undermined produc-tivity and efficiency; and the masses of the people were deeply alienated from a system that they were supposed to control but did not.

Furthermore, Soviet communism failed to incorporate the gains of the bourgeois revolutionary traditions which Marx and the classical Marxists believed were an indispensable part of the socialist heritage. As noted, many classical Marxists saw the need for genuine democracy in order to have gen-uine socialism. Furthermore the very experience of the Soviet Union suggests to me that in addition to popular sovereignty being valorized as a key com-ponent of genuine democracy, the bourgeois concept of a division of power (Montesquieu) and a system of checks and balances should also be seen as key components of genuine democracy. Soviet communism was thoroughly totalitarian, with the state controlling everything. With power centralized in the state apparatus, society grew stagnant and atrophied. There was no social-ist public sphere, no civil society, no economic freedom, no cultural freedom, and so stagnation set in and the people and society suffered accordingly.

Division of power and the creation of a socialist public sphere thus seem to be integral parts of a genuinely democratic and socialist society. It was the tragedy of Gorbachev's administration that he responded to the failures of the Soviet system and the struggles for change with measures that were too little and too late. Gorbachev lacked the historical vision and imagination to revivify the Soviet system, though glasnost (i.e., cultural freedom and open-ness, experimentation in arts, criticism and intellectual freedoms) was obviously needed for the system to survive, to regenerate itself. Likewise, per-estroika (i.e., a systematic process of economic, political, and social restructuring) was obviously necessary for the Soviet Union to survive, but Gorbachev and his followers were unable to carry through the necessary restructuring, and some critics claim that Gorbachev himself ultimately opted for an authoritarian model of change from above, replicating the "Bonapartism" that Marx had criticized as early as the 1850s (see Callinicos 1991, 48ff.).

The collapse of Soviet communism suggests not that socialism is dead but that only democratic socialism can work and that only with genuine democracy can socialism provide a real alternative to the democratic-capitalist societies of the West and East. Socialism requires workers' self-management and democratic participation in all affairs of society and the polity or else it is but another economic system, merely a means of rationalizing and modernizing the economy. The lesson of the collapse of communism is that only democratic socialism can succeed to win the allegiance of its citizens. Consequently, it is the democratic socialist and revolutionary Marxian tradition that has the resources to construct positive alternatives to both capitalism and state communism for the present age.

I would also argue—against postmodern critiques that proscribe global and totalizing theories—that making sense of the momentous collapse of Soviet communism proves the need for Marxian theories to describe the epochal restructuring of the post-Cold War world now occurring, with its attendant problems and crises. The role of the masses in overthrowing communism suggests the continued viability of mass politics and confirms certain Marxian theories about the circulation of struggles and the importance of mass insurrections. In 1848, Marx and his generation experienced a series of mass upheavals, leading Marx to theorize a process of world revolution. In certain respects, 1989 was the most significant year since 1848 and in similar fashion exhibited a succession of revolutions, originating from below and circulating from one country to another in the Soviet bloc and eventually to the Soviet Union itself. The events of 1989 fit in with the heritage of revolutionary struggle of 1789, 1848, 1870, 1905, and 1917–1918, and they show the continued viability of Marxian theories of mass politics, insurrection, and revolution.

Thus, from a Marxian class and revolutionary perspective, revolts emerged against Soviet-style communism because it had failed to incorporate the progressive heritage of both the bourgeois revolutionary traditions and the Marxian revolutionary socialist heritage into its system. The Marxian theory, however, both can explain these events and finds key elements of its political theory vindicated. Thus, I believe that the Marxian theory continues to be useful today, even if there are problems with certain aspects of its theory of history and political analysis, aspects of which now appear problematical in the light of contemporary developments. Yet I shall argue that Marxism continues to provide indispensable resources for the radical project, though I also argue that we need new thinking in our radical theory and politics. However, this idea is completely consistent with the critical and historical impulses of the Marxian theory itself and portends its development and reconstruction and not its obsolescence and abandonment.

THE END OF ORTHODOX MARXISM

I have argued so far in this chapter that the most recent crisis of Marxism has not been terminal and that Marxism still has the theoretical and political resources to provide an account of contemporary history and strategies for radical social transformation. In a sense, Marxism is always in crisis as new events emerge that require revision and development of the theory. Marx himself and subsequent Marxists were always revising and reconstructing the theory to take account of historical developments and to fill in deficiencies in the original theory. In this sense, "crises of Marxism" are not so much signs of the obsolescence of the Marxian theory as a typical situation for a social theory facing anomalies or events that challenge its theories.

It is therefore not unusual for Marxism to be in crisis and for Marxists to reconstruct the theory in response to crisis. This was the life work of Herbert Marcuse, and many other Marxists have also responded to crises of Marxism with important, sometimes spectacular, developments of the theory.[12] In general, crises for the Marxist theory become an opportunity for its development. Crises bring about a challenge to a social system or theory that may lead to its weakening and collapse or to its improvement and strengthening. Crises of Marxism are among the periodic events that global sociohistorical theories continually undergo when events belie forecasts, or historical changes appear that force development or revision of the theory. When theories like Marxism are put in question during a crisis, debates ensue that frequently improve the theory. Consequently, crises of Marxism do not necessarily refer to failures of Marxism that portend its collapse and irrelevance but rather point toward opportunities to expand, develop, and strengthen the theory.

And yet the collapse of Soviet communism is such an epochal event that perhaps one can say that a certain version of Marxism is now at its end. I am speaking of that version of "orthodox Marxism" that claimed to be theorizing the very movement of history and held that history guaranteed the triumph of socialism and that the collapse of capitalism and transition to socialism and communism were inevitable. This form of Marxism claimed to be grounded in a "scientific" analysis of history and exhibited features of certainty, dogmatism, and orthodoxy. Orthodox Marxism was systematized in the Soviet Union and transmitted in different versions all over the world. It was rooted in doctrines concerning the revolutionary vocation of the proletariat and the certainty that capitalism would be overthrown by a revolutionary proletariat. Orthodox Marxism claimed that such a form of socialism was being produced in the Soviet Union and that the triumph of socialism on a world scale was guaranteed by the success of Soviet communism. This version of orthodox Marxism had dire consequences for the construction of socialism. Belief that history itself was leading to socialism and that one was part of the flow of history led to submission to historical trends and the dictates of party leaders who could claim to read the direction and flow of history. It created arrogance and dogmatism and produced a version of Marxism that could be used to legitimate oppressive societies. This version of orthodox Marxism is now totally obsolete and in turn discredits the Marxism-Leninism and "scientific Marxism" that are associated with it. Yet I would argue that a critical Marxism that remains open, nondogmatic, more modest, and tentative continues to provide theoretical and political resources to develop a critical theory and radical politics for the present age.[13]

In sorting out "what is living and dead" in Marxism, one should distinguish between the Marxian method and theory and recognize that the theory contains both an overarching system and specific theoretical and political positions. As I have suggested, the Marxian method of inquiry is a highly historical method, so development of the Marxian concepts and theories is itself prescribed by the method. It would go well beyond the limits of this chapter to lay out in detail the Marxian method and to specify its continuing relevance,[14] but I will simply state here that it is not clear how any historical events could render obsolete a method of inquiry, so it is not necessary for the purpose of this article to demonstrate the continuing relevance of the Marxian method. I would simply assert that at least some versions of the Marxian method continue to be of use, while aspects of the Marxian theory and a certain version of classical Marxism are now obsolete.

There is an impressive unity between theory and practice and all of the specific elements of the theory in classical Marxism. The critique of capitalism, theory of society and history, method of analysis, concepts of socialism and revolution, and relation between theory and practice all neatly fit together in classical Marxism. It is precisely this classical synthesis that now appears problematical and historically irrelevant as well as aspects of the Marxian theory, such as the theory of proletarian revolution, which was the linchpin of the classical Marxian theory.[15] Since the Frankfurt School work in the 1930s (see Kellner 1989a), Marxists have put in question the concept of proletarian revolution and attempted to reconstruct the Marxian theory in the light of existing historical realities and struggles and the failure of movements like Soviet communism that adopted, perhaps illicitly, the name of Marx and socialism.

It is precisely the reconstruction and rethinking of Marxism in the light of contemporary realities that is necessary today. The particular challenge and opportunity for critical Marxism is to provide an account of the restructuring of capitalism and new system of technocapitalism that is now emerging (see Kellner 1989a). I would argue that the Marxian theory provides the best perspectives and resources for this monumental task and that the Marxian theory continues to provide powerful resources to develop a social theory and radical politics for the present age. For the Marxian theory is at bottom a theory of capitalism, rooted in the political economy of the existing social system. If the economy is undergoing changes, and if economic factors continue to play a key role in all aspects of social life, then a theory of capitalism is a necessary component of radical social theory. Because no competing economic theory or critique of capitalism has emerged to replace Marxism, it is still an indispensable part of radical social theory.

Yet it is necessary for the Marxian theory to develop new categories and analyses in order to theorize the current restructuring and crises of capitalism. Although this process has appeared to signify a disorganized capitalism for some theorists (e.g., Offe 1985, Lash and Urry 1987), it also involves a reorganization of capitalism, sometimes described as "post-Fordism," which requires new analyses. Many Marxists are indeed providing these analyses, thus updating Marxian political economy. In addition, it has been well documented in the past decades that there have been tremendous advances in Marxian social theory, cultural theory, and philosophy and within every conceivable academic discipline providing new Marxian analyses of all domains of social life (see Ollman and Vernoff 1982, 1984 and 1986). These efforts provide indispensable components of a reconstructed Marxism for the present age.[16]

Indeed, from this perspective we can see the limitations of the fashionable postmodern theories that have accumulated a certain degree of cultural capital and influence by critiquing Marxism and other modern theories.[17] Such critiques proclaimed "the end of history" at the very moment that communism was collapsing, the capitalist system was restructuring itself, and new possibilities and problems were appearing on the historical scene with increased acceleration and urgency. To say that "history" has ended in such a situation is totally absurd. Baudrillard's concept of "the end of political economy" is equally absurd at a time when capitalism is restructuring itself on a global level. Indeed, the attack on macro and systemic theories is equally disabling at the very moment when we need new theories and politics to conceptualize the new socioeconomic, political, and cultural configurations of the moment and to seek solutions to the political problems of the present age, which are increasingly global in nature (e.g., global debt crisis; global ecological crisis; and the globalization of local political conflicts such as the Gulf war and the crises in the former Yugoslavia, the former Soviet Union, and other parts of the world). Thus I would argue that Marxism contains the resources to develop a critical theory of the present age and that renouncing it because of the political collapse of Soviet communism, which arguably was a distortion of Marxian theory in the first place, is simplistic and unproductive.

RETHINKING SOCIALISM

Only the most ideological enemy of Marxism, or uninformed pseudointellectual, could seriously maintain that the Marxian theory is obsolete. But what of Marxian politics? While Marxism is arguably alive and well as a theory, Marxist politics seem nonetheless to be floundering. It is a curiosity of the fate of Marxism today that in the past decades, while there has been a tremendous development of theory, there has been a steady decline in Marxist politics as well as a declining role for Marxist discourse and practice in contemporary political movements. Some Marxist radicals have urged that the discourse of socialism be abandoned in the present context, and socialist parties in the Western capitalist countries seem to be rapidly declining in power and influence. Labor struggles and the sort of class politics classically associated with Marxist theory also seem to be in decline, so the question arises whether the very discourse of socialism and revolution should be abandoned.

In the following discussion, I will concede that socialism and social change need to be reconsidered, but I will also argue that Marxian political theory is not obsolete. In part, its continuing political relevance is due to its intense and resolute focus on class. The class theory of politics, I believe, constitutes

both an enduring contribution of the Marxian theory and an obdurate limi-
tation. During the past twelve years in the United States, and more or less
elsewhere throughout the world, there have been growing class divisions
between rich and poor, haves and have-nots. To proclaim the obsolescence
of social classes and class struggle is absolutely wrong in the face of the
unpalatable reality of class.

Yet the class privileged by the classical Marxian theory of revolution, the
proletariat, or industrial working class, is a declining class sector in the
Western industrial countries (though not in the Third World, where industrial labor is increasingly exported). Beginning with the Frankfurt School,
Marxian theorists questioned whether the proletariat could serve as a revolutionary subject, as it did in the original revolutionary theory of Marx
(Kellner 1984 and 1989a). It is also widely accepted that classical Marxism
exaggerates the primacy of class and downplays the salience of gender and
race. Clearly, oppression takes place in many more spheres than just the economic and the workplace, so a radical politics of the future should take
account of gender and race as well as class.

Nonetheless, it would be wrong to ignore the centrality of class and the
importance of class politics. But a radical politics today should be more multicultural, race and gender focused, and broad-based than the original
Marxian theory. Thus, a form of Marxism seems to have come to an end: the
Marxism of the industrial working class, of proletarian revolution. Marxism
has been identified since its beginnings with working-class revolution, and
Marxian-inspired revolutions have been legitimated by defining themselves as
working-class revolutions. No doubt a future Marxism will have to distance
itself from its concept of the proletariat and privileging of the industrial working class as the subject of revolution and the construction of socialism. For as
new technologies expand and the industrial proletariat shrinks, new agents
of social change must be sought.[18]

But, still, the question arises whether the collapse of the Soviet empire and
of communism in the Soviet Union signifies the end of Marxism as a world-
historical political force and shaper of political reality. Are these series of
dramatic events the finishing blow, the crisis from which Marxism cannot
recover, the historical episode that refutes and ends Marxism as a political
force once and for all? Does the collapse of communism prove that Marxian
politics simply do not work?

We need to theorize the failure of Marxian politics over the past decade—after a series of spectacular triumphs from the late 1950s through the late 1970s—and draw appropriate lessons from recent history. But it is premature to describe a series of setbacks as evidence for the collapse of Marxist politics per se. In the long term, we still don't know if the collapse of the Soviet Union and its empire was positive or negative for the Marxian project. It was certainly a negative event in that it provided for an ideological celebration of capitalism and a market economy as the best economic system as well as bringing about the actual dismantling of state communist societies and the implementation of market economies in the previous Soviet empire. Thus the economic and political counterweight to capitalism, an alternative world system, disappeared, leaving the capitalist economy triumphant.

Yet one could argue that the collapse of Soviet communism will create new conflicts and crises for capitalist countries. The capitalist economy on a world scale was fueled by the tremendous military spending legitimated by the Cold War. With the end of the Cold War and the communist enemy, such a level of state-administered spending will no longer be justified, and, with the increased pressure of gigantic national deficits and capital shortages, its end may cause new crises of capitalism. In addition, it was the common communist enemy that united, at least to some extent, the capitalist countries, whose rivalries may now explode and produce a new era of intracapitalist conflict and crisis as well as the explosions and instabilities evident in the former Yugoslavia and Soviet Union after the breakup of the communist empire.

Furthermore, the passing away of a social system that fundamentally distorted Marxian theory opened the way for a new type of socialism that could enhance freedom, democracy, and human happiness. In this context, it is premature to jettison the concept of socialism when really existing capitalist societies are in need of such profound transformation. I would argue that one can still use the concept of socialism as a practical guide to inform policies in democratic capitalist societies and to make specific policy demands: full employment; health care; shortening the work week; democratizing the work place, the media, and other domains of society. One can also use socialist ideas to call for more radical democratization, yet one should perhaps argue that with a genuinely democratic socialism, all classes of society will participate in self-management, and thus there should be no privileging of the working class or any other class as in some versions of classical Marxism.

Secondly, Marxian concepts can be used to demonstrate the problems of an unrestrained capitalism and can be used to justify regulation and social control of capitalism. During an era in which "free markets" are being touted as the source of economic prosperity and human freedom alike, the Marxian critique of market capitalism shows their limitations. Capitalism has produced incredible suffering all over the world, and Marxian critiques can be used to point to its limitations, the need for regulation, and ultimately for a better organization of society. Putting the imperative to maximize the accumulation of capital over the needs of people is one of the structural limitations of capitalism that radical discourse could attack in efforts to legitimate social change that could win the favor of large numbers of people.

Perhaps most important, the Marxian vision of emancipation could continue to animate struggles for a freer and more democratic society. The Marxian demand for shortening the workday and increasing the realm of leisure is especially relevant during an era when technology makes less work possible, yet capitalism continues to impose more work.[19] Marx's vision of emancipation and full development of the individual is appropriate to the present level of technological development and can provide a critical standpoint to denounce continued societal oppression. Its emphasis on the democratization of social life is appropriate when the democratic revolution seems to have triumphed, or to be at least possible, on a worldwide scale.

The Marxian vision of democracy and freedom, I would argue, is preferable to the liberal version in that it has a more comprehensive vision of democracy that encompasses all realms of social life. The popular sovereignty exercised in the Paris Commune and celebrated by Marx and Engels as a model for the self-management of society would involve genuine popular sovereignty on the social and political level as well as economic democracy. While the really existing socialist societies never developed social democracy, there existed a modicum at least of workplace democracy. In the liberal capitalist countries, by contrast, democracy is effectively curtailed to periodic voting, and there is little real popular sovereignty in the social realm or democracy in the workplace.

Thus, classical liberalism's notion of representative democracy, its equation of democracy with voting, severely restricts the conception, yielding but a weak democracy that is easily manipulated by conservative forces who use their wealth and power to control electoral processes. The classical liberal concept of freedom is also truncated, often limiting freedom to individual freedom of choice in the market and political popularity contests. The question also arises as to whether the vast majority of the population is really free in capitalist societies that do not provide the economic basis to live a free life. How can one be said to be "free" when one is suffering constant anxiety about employment, hopelessness, health care, environmental crisis, and the possibility of economic collapse? Theodor Adorno's demand for a life without anxiety is relevant as a critical marker against really existing capitalist insecurity and anxiety.

Yet it must be admitted that the former communist societies never incorporated the bourgeois tradition of rights, individual liberties, and democracy to the extent stressed by some of the Marxist classics. Failure to adequately appropriate the progressive heritage of liberalism into the Marxian political theory rendered it vulnerable to liberal critiques and the belief that only liberalism provided genuine freedom and democracy. Marxism should have established itself as the champion of these political values, but an underdeveloped Marxian political philosophy and really existing political oppression of the socialist regimes created an identification of Marxism with oppression and liberalism with freedom and democracy.

Finally, against liberalism's individualism—as well as some so-called postmodern politics that stress micropolitics—one could argue that Marxian concepts of mass politics that call for mass struggle, radical systemic change, and fundamental restructuring of the system were instantiated by the very struggles in Eastern Europe and the former Soviet Union that were previously claimed to have invalidated the Marxian theory. The dramatic mass struggles and upheavals in these regions caused fundamental social change (which may, however, turn out to be regressive in many ways.) Although micropolitics may contribute to such a process, it is premature to claim that the era of mass politics, associated in part with Marxism, is over.

Indeed, Marxian political theory articulates and grounds those values that can help produce coalitions between disparate political movements. Championing "new social movements" per se as the contemporary agents of change covers the fact that some of these movements are reactionary, some are at best liberal, and some are genuinely progressive. We need broad political perspectives to judge between contending political movements and to provide values and ideals that might unite specific movements for specific goals. As Jesse Jackson reminds us, coalition politics requires discovering that common ground that might unite progressive movements, which then together can move to the higher ground of democratic political transformation.

Yet questions emerge as to whether the Marxian theory of social change should presuppose the collapse of capitalism as a necessary condition for the triumph of socialism. Capitalism has experienced severe crises for decades, but it has often emerged stronger than before and now appears far from collapse in its problematical triumph after the collapse of communism. And yet it may also be premature to sound the death knell of the Marxian theory of revolution. Why should one believe that capitalism itself, capitalism in the most "advanced" capitalist countries such as the United States and Japan, might not collapse? Japanese capitalism is in severe crisis, and it is not clear that U.S. capitalism has any solutions to its deficit and debt problems; its banking and financial crises; and the crisis of life in decaying cities marked by growing crime and violence, illness and lack of health care, and a pervasive sense of hopelessness. And, finally, the very environment in which we live, nature itself, may revolt against capitalist misuse and require another mode of social organization to guarantee the very survival of the species on planet Earth.

Capitalism could thus collapse, or at least not work in many parts of the world, which may well turn to socialism as an alternative—but this time a democratic and multicultural socialism, or new forms of socialism that have not yet been theorized and perhaps will emerge only through a process of historical experimentation. The failure of market capitalist experiments in Eastern Europe and the former Soviet Union may yet reinvigorate new socialist experiments, which may yet contain many solutions to acute problems of the present age.

In regard to these problems and crises of capitalist society, we can still use Marxian theory to confront the capitalist organization of society and accumulation process. We need to rethink markets and how to tame their destructive effects as well as developing resolute critiques of state communism and its problems with bureaucracies. We also need a resurgence of socialist internationalism, with new emphasis on the need for internationalist thinking in the face of capitalist internationals. Not only the Trilateral Commission but Masterricht and the General Agreement on Tariffs and Trade (GATT) appear to be organs of the international capitalist class to promote its interests. Similarly, socialists and other progressives must organize on an international level and think globally to deal with the problems of the economy, environment, and everyday life and to come up with attractive alternatives to capitalism.

Yet, in conclusion, I would argue for the need for new thinking and politics. Events in the communist world of the last few years refute both Cold War anticommunist myths and communist dogma and require new political thinking. Most conservative, liberal, and Leftist thinking failed to anticipate the dramatic upheaval in the communist world. Furthermore, it is not clear that any one political ideology has the answers to the mind-boggling problems of the present era. In view of the dramatic changes of the past years and the enduring and even intensified problems, we need new political thinking, we need to dispense with a lot of old thinking, and we need to theorize the new and still changing political realities of our time.

Thus, we perhaps need to rethink and reconstruct the concept of social-ism. Certainly, the concept of socialism maintained in what I am calling a now-obsolete orthodox Marxism must be abandoned: socialism as guaranteed by history, socialism as inevitable, socialism as the telos of history. Perhaps socialism should be seen more as a normative ideal than as a historical force; more as a model or regulative ideal to provide critical alternatives to the existing society than a tendency in history. This model of socialism, as my analysis suggests, could be used to criticize existing capitalist societies, to provide policy guidance and justification of certain policies, and to provide a radical alternative to the existing organization of society. Socialism must be rethought in the light of historical developments in order to retain its potential to generate progressive social change.

RECONSTRUCTING MARXISM

I am ready to concede that we need new post-Cold War political theory and practice to deal with the problems of the present age and that Marxism can only be a part of such new theories and politics. Yet we need to build on viable political and theoretical perspectives and resources of the past, and I would argue that Marxism continues to provide vital resources for radical theory and politics today. I would also argue, against postmodernists, that the Enlightenment tradition provides important resources for the present, though developing this position would constitute the basis of another essay. In sum, I believe that we need new theoretical and political syntheses, drawing on the best of classical Enlightenment theory, Marxian theory, feminism, and other progressive theoretical and political currents of the present. Key aspects for such new syntheses, however, are found in the Marxian tradition, and those who prematurely abandon it are turning away from a tradition that has been valuable since Marx's day and will continue to be so into the foreseeable future. Consequently, Marxism is not yet obsolete. Rather, the Marxian theory continues to provide resources and stimulus for critical theory and radical politics in the present age.

Whither, then, Marxism? Certainly not a master theory and narrative, as it appeared in its classical forms. However, it continues to be an important method of social research and set of theoretical perspectives, concepts, and values that can still be used for critical social theory and radical politics today. We continue to live in a capitalist society, and as long as we do, Marxism will continue to be relevant. A reconstructed Marxism, a Marxism without guarantees, teleology, and foundations, will be more open, tolerant, skeptical, and modest than previous versions. A Marxism for the twenty-first century could help promote democracy, freedom, justice, and equality, and counterattack conservative ideologies that merely promote the interests of the rich and powerful. As long as tremendous class inequality, human suffering, and oppression exists there is a need for critical theories such as Marxism and the visions of radical social change that the tradition has inspired. Marxism will disappear either when the nightmare of capitalism is finally over or when a democratic and free society emerges that will produce its own philosophy and way of life. If Marxism has inspired such a project, then the doctrine can pass on to a happy obsolescence and the sufferings and struggles of those in the Marxian tradition will be redeemed.

This notion points to a final reason to hold onto and reconstruct Marxism once again in the present era: loyalty to those who have given their lives for the genuinely progressive hopes and dreams of the Marxian heritage. Loyalty to the radical tradition suggests building on its insights, learning from its errors and failures, and reconstructing one's radical theories and politics accordingly. The fashionable postmodern nihilism that cuts itself off from the theoretical and political resources of the past not only disables contemporary theory and politics but arrogantly, in quasi-Stalinist fashion, relegates to the "dustbin of history" those ideas, political struggles, sacrifices, and heroism of the past. Instead of such absolute negation, the dialectical negation and sublation practiced by Hegel and Marx (*Aufhebung*) continues to be a more productive way of relating to tradition and reconstructing our radical theories and politics in the contemporary era.

notes

1. Habermas notes that the term "crisis" in the medical sense "refers to the phase of an illness in which it is decided whether or not the organism's self-healing powers are sufficient for recovery" (1975, 1). A crisis in this sense thus threatens the survival of a phenomenon and suggests that if it does not survive the crisis, it will cease to exist.

2. U.S. State Department neo-Hegelian Francis Fukuyama proclaimed the "end of history" after the fall of the Berlin Wall and the collapse of the Soviet empire. He declared "the ultimate triumph of Western liberal democracy" and "the unabashed victory of economic and political liberalism" (1989, 3). As Derrida reminds us (1993), such claims have been made regularly from the 1950s throughout the Cold War. The question arises, however, whether the collapse of communism in the Soviet Union portends the obsolescence of Marxism.

3. For descriptions of these crises of Marxism and the ways that Western Marxist theorists responded to the crises, see my book on Herbert Marcuse (Kellner 1984), who attempted to reconstruct the Marxian theory in response to a series of crises of Marxism.

4. On Baudrillard, see Kellner 1989b.

5. See Callinicos 1991, 21–37, for a sketch of the historical differences between Bolshevism and Stalinism, concluding with a quote from Lewin, who notes: "'the party became an organization of an unprecedented type: a bureaucratic-political administration, highly centralized and geared to mobilization, regimentation, and control, entirely different from what it had been under Lenin" (37).

6. Callinicos (1991) argues that the establishment of the Congress of People's Deputies in March 1989 "involved an appeal by the reformers for popular support in their struggle against the conservatives. This step, the decision to take the differences within the apparatus to a larger audience, marked the real turning point in the process of *glasnost*, the moment at which the revolutionary over-

throw of the Stalinist regimes became a real possibility" (49). Perhaps a moment of genuine radical reform did exist during the Gorbachev era, but it might also be the case that the system was corrupted beyond reform and that sufficiently revolutionary forces did not exist to overthrow it — an argument bolstered by the failed communist coup of August 1991 and the subsequent collapse of the Gorbachev regime and ascendancy of Yeltsin and his reformers, who renounced Marxism and socialism.

7. Della Volpe (1978), for instance, stresses the closeness of Rousseau, Marx, and the socialist tradition; while Miller (1984) stresses the importance of Rousseau for democratic theory and politics.

8. Marx concludes: "The absence of freedom of the press makes all other freedom illusory. One form of freedom governs another just as one limb of the body does another. Whenever a particular freedom is put in question, freedom in general is put in question. Whenever one form of freedom is rejected, freedom in general is rejected and henceforth can have only a semblance of existence, since the sphere in which absence of freedom is dominant becomes a matter of pure chance.... Freedom remains freedom whether it finds expression in printer's ink, in property, in the conscience, or in a political assembly" (Marx and Engels 1975, 180–181). One could object that this fulsome defense of the freedom of the press was an idealistic residue of the early Marx, but in fact Marx supported himself through journalism in the 1850s and 1860s and never failed to advocate freedom of the press. In writing on the Paris Commune in 1871, he praised the Communards for publishing accounts of their deliberations and their proclamation of freedom of the press, and this issue remained a lifelong concern and commitment of Marx.

9. For example, see the discussions in Callinicos 1991 and in Blackburn et al. 1991.

10. This argument was made as early as the 1940s by Max Shachtman and others.

11. As I point out in an introduction to the 1985 Columbia University Press reprint of *Soviet Marxism*, Marcuse was the first member of the Frankfurt School to systematically analyze and critique Soviet Marxism and its divergences from classical Marxism. He also foresaw the "liberalizing trends" brought about by Gorbachev, though he did not anticipate Soviet communism's collapse.

12. This was a major theme of my book on Marcuse (Kellner 1984) and on the critical theory of the Frankfurt School (Kellner 1989a).

13. On the difference between scientific and critical Marxism, see Gouldner 1980.

14. For one thing, there are many different versions of the Marxian method, which

are more or less defensible; see, for example, Gouldner (1980), who contrasts the methods of critical and scientific Marxism. See Kellner 1989a for a systematic defense of the relevance of the Marxian method of social inquiry as elaborated by the Frankfurt School; I also called attention to the limits of the Frankfurt School appropriation of Marxism.

15. For delineation of the contours of the classical Marxian theory and its dependence on a theory of proletarian revolution as its centerpiece, see my book *Karl Korsch: Revolutionary Theory* (Kellner 1977).

16. See the three volumes assembled by Ollman and Vernoff (1982, 1984, and 1986), *The Left Academy,* for documentation of contributions to the development of Marxian theory in many academic disciplines during the past two decades.

17. On postmodern theory, see Kellner 1989b and Best and Kellner 1991.

18. This problem was the dilemma of the Frankfurt School. For discussion of the political implications of this impasse, see Kellner 1989a.

19. See Schor 1992 on "the overworked American" and Gorz 1982 and 1985 on why it is so ridiculous to continue to organize society around work.

references

Bahro, Rudolf. (1978) *The Alternative in Eastern Europe.* London: New Left Books.

Baudrillard, Jean. (1974) *The Mirror of Production.* Saint Louis: Telos Press.

––––––. (1976) *L'echange symbolique et la mort.* Paris: Gallimard.

Best, Steven, and Douglas Kellner. (1991) *Postmodern Theory: Critical Interrogations.* London and New York: Macmillan and Guilford Press.

Blackburn, Robin, et al. (1991) *After the Fall.* London and New York: Verso.

Callinicos, Alex. (1991) *The Revenge of History.* University Park: Pennsylvania State University Press.

Della Volpe, Galvano. (1978) *Rousseau and Marx.* London: Lawrence and Wishart.

Derrida, Jacques. (1993) "Spectres of Marx: The State of the Debt, the Work of Mourning and the New International," paper presented at "Whither Marxism?" conference, University of California at Riverside, April 1993.

Fukuyama, Francis. (1989) "The End of History?" *The National Interest.* 16 (Summer), 3–18.

––––––. (1992) *The End of History.* New York: The Free Press.

Gorz, André. (1982) *Farewell to the Working Class.* Boston: South End Press.

————. (1985) *Paths to Paradise*. Boston: South End Press.

Gouldner, Alvin. (1980) *The Two Marxisms*. New York: Seabury Press.

Habermas, Jürgen. (1975) *Legitimation Crisis*. Boston: Beacon Press.

Kagarlitsky, Boris. (1990) *The Dialectic of Change*. London: Verso.

Kellner, Douglass. (1977) *Karl Korsch: Revolutionary Theory*. Austin: University of Texas Press.

————. (1984) *Herbert Marcuse and the Crisis of Marxism*. London and Berkeley: Macmillan and University of California Press.

————. (1989a) *Critical Theory, Marxism, and Modernity*. Cambridge and Baltimore: Polity and Johns Hopkins University Press.

————. (1989b) *Jean Baudrillard: From Marxism to Postmodernism and Beyond*. Cambridge and Palo Alto: Polity and Stanford University Press.

Lash, Scott, and John Urry. (1987) *The End of Organized Capitalism*. Cambridge: Polity Press.

Lyotard, Jean-François. (1984) *The Postmodern Condition*. Minneapolis: University of Minnesota Press.

Marcuse, Herbert. (1985 [1958]) *Soviet Marxism*. New York: Columbia University Press.

Marx, Karl, and Friedrich Engels (1975) *Collected Works*. New York: International Publishers.

Miller, James. (1984) *Rousseau: Dreamer of Democracy*. New Haven: Yale University Press.

Offe, Claus. (1985) *Disorganized Capitalism*. Oxford: Basil Blackwell. Ollman, Bertell, and Edward Vernoff. (1982, 1984, and 1986) *The Left Academy: Marxist Scholarship on American Campuses*. Vol. 1, New York: McGraw-Hill; Vols. 2 and 3, New York: Praeger.

Popper, Karl. (1963 [1945]) *The Open Society and Its Enemies*. New York: Harper and Row.

Rousseau, Jean-Jacques. (1987 [1762]) *The Social Contract*.

Schorr, Juliet. (1992) *The Overworked American*. New York: Basic Books.

ABDUL JANMOHAMED

refiguring values, power, knowledge

or foucault's disavowal of marx

1

In responding to the question posed by the conference, "Whither Marxism?",
I would like to bracket the questions about the future directions of Marxism as
theory and praxis and focus instead on the fate or contemporary reception of
Marxian thought, not so much as a consequence of the debacle of communism in the ex-Soviet Union, China, and their colonial satellites, but within
the context of the Western "analytic tradition," where Marxism has enjoyed a
more critical if not entirely integrative response. I would like to examine the
"withering" of Marx(ism) via Michel Foucault's unacknowledged appropriation of Karl Marx's ideas and read this appropriation as a symptom of the
current status of Marxian ideas and methodological procedures in the West,

the latter to be understood not so much as a geographical but as a cultural and epistemic space.

Foucault's relation to Marx bears scrutiny not only because of the former's unimpeachable credentials as a radical, provocative, and influential thinker but also because that relation is marked by a double anxiety. The first of these anxieties, which will constitute the center of this essay, consists of the tension that surrounds Foucault's few explicit comments about, and his ample but unacknowledged references to, the work of Marx, particularly in Foucault's theory of power. Indeed, it is my contention that Foucault's theory or "analytics" of power is profoundly indebted to and modeled on Marx's labor theory of value and that Foucault's refusal to acknowledge this relation, which is itself a fascinating instance of relations of power/knowledge, constitutes a disavowal symptomatic of a hasty "post-Marxism" that has never adequately come to terms with Marx. The second instance of this anxiety is precisely the uneasiness that Foucault's disavowal causes within circles that explicitly acknowledge themselves as Marxist or post-Marxist.

Both forms of apprehension are best revealed in Duccio Trombadori's interviews of Foucault (Foucault, Michel. *Remarks on Marx: Conversations With Duccio Trombadori/Foucault.* New York: Semiotext(e), 1991). The editor's ardent desire to connect Foucault to Marx manifests itself in the title, "Remarks on Marx," which insists on the connection in spite of Foucault's refusal to reflect or comment on his relation to the thought of Marx except in the most cursory and indirect way. Foucault does briefly discuss the Frankfurt School and his own relation to the French Communist party (PCF), but he only refers to Marx by way of defending his earlier argument that Marx was confined by nineteenth-century epistemology.[1] The title's insistence can be read as an index of a rather urgent feeling among certain circles that a substantive connection between Foucault and Marx needs to be made or, at least, systematically examined.[2]

The pressure of these interviews also indirectly reveals some of Foucault's anxieties about the genealogy of his work. The discussions gradually disclose Foucault's willingness to acknowledge clearly and unequivocally only one of the three most important genealogical antecedents of his own work that are explored in these interviews. Friedrich Nietzsche and his mediators and interpreters (Blanchot and Bataille are mentioned repeatedly) constitute a group unhesitatingly embraced as the major line of descent. By contrast Edmund

Husserl and Marx, on whose work Foucault never comments explicitly and directly, are dismissed as part of the prevailing Western humanistic epistemology that must be overcome; in fact, the two intellectual movements, phenomenology and Marxism/communism, spawned by these thinkers are severely criticized by Foucault. The strong rejection of these movements in conjunction with Foucault's refusal to comment in any specific manner on the work of the two authors is noteworthy particularly because his own writing manifests such a strong, but unacknowledged, influence by Husserl and Marx.[3] Indeed, Foucault's diffident comments about Louis Althusser, who, as I shall argue at the end of the essay, is for Foucault as important a mediator of Marx as Blanchot and Bataille are of Nietzsche, seem to be part of this disavowal.

Reading these interviews in conjunction with Foucault's historical and theoretical publications, one can begin to discern a categorical difference between that which he acknowledges and that which he rejects. The influence of Nietzsche functions in Foucault's work predominantly at the level of content and telos rather than in terms of form: what Foucault retains from the Nietzschean project is the imperative to overcome "man," the need to annihilate "subjectivity" as formulated thus far by Western culture, and the obligation to clear an epistemological space for posthumanist thought. In formal terms Foucault's work is scrupulously historical and far more systematically theoretical than is Nietzsche's.[4] By contrast the teloi embedded in Husserl's and Marx's projects, contaminated as they are by enlightenment-based notions of subjectivity and rationality, are soundly rejected by Foucault. What Foucault retains, but never adequately acknowledges, are some of the powerful methodological tools and procedures of Husserl and Marx. That is, Foucault's historical method is profoundly phenomenological at some level, and his theory or analytics of power are profoundly Marxian in some ways.

Foucault signals his own hazy, hesitant, ambivalent, and somewhat incredulous awareness of this complex and uneasy combination of Nietzschean and Marxian genealogical lines in defining the motives that led him to join the CPF. "For many of us as young intellectuals (inspired by a "need for the total rejection of the world in which we found ourselves living"), an interest in Nietzsche or Bataille didn't represent a way of distancing oneself from Marxism or communism." Thus Foucault becomes what he calls "A Nietzschean Communist!": "Something really on the edge of 'liveability.' And, if you like (I too knew it) something a bit ridiculous, perhaps" ("Remarks," 51). The implied combination is not as ridiculous as it might seem. In fact, what Foucault has produced in his corpus is simultaneously Nietzschean and Marxian: substantively inspired by Nietzsche, he investigates and articulates the mechanisms of power in a manner that is historically systematic and empirical in methodology quite unlike the approach of Nietzsche; formally inspired by Marx, he insists on investigating the mechanisms of power in their capillary manifestations and in the processes of social exchange while eschewing the utopian humanism as well as the "scientific" pretensions of Marx. However, his syncretism is diffident; the disavowal of Marx is too strong to permit a more deliberate and open synthesis. Foucault's anxiety is an unfortunate one, for if he had not felt the need to disavow Marx, then he could have developed a more systematic political "economy of power relations," the need for which he acknowledged toward the end of his life (Dreyfus, Hubert and Rabinow, Paul. *Michel Foucault: Beyond Structuralism and Hermeneutics.* Chicago: University of Chicago Press, 1982, p. 210). At the end of this chapter I would like to examine Foucault's disavowal of Marx,[5] or, more accurately, to draw out the tension in the Marx-Foucault relationship between the register of political psychosis (i.e., disavowal) and political neurosis (i.e. repression). Provisionally, however, the relationship can be defined simply as a form of veiled recognition, a simultaneous movement of acceptance and rejection.

The specific aspect of the Marx-Foucault relationship to which I shall devote the bulk of this chapter will consist of a cross-reading of Marx's labor theory of value and Foucault's exchange theory of power. In order to delineate the terrain more precisely it may be useful to emphasize what I will not investigate. On the Foucaultian side, I am not interested here either in his concrete, historical descriptions of how power operates in various discursive formations or in his persuasive suturing of power and knowledge. His empirical descriptions of the emergence of modern modalities of power, his demonstration that power is "productive" and not merely limiting, his critique of the juridico-discursive model of power and hence of the repressive hypothesis and state-centered political practice, his articulation of disciplinary forms of power predicated on the experts' command of truth and knowledge, and his focusing of our attention on the microphysics of power and hence on the body and everyday life: all of these are enabling and furnish very substantive and apposite critiques of liberalism and Marxism. Nor, indeed, do I wish to underestimate Foucault's "nominalism" in the analysis of power, the value of which Etienne Balibar, Gayatri C. Spivak, and others have articulated, except to note that whereas Marx's nominalism is accompanied, according to Althusser's well-known analysis, by his systematic thinking through of the "concept" of value, Foucault seems to refuse such a step.[6] On the Marxist side, I wish to defend neither the base-superstructure model with its implicit notion of a mechanical economic determinism; nor the Marxist faith in radical historical determinism; nor the Marxist pretensions to scientificity; nor the privileging of the proletariat (and its vanguard) as the locus of revolutionary conscious- ness; nor the class struggle as the privileged avenue to social, political, and economic transformation; nor Marxism's faith in an ontology of the Real; nor, finally, its (ultimately) ethical investment in the liberating power of truth, implicit in the definition of ideology as "false consciousness" and predicated on versions of "mechanical" and "expressive" causality.

What this chapter will undertake is a cross-reading of Marx and Foucault at the points where, so to speak, the former begins and the latter leaves off (though neither one of them works in a unilinear or univocal manner). Post- Foucaultian readings of power relations within Marxist analyses of "macro" structures—class relations, function of the state, and so on have demonstrated that at this level Marx was as concerned with forms of power as was Foucault, and that he anticipated the latter in some ways.[7] By contrast, I wish to focus on the capillary level, on the microphysics of Marx's description and analysis of the functioning of capitalist political economy, on the productive and exchange mechanisms through which that economy generates "commodities," labor-power," "capital," and, most importantly, "value," that is, on elements that Althusser has identified as central to the epistemological break produced by Marxian theory.[8] While the macrostructures of Marxian analyses and prax- is were clearly subject to various aspects of nineteenth-century epistemology, as Foucault has argued, Marx's analysis and theorization of the microphysics of capitalist political economy were not, as Althusser has amply demonstrat- ed. What Marx examines is not a "command" economy directed by some juridico-discursive center but precisely a mundane discursive practice "con- trolled" by the accepted "truths" and the "knowledge" of an "autonomously" functioning "market." In other words, he describes a disciplinary formation, one that, as Foucault himself admits, operates in conjunction with other disciplinary formations to produce modern society. It is thus Marx's microphysical analysis of political economy that I would like to read against Foucault's theory of power. For whereas Foucault's historical and empirical descriptions of the nature and function of power in various discursive practices and disciplinary formations are profoundly enabling, his "theorization" of that power shies away from the kind of rigor that clearly characterizes Marx's theoretical elaboration of the nature and function of value.

Marx's labor theory of value, that is, his microphysical analysis of the capitalist political economy, is precisely analogous to Foucault's empirical descriptions and analysis of the microphysics of synchronous discursive practices and disciplinary formations. It seems to me that because the latter are modeled on the former, Foucault, in the final analysis, grounds his theory of power in "activity," just as Marx grounds his theory of value in "labor." Throughout this chapter "labor" must be understood in its broader implication, not just as activity that transforms "nature" for human consumption but also as activity that consequently (trans)forms all aspects of human society. "Labor" is often interpreted exclusively to designate either the category of the proletariat, which is then designated as the privileged agent of historical change, or the activity that transforms nature, which is then defined as qualitatively different from other kinds of activity. But it can be argued that for Marx "labor" includes all "activity" that "produces" material and cultural components that constitute society. Thus the "elementary factors of the labour-process are 1, the personal activity of man, i.e., work itself, 2, the subject (i.e. object) of that work, 3, its instruments."[9] As Marx elaborates, the instruments or means of labor are themselves the products of previous labor, as indeed is the object of labor, including "raw material." There is not a single product of human society that is not always already saturated with labor, which then must be seen as including what Althusser defines as "theoretical production." The category of "production" too is to be understood in its broader form, as incorporating moments of consumption (what Marx calls "productive consumption") and exchange (for instance, of the means of labor or of labor-power between the owner of capital and the laborer, etc). While the problem cannot be examined here, it seems to me that the privileging of certain kinds of labor over others or of production over consumption and distribution are not so clearly entailed in the work of Marx.[10] It is in terms of Marx's theory of value, and particularly in terms of the broader definitions of labor and production, then, that I wish to interrogate Foucault's theory of power and to ask why, given the affinity between the two theories, Foucault disavows this facet of Marx.

Thus in addition to exploring the question of disavowal, this chapter constitutes a Foucauldian rereading of Marx as much as a Marxian reading of Foucault. The essay is not to be construed, above all, as being in the service of Marxism; indeed, by drawing an implicit distinction throughout this essay between Marx*ian* and Marx*ist*, the former denoting the works of Marx and the latter the movement that has built itself up around his name, I hope to make a case, at least indirectly, for the need to reread Marx in a context free from the quasi-deification (and hence quasi-religious incarceration) to which the "communists" and some Marxologists have subjected him, as well as free from the irrational demonization (and hence quasi-religious excommunication) to which bourgeois capitalist cultures have subjected him. Foucault's disavowal of Marx is, I think, an important instance of the latter process.

II

One of the most obvious signs of Foucault's anxiety about his relation with the work of Marx occurs in those situations where he feels obliged to mention the field of political economy. Take, for instance, the following remark: "Now, it seems to me that economic history and theory provided a good instrument for relations of production; that linguistics and semiotics offered instruments for studying relations of signification; but for power relations we had no tools of study" (Dreyfus and Rabinow. 209). What seems remarkable about such statements is Foucault's unwillingness to consider, even momentarily, the possibility that "relations of production" as theorized by Marx may furnish a particular form of power relations; if not the privileged form, as Marx insisted. In such instances Foucault never pauses to inquire whether the kinds of struggles between individuals as well as groups that Marx describes as taking place in the processes of production may be similar to his descriptions of power relations or, if they are significantly different, what the differences might reveal about the nature of power. While such instances of avoidance provide ready indices of his anxiety, instances where Foucault displaces Marx's work furnish signs of even deeper anxiety.

Foucault's primary tactic in criticizing the Marxist notion of political power is to link it with a liberal view of power. In spite, "and even because of (the) difference (between the two views), I consider there to be a certain point in common between the juridical, and let us call it, liberal conception of political power (found in the *philosophes* of the eighteenth century) and the Marxist conception, or at any rate a certain conception currently held to be Marxist. I would call this common point an economism in the theory of power" (PK, 88). But the nature of this "economism" differs. The liberals, according to Foucault, treat power as a "commodity" that an individual or group can possess and than can be transferred or alienated, through acts that are in fact or implicitly legal in character, such as contracts. It is the transfer or appropriation of this power-as-object that leads, within this conception of it, to the establishment of sovereignty. By contrast, within the Marxist conception, the economism is one of "functionality": that is, for Marxists "the historical *raison d'être* of political power and its concrete forms and actual functioning, is located in the economy" (PK, 89).

To the extent that Foucault is critical of crude or refined versions of the base-superstructure model, where the former determines the latter totally, he is of course correct. Yet, as Bob Fine has pointed out, his critique, when applied to the work of Marx, is not totally persuasive.[11] Foucault himself is aware of the problems involved in his conflation of Marx and Marxism and in the hasty skirting of Marx's notion of the function of power within the sphere of political economy. Thus in his critique of economic functionalism he implies a tacit distinction between Marx and "certain conceptions currently held to be Marxist," but he never returns to examine explicitly what lies behind the current and, by implication, mistaken notions. More importantly, Foucault acknowledges that one might better understand the structuration and the function of the body and subject if they are examined in the complex intersection between the realms of political economy and discursive practices (the distinction between these two realms to be understood purely as a provisional one that facilitates analysis):

> This political investment of the body is bound up, in accordance with complex reciprocal relations, with its economic use; it is largely as a force of production that the body is invested with relations of power and domination; but, on the other in hand, its constitution as labour power is possible only if it is caught up in a system of subjection (in which need is also a political instrument meticulously prepared, calculated and used); the body becomes a useful force only if it is both a productive body and a subjected body. (Foucault, Michel. *Discipline and Punish*. New York: Pantheon Books, 1977, pp. 25–26).

Foucault here acknowledges the link between his notion of power and Marx's notion of labor power. But he seems content to rely on an Althusserian position regarding the simultaneity and in some sense the equivalence of the cultural processes of subjection and the economic processes of production and exchange. By thus avoiding the issues of causal relations and priority between labor power and what he quite simply (too simply) calls power, and by confining himself to a relatively simple notion of "exchange," Foucault sidesteps the possibility of articulating a theory or an "analytics" of power based on a more rigorous Marxian description of the processes of labor, production, exchange, and accumulation—in short, on Marx's theory of value.

However, the depth of Foucault's disavowal of the entire analytic apparatus that Marx uses to articulate his theory of value is most thoroughly revealed in a juxtaposition of the two poles, the negative and the positive, of Foucault's various statements defining power. At the negative end, power, according to Foucault, is not a "commodity." At the positive end, in Foucault's most definitive, and yet most abstract and totalizing statement, power is defined as "action": "A set of actions upon other actions" (Dreyfus and Rabinow, 220). As I will elaborate, in its abstraction this definition of action as the basis of power can be read as a variation on Marx's definition of labor as the basis of value. For Marx the analysis of political economy dialectically oscillates through various categories between commodity and labor; for Foucault the analysis of the "economy of power" oscillates between "non-commodity" and action. The parameters of the analysis are identical in both cases, except for the difference over "commodity," which is really only an apparent one and which, in revealing Foucault's misunderstanding, demonstrates the depth of the anxiety behind his disavowal.

The context in which Foucault uses the term commodity to define power negatively shows a metonymic displacement characteristic of repression/disavowal. In the earlier passage in which Foucault links the liberal conception of power with the Marxist version through the economism that is common to both, he uses the term "commodity" (along with the terminology of "contracts") to describe the liberal view, without, however, commenting in any way on what this category may mean within the Marxian framework. This slippage—inattention or oversight—is remarkable, particularly in view of his insistence that power is constituted *only* in the processes of social "exchange," since these are also the processes that Marx identifies as being absolutely fundamental for the constitution of "commodities." In other words, Foucault can only use the term "commodity" in the manner he does if he ignores the Marxian definition and means by "commodity" a "natural" (i.e., entirely nonsocial) or a totally reified object: that is, not constituted by and subsequently modified in the process of exchange and circulation or an object that does not constitute and modify (i.e., function) the subjects who are the agents of exchange and circulation. To the extent that the processes of exchange constitute the commodity as a form and simultaneously constitute both the value of the object exchanged and the agent of exchange—for labor, and hence the individual agent of labor, too, becomes a commodity in the circuit of exchange—commodity is exactly a form that mediates social relations of power, albeit economic power. It is precisely through such a dual process of constitution that Foucault defines the functioning of power. Power, accordingly, is employed and exercised through netlike organization: " And not only do individuals circulate between its threads; they are always in the position of simultaneously undergoing and exercising this power. They are not only its inert or consenting targets; they are always also the elements of its articulation" (PK, 98). It would appear that Foucault *seems* to ignore not only Marx's definition of commodity but also his theorization of exchange and value. The latter is definable and can manifest itself only through the production and exchange of commodities, in other words, through mundane social relations, through the microphysics of a political economy, just as power, according to Foucault, can also manifest itself ultimately only through specific and mundane social relations.

A closer scrutiny of the function of commodity and exchange within the Marxian description of the relations of production can clarify its similarity to Foucault's description of the relations of power and, indeed, render the latter more complex and discriminating. Commodities are, in the first place, the form products take only when they are involved in social exchange, much as power constitutes and manifests itself only in exchange. As Marx put it, "Whoever directly satisfies his wants with the produce of his own labour, creates, indeed, use-values, but not commodities. In order to produce the latter, he must not only produce use-values, but use-values for others, social use-values" (C, 1, 40–41). Secondly, commodities are the crystallizations of values:

> Commodities come into the world in the shape of use-values, articles,
> or goods.... They are, however, commodities only because they are
> something two-fold, both objects of utility, and, at the same time, depos-
> itories of value. They manifest themselves therefore as commodities or
> have the form of commodities, only in so far as they have two forms, a
> physical or natural form, and a value-form. (C, 1,47)

As depositories of value, they are also the bearers of whatever power relations
have been invested in their production and exchange. And, finally, the value or
the power that is crystallized or constituted in the commodity form can "manifest itself or be expressed" only through the *form* of exchange-value (C, 1, 38).
Value, like power, constitutes itself only through the processes of production
and exchange.

Because Marx's theory of commodity expresses the fundamental categories
within which the entire capitalist mode of production—and the categories
used to understand social/power relations within that world (capital, the commodity, money, purchase, sale, and various subsidiary forms of value)—can
be described and analyzed, Foucault's rejection of power-as-commodity
amounts to a refusal to acknowledge the utility and value ("use" *and*
"exchange" values) of Marxian analysis. But if commodity is seen as bearer
and crystallization of power relation, then the entire analysis of value can be
seen as a mapping of power relations. This is particularly so when Marx's definition of labor is taken into account. As I will elaborate, because Marx's
analysis of commodity constitutes the basis for the theory of abstract labor—
and in particular of the fact that labor appears on the market as commodity
even though labor power is not produced as commodity, nor does its value
arise directly from the labor expended in producing it—his investigation of
labor also elucidates the positive pole of Foucault's definition of power as
activity that affects the activity of others.

Perhaps what Foucault had in mind, in avoiding the concept of commodity
for the definition of power, is the form of commodity that has been thoroughly "fetishized"—that is, the products of human labor that are only com-
prehended as an independent and uncontrolled reality apart from the people
who have created them—or reified—that is, products that are seen as bearers not of social (power) relations but of relations between things. However,
even if Foucault's intention is to disabuse us from perceiving power in these
fetishized or reified forms, a closer examination of Marxian theorization of

these phenomena would produce greater clarity. For Marx the "appearances" produced by fetishism and reification are not entirely false: they exist in reality but conceal another feature of that relationship, namely the direct social relations between producers; "the relations connecting the labour of one individual with that of the rest appear, not as direct social relation between individuals at work, *but as what they really are*, material relations between persons and social relations between things" (C, 1, 73). If commodity fetishism and reification produce this "inversion" in mundane human perception under capitalist (i.e., modern in Foucaultian terms) relations of production, then we need to consider how such an inversion is itself further involved in the production of power/value. This inversion can be seen as one that induces the modern subject to "invest" social relations in object relations, and the investment can in turn be understood as a form of the crystallization of power relations in a society whose political economy is defined by the production and exchange of commodities. Thus reification and fetishism are not, as popular interpretations of Marx would have it, just forms of alienation, ones that rob people of their "natural liberty" or "truth," but are also *productive*: they produce a certain type of behavior by encouraging further consumption and production; the greater the sense of alienation from other people, the greater the tendency to fill the lack with commodities that are in fact inverted condensations of social relations.

The increasing acquisition and consumption of commodities then come to be defined as a form of power that in turn plays a central role in the constitution of modern subjectivity. These forms of alienation can thus be understood as a part of the "disciplinary" mechanism of capitalist political economy, productive of modern subjectivity that is indeed encouraged to see and consume social relations/relations of power in the form of commodities: the comodification of power relations is one of the forms through which the modern subject is "governed" and "governs itself," and such conduct can be understood as *"empowering"* for the subject within capitalism, that is, as furnishing the terms according to which the subject can constitute itself within the capitalist regime of truth. Thus the inverted investment of social relations in commodities can be read as a discursive practice that is essential for capitalist relations of production and modern relations of power. If Foucault is truly interested in describing the surfaces of discursive practices, then various forms of power must be seen, at least in part, literally as commodities.

Foucault's most explicit (though not concrete) and positive definition of power also demonstrates an entanglement with Marxian theory. Power, Foucault claims,

> is a total structure of actions brought to bear upon possible actions; it incites, it induces, it seduces, it makes easier or more difficult; in the extreme it constrains or forbids absolutely; it is nevertheless always a way of acting upon an acting subject or acting subjects by virtue of their acting or being capable of action. A set of action upon other actions (Dreyfus and Rabinow, 220).

This most abstract and minimalist definition is elaborated by the double valence of "governmentality" (conduire/se conduire), which then involves a set of distinctions between relations of power as such and other relations that may overlap and merge with power relations but are not in themselves necessary for power relations. Crucial to these distinctions is Foucault's insistence that relations of power are predicated on the recognition of the freedom of other subjects, and that the actions that constitute power be such that they do not totally foreclose the field of possibility for the other. "Power is exercised only over free subjects, and only in so far as they are free. By this we mean individual or collective subjects who are faced with a field of possibilities in which several ways of behaving, several reactions and diverse compartments may be realized."[12] Predicated on the freedom of the subjects involved, power relations do not necessarily entail relations based on violence or consent: neither slavery nor contractual relations in themselves constitute power relations for Foucault.[13]

While the negative pole of Foucault's definition of power attempts to displace the Marxian notion of commodity, the positive pole appropriates, without acknowledging it, the foundation of Marxian theory of value. Just as activity and freedom are central to Foucault's description and definition of power, so labor and freedom are equally central to Marx's description and definition of value. Labor-power, for Marx, much like power for Foucault, "becomes a reality only by its exercise; it sets itself in action only by working" (C, 1, 171). Once one moves beyond the hypothetical moment of "primitive" production—the unskilled gathering of food for the purposes of subsistence—that is, once either a division of labor or an accumulation and dissemination of productive skills is introduced in human society, the activity of labor becomes a form of action that necessarily impinges on the activity of other acting subjects. Not only is labor-power a perfect instance of Foucault's notion of power, but the manifestation of labor-power in the modern/capitalist political economy, which is properly speaking the moment at which labor-power comes into being as a commodity, is predicated just as much on the freedom of the subjects involved as is Foucault's power. Suffice it to cite Marx's well-known statement on this topic:

> [The market where the sale and purchase of labour-power goes on] is in fact a very Eden of the innate rights of man. There alone rule Freedom, Equality, Property, and Bentham. Freedom, because both buyer and seller of a commodity, say labour-power, are constrained only by their free will. They contract as free agents, and the agreement they come to, is but the form in which they give legal expression to their common will. (C. 1, 176)

Marx goes on in this sarcastic fashion to show that each individual subject in the market engages in such trade because he gains something from it, that this form of exchange in fact gives each party some form of "power." Of course, precisely how this power can be theorized in terms of a substance-appearance binary still remains an open question.

Like Foucault, Marx understands that the subject is both the effect and the vehicle of power. In the first place the freedom of the laborer, the agent of Foucault's activity, consists of a complex tension between freedom and necessity: for conversion of his money into capital, the owner of the money "must meet in the market with the free labourer, free in the double sense, that as a free man he can dispense of his labour-power as his own commodity, and that on the other hand he has no other commodity for sale, is short of everything necessary for the realization of his labour-power" (C. 1, 169). More crucially, it is absolutely necessary that this freedom be perceived as such in order for capitalism and the commodity structure of production to develop:

> The historical conditions of [capitalism's] existence are by no means given with the mere circulation of money and commodities. It can spring into life, only when the owner of the means of production and subsistence meets in the market with the *free* labourer selling his labour-power. And this one historical condition comprises a world's history. Capital, therefore, announces from its first appearance a new epoch in the process of social production. (C, 1, 170)

Marx goes on to add in a footnote that the "capitalist epoch is therefore characterised by this, that labour-power takes in the eyes of the labourer himself the form of commodity which is his property; his labour consequently becomes wage-labour. On the other hand, it is only from this moment that the product of labour universally becomes a commodity." Thus the commodity, which, through the processes of exchange, becomes an object-ification, a bearer of social relations, is as much an index of power as is the activity that constitutes labor. It is indeed on the two poles of commodity and labor that Marx builds his theory of value, and in a moment I will propose a synthesis in which the equivalents of the mediating categories he develops and employs in articulating his theory can be used to further articulate Foucault's theory of power.

III

First, however, in order to complete this cross reading of Marx and Foucault and further articulate the isomorphism between the theories of the two, it is necessary to trace the structural homology between the Marxian and Foucaultian corpus that lies in their fundamental hermeneutic procedures. In spite of Foucault's insistence that his work describes discursive formations that are not hidden but always already on the surface, in other words, in spite of his attempt to eschew the depth model of analysis, his analytics of discursive formations cannot avoid articulating the latter in terms of vertical spatiality. For instance, in *Discipline and Punish* Foucault claims that he does not wish to explore the processes of the formally egalitarian parliamentary democracies through which the bourgeoisie came to power in the eighteenth century because these processes constitute a mask for other disciplinary practices that ensured their hegemony. Instead, he wishes to explore "the development and generalization of disciplinary mechanisms [which] constituted *the other, dark side* of these processes" (*Discipline and Punish*, 222, emphasis added). Foucault's terminology, "the other, dark side," attempts to represent spatial relation between the democratic structures and the disciplinary mechanism in horizontal rather than vertical terms, but this does not avoid the problem because any object with two sides implies a space in between that constitutes a depth, however shallow. In fairness to Foucault it must be said that he does succeed in avoiding the allegorical reductions that haunt the depth models of Nietzsche, Marx, and Freud. But, as he himself

implies, we are all still caught up in the fundamental hermeneutics procedures that these three individuals inaugurated.[14]

The Marxian project too was motivated by the desire to define the underlying complexity of a surface political economy, just as the Foucaultian project
seeks to map the underlying political economy of discursive formations. As
Bob Fine put it, Marx's method can be seen by drawing an analogy with his
critique of the economic forms of value or capital; in each case, what appears
on the surface is the process of 'personification,' that is, the manner in which
value and capital impose their laws on the 'bearers' of these relations. What
remains concealed from view (and what Marx seeks to reveal) is the reverse
process: namely the reification of social relations into the form of value and
capital. (Fine, 80)

Similarly, he argues, Foucault's description and theory of power attempt to
show that what he calls the crystallized forms of power, e.g. juridical structures, are reified forms that mask the microphysics of power, which are formed
by and manifested In more mundane social relations. In short, what Marx
attempted to do in the realm of political economy, Foucault attempted to do in
the realm of discursive formations.

At a more specific level, the isomorphism between the procedures of
Foucault and Marx is particularly striking when one begins to compare the
former's methodological precautions with the latter's strategies. As one moves
back and forth with Marx through the dialectical procedures that he uses to
trace the complex nexus of relations that form value (working from commodity, through the binary oppositions of use and exchange values, the relative and equivalent values, the total or expanded form of value, to the general
form of value and the universal equivalent), and then as one reads Foucault's
precautions for the analysis of power, the strategies employed by the two men
begin to reveal some fascinating similarities. The isomorphism cannot be
explored in complete detail here, but the salient features must be outlined.

According to Foucault's first precaution, one should focus on how "power
[operates] at its extremities. In its ultimate destination, with those points
where it becomes capillary . . . one should try to locate power at the extreme
points of its exercise, where it is always less legal in character" (PK, 96–97).
If one were to treat Marx as a student of Foucault and to examine his procedures, the former would indeed qualify as a faithful disciple of the latter. For
instance, Marx insists on commencing his analysis of the entire capitalist polit-

ical economy by investigating the commodity, which must be understood not as random and heterogeneous objects, but as a social form. And surely, if his analysis has any validity at all, it should establish quite persuasively that the commodity is indeed the capillary point of that political economy. In other words, a plethora of complex social, economic, and political *relationships* manifest themselves in mundane practices in the form of the commodity, which is fundamentally defined by relations of exchange. The exchange of commodities is in a sense the "ultimate destination" of the capitalist political economy, and it is not governed by a juridical apparatus.

According to the second precaution, instead of inquiring into the intentions of those who are thought to possess power, one should study "power at the point where its intention, if it has one, is completely invested in its real and effective practices" (PK, 97). Even though Marx, permitting his imagination to run free in a rather Dickensian manner, is fond of personifying various agents in the capitalist drama and habitually speculates about the intentions of the capitalist, he never tires of saying in response to his critics that his analyses begin with real and effective practices as these are crystallized in the commodity form. His claims about the intentions of various individual and collective agents are anthropomorphic projections based on his analysis of the intentions manifested in the real and effective economic practices of production and exchange at the capillary level.

According to the fourth precaution, "One must conduct an *ascending* analysis of power, starting, that is, from its infinitesimal mechanisms, which each have their own history, their own trajectory, their own techniques and tactics, and then see how these mechanisms of power have been—and continue to be—invested, colonized, utilised, involuted, transformed, displaced, extended, etc., by ever more general mechanisms and by forms of global domination" (PK, 98–99). Again, Marx seems to have taken Foucault quite seriously, for he begins his analysis with the mundane processes of exchange of objects, defines the form taken by the exchange of these objects, and then gradually builds up his analysis to include the complicated procedures and forms that eventually lead to an understanding of the function and power of capital, and then, finally, to an analysis of different historical modes of production. Examples of Marx's practice of examining the intentions that are manifest "in real and effective practices" and of conducting an ascending analysis of power abound in his work. His analyses of the "working day," chapters X and XVII in the first volume of *Capital*, furnish excellent examples of how Foucault's second and fourth precautions can be put into practice.

Finally, as is well known, Foucault insists, in his third precaution and in other essays, that "Power must be analyzed as something that circulates, or rather as something which only functions in the form of a chain. It is never localized here or there, never in anybody's hands, never appropriated as a commodity or piece of wealth" (PK, 98). Again, the Marxian procedure is faithful. The commodity is for Marx a form that is determined precisely by the market processes of exchange and circulation. Just as Foucault arrives at the definition of power by investigating mundane discursive practices, so Marx arrives at his definition of value (and his labor theory of value) by scrutinizing mundane economic practices involved in production and exchange.

The isomorphism of these procedures used by Marx and Foucault yields, not surprisingly, results that are remarkably similar: neither power nor value can exist outside the circuit of exchange; neither can be possessed or stored outside the circuit; power and value are both dynamic, transformative matrices that simultaneously constitute individuals and make them their vehicles and that constrain and empower individuals. However, there is one major difference between the two theories that I will elaborate later at greater length: for Marx, value can indeed be accumulated and can exist as a "possession"-within-the-circuit, whereas Foucault simply contends that power can never be possessed, without articulating what happens to the power that is generated by exchange.

If we set aside Foucault's disavowal of Marx and see him as someone whose work follows rather than precedes Marx's, then we can better appreciate some of the limitations of his theorization of power. For Instance, as Bob Fine has pointed out, "Foucault's location of the fundamental contradiction behind bourgeois power as resting in the opposition *between* discipline and legality, rather than (as was the case with Marx) *within* each modality, gives rise to a formalistic conception of legality (Fine, 83–84). That is, Foucault does not explore the contradictions within legality and thus does not address the inequality that provides the *content* of equal rights. So anxious is Foucault to eschew the juridical model that he tends to reify the entire juridical process. Thus he does not tire of repeating that power is not to be defined on the model of the "contract." Yet if we take seriously Foucault's own reversal of the Clausewitz axiom—power, says Foucault, is war carried on by other means—then it is possible to argue that a contract is also war carried on by other means, or, more precisely, that a contract merely marks a hiatus, a temporary truce, in the perpetual struggle of power, that a contract is always temporary, valid only until one party needs to negate or to renegotiate it.[15] Much the same can be said for Foucault's rather hasty disclaimer about "territory" or even "wealth."

IV

Finally, in order to complete this homology between the Foucauldian and Marxian articulations, we need to compare the concepts of power and value as such. A juxtaposition of the similarities and differences between these two concepts should be useful in revealing the limitations of Foucault's ultimately rather vague theorization of power and, more importantly, in suggesting strategies for articulating power more precisely so that its potential usefulness can be realized.

Foucault insists that power as such does not exist outside the circuit of social interaction: "something called Power, with or without a capital letter, which is assumed to exist universally in a concentrated or diffused form, does not exist" (Dreyfus and Rabinow, 219). However, as I have argued elsewhere,[16] Foucault's tendency to bracket his circuit of exchange at both the macro and micro ends—at the macro level, he is content to characterize institutional apparatuses as only the "terminal" forms of power, and at the micro level, he defines power as that which can never be possessed but only exercised—seems to be a necessary closure, a blindness that enables him to demonstrate brilliantly how power functions in the circuit of discursive exchange. Now, for Marx too value cannot exist outside the circuit of production, exchange, and consumption. In contrast to Foucault, Marx takes great pains to articulate the operation of the entire circuit and, more importantly for this comparison, carefully dissects value in order to show how its different components are generated by and interact in the processes of production and exchange.[17]

At first glance, particularly, given a certain popular conception of Marx's definition of value (which would seem to be Foucault's model), the definitions of power and value appear to be exactly homologous. In its reduced form the homology could be stated as follows:

actions that act on the actions of others = power

labor = value

Such an equation becomes more appreciable if we keep in mind that labor, as I have already mentioned, is always (beyond the point of so-called primitive production) an activity that acts on the activity of others in that whatever tools, skills, resources, and so on are used in the act of labor/production are always already the manifestations of the activity of others. A given moment of labor is thus one moment in a cycle of activities that act on the actions of others. It would seem, then, that Foucault's definition of power is identical to Marx's definition of value.

However, as I. I. Rubin so carefully demonstrates, the above definition of Marx's analysis of value (i.e., that labor = value) is too simple and misleading:[18] Value is not simply labor or "activity-in-circuit." In order to do justice to its complexity, Marx breaks down the concept of value into three components: the substance or content of value, which is labor; the magnitude of value, which is labor-time; and the form of value, which is exchangeability as such.[19] This distinction between content and form of value permits Marx to articulate value as a relational concept, which Rubin sums up as follows:

> Now when we have considered value in terms of content and form, we relate value with the concept that precedes it, abstract labor (and in the last analysis with the material process of production), the content. On the other hand, through the form of value we have already connected value with the concept which follows it, exchange value. In fact, once we have determined that value does not represent labor in general, but labor that has the "form of exchangeability" of a product, then we must pass from value directly to exchange value. In this way, the concept of value is seen to be inseparable from the concept of labor on the one hand, and from the concept of exchange value on the other. (Rubin, 122–123)[20]

Thus value is constituted by two poles that mark the relationship: the "internal" moment of production and the "external" moment of exchange. Variation in either of these moments will cause value to fluctuate, so that either improvement in productivity or changes in the "relations of exchange" with other commodities will alter the relative value of a given commodity. As a relational concept, value is also determined by the interaction of two subcategories: relative value and equivalent value, which are hypothetical moments in the conceptual articulation of value and which in practice are obviated by the prior existence of the general equivalent of value, which rapidly mediates between the two.

If labor, as the content of value, is to be defined as activity acting on the action of others, then the differential "production" or generation of another facet of value, namely surplus value, also needs to be examined. Within the Marxian framework surplus value is produced by the difference between the cost of labor-power and the value generated by that labor which, in successful enterprises, usually exceeds its cost. It is precisely the eventual conversion of this surplus value into capital that allows the capitalist then to "act" (again) by buying more "labor-power," that is, to buy the activity of the laborer in order eventually to produce more surplus value, and so on. Thus the relation between capital and labor becomes the primary, indeed *the* paradigmatic, instance, within the realm of political economy, of Foucault's definition of power. And yet he ignores it, or at least seems to.

The point of this brief excursion on value is not only to emphasize that Marx's mapping of the specificity of the processes and forms involved in the generation of value in the circuits of production and exchange is far more complex than Foucault's similar mapping of power, but also to suggest that had Foucault been able to avoid his anxiety and appropriate Marxian analysis more consciously, deliberately, and explicitly, he would have been able to theorize power in a more systematic manner. The homology between the two political economies can be fruitfully extended by the following kinds of questions. If power is constituted by "activity-in-exchange," then the precise and intermediate steps and forms that define "relations of power" need to be mapped. What, for instance, in a given social relation that produces power, constitutes "relative power" in contrast to "equivalent power"? Or, if power is "produced" by "relations of exchange," then how are we to distinguish the internal moment of production from the external moment of exchange? To the extent that power generates itself because "it incites, it induces, it seduces, it makes easier or more difficult...etc.," how does the variability in the "seduceability" (or, alternately, the "resistance") of a given subject that is the locus of a given instance of power relation affect the magnitude of power generated, in contrast to the variable value of similarly generated power effects in discursive practices that are contiguous, and hence determine to some extent the exchangeability, or value, of the initial power effect?

Answers to questions such as these, it seems to me, can be best approached through a thorough appreciation of Marx's definition of value. A clear articulation of the social form of value (i.e. of value-as-form) permitted Marx to complete the Möbiuslike circuit of his analysis of production and exchange (a completion in which the structure of Marx's logic repeated the circuit of the political economy). In a very specific sense, the social form of value is reified labor, that is, labor that has been "reduced" to a commodity (which is the point at which Marx begins his analysis). Rubin again provides a succinct articulation of this relation:

> The product of labor is "reified," it acquires the "form of value," i.e., the form of property attached to things and which seems to belong to the things themselves. This "reified" labor (and not social labor as such) is precisely what represents value. This is what we have in mind when we say that value already includes within itself the social 'form of value.' (Rubin, 115)

Given the linkage in Marxian analysis between the complex social and categorical relations that are used to define value and the clear and convincing identification of its social form, one is led to ask what is/are the social form/s of power. Foucault does, of course, make large distinctions in the forms of power, thus providing us with the fundamental distinction between traditional and disciplinary forms of power. But these are analogous, indeed parallel, to Marxian distinctions between different modes of production. The question still remains: Within the disciplinary mode of power, for instance, what is the social form taken by power? What is the equivalent of reified labor (i.e., that which manifests itself as commodity) in Foucault's field of power? How does power, generated by social exchange with the discursive practices functioned by a given regime of truth, manifest or register itself in social practice? Without a more rigorous definition, power remains a relatively vague category, useful for criticism that wants to be progressive but that in effect eschews the political dimension of power.

While the isomorphism between the theories of power and value that I have been articulating in this essay is designed to suggest that a synthesis between them would result in a formulation that can be more productive than either theory functioning alone, a suturing of the two cannot be undertaken in the space available here. Nevertheless, it may be useful to provide a sketch of the possibilities. It seems to me useful to begin by supplementing Foucault's suture of "power/knowledge," with a more complex Marxian/Foucauldian suture of "value/power/knowledge," wherein power would be understood as being determined and functioned by value on the one hand and knowledge on the other, much as Marx's definition of value is determined and functioned by labor on the one hand and exchangability on the other.[21] The connections between these three elements must be understood as being essentially similar to the link between power and knowledge as defined by Foucault: "Between techniques of knowledge and strategies of power, there is no exteriority, even if they have specific roles and are linked together on the basis of their differences" (PK, 98). As Rubin takes great pain to demonstrate, in the Marxian analysis of value there is also no exteriority between labor, value, and exchangeability. Value and power seem to demand fusion primarily because separately or together they constitute a fundamental "matrix of transformation."

While the full implications of such a synthesis remain to be worked out, it may be useful to provide a few significant illustrations. The isomorphism between the two political economies raises questions about the possible homology between the production of "surplus value" and that of "surplus power." What, in the realm of discursive practices, are the equivalents of the differential between the cost of labor-power and the value produced by that labor? Foucault acknowledges but refuses to develop further this homology or, more specifically, the structural similarity that underlies the intentional logic of political economy and discursive practices of the same period. An important component of the "genius of the bourgeoisie," he admits, "is precisely the fact of its managing to construct machines of power allowing circuits of profit, which in turn re-enforced and modified the power apparatuses in a mobile and circular manner.... The power of the bourgeoisie is self-amplifying, in a mode not of conservation but of successive transformation" (PK, 161).[22] Thus Foucault here assumes what Marx is very clearly aware of and what Marx therefore privileges: that the respective economies they are investigating are structured by logics of accumulative desire. Thus where Marx is anxious to demonstrate precisely how accumulation takes place, Foucault once again shies away from the logic of his own analysis and theory and fails to articulate the forms and processes through which surplus power is identified, siphoned off, accumulated, and reinvested in the further production of power.

Indeed, more often than not, in the anxiety of his disavowal he tends to contradict this logic by claiming that various political formations—the state, the juridical apparatus, "social hegemonies"—"are *only* the *terminal* forms power takes" (Foucault, Michel. *The History of Sexuality.* New York: Random House, 1978, pp. 92, 93 emphasis added). But in fact these crystallized political forms are no more "terminal" than is capital. Surely, in modern/capitalist society the primary function of these "terminal" forms is precisely to reinvest the material/symbolic capital/power that they have accumulated. Foucault's historical studies do in fact examine the entire circuit, but in theorizing power he tends to avoid these logical conclusions.

While the political economy of the accumulation of power at the macro level of the formation of various institutions, class struggles, and state apparatuses has received some attention from a Marxian viewpoint, the accumulation of power at the micro level of the individual subject needs some comment, particularly because it is at this capillary level that Foucault's theory of power seems weakest and could most benefit from the kind of synthesis proposed above. The problems with the Foucaultian formulation of power at this level, i.e., that power can only be "exercised," never "possessed," become readily apparent once the temporal structures of exercise and possession as well as of subjectivity as such are probed. Exercise and possession, as activities, can be characterized by relatively long or short durations: the ability to exercise power can endure over a long period of time, for decades and—in terms of group authority, rights, and so on—for centuries; conversely, possession can be fleeting. How is one to distinguish power that is exercised over a long duration from that which is possessed? The problem, it must be emphasized, is not simply a product of terminological ambiguity. The temporal structure of subjectivity implicit in Foucaultian epistemology and ontology creates insurmountable problems for his theory of power. The assumption of a radically decentered subject, particularly one that possesses no *diachronic* identity or coherence, seems entirely unfeasible within the Foucaultian structure: discursive practices can only form and deploy subjects in the manner that they are supposed to if they function the latter through some form of mnemonic continuity; without the assumption of mnemonic continuity, discursive practices cannot have their supposed effects.

Similarly, the agency of a subject must endure beyond a given moment for it to be meaningful. In short, empirically and theoretically, the subject endures.

And if it endures and is involved in social exchange over a period of time, then the subject must have some form of "control" over its actions, which in turn implies some form of "(self-)possession" over its ability to act, and because action is central to Foucault's definition of power the subject must be capable of possessing power in order to be a subject. Discursive practices cannot empower subjects if they cannot permit the latter to possess some aspect of that power. This is particularly the case if, as Foucault insists, the subject's engagement in relations of power is predicated on its freedom. In short, within the logic of Foucaultian epistemology and ontology the relationship between power and the subject is not contingent but structural: the subject is constituted by power relations, and if the subject is free, its freedom cannot be divorced from its ability to possess its freedom as a form of power.

This apparent contradiction or opposition between the exercise and the possession of power can be "overcome" through the synthesis of power and value. If power can only be exercised and is not possessable, then the question arises whether or not power is totally "expended" in the process of exchange. If so, then the subject is left powerless, which is a proposition that Foucault would not accept. If power is not totally expended, then it is possible some power is retained in the process of exchange. Indeed, like capital, power seeks to reproduce and augment itself in the processes of expenditure and exchange. To the extent that power reproduces itself in this manner, it can do so only by generating sufficient surplus power so that the subject remains empowered while the circuit of exchange siphons off the surplus. Gayatri C. Spivak's elaboration of "labor-power" as the materialist predication of the subject underscores this point: "It is in the full account of value-formation that the textuality of Marx's argument…and the place of use value is demonstrated, and the predication of the subject as labor-power *(irreducible structural super-adequation—the subject defined by its capacity to produce more than itself)* shows its importance."[23] It is the emergence of this structural superadequation of the subject that enables the development of an economy that can appropriate the subject's production of surplus, of the value/power that is "more than itself" while "permitting" the subject to "retain" sufficient value/power so that it can continue being "itself."

A fusion of value and power allows us to rearticulate more precisely Foucault's description of the dual function of the subject in the circuit of power generated by discursive practices. As I have already mentioned, individual subjects for Foucault "are always in the position of simultaneously undergoing and exercising this power;" they are not only its "inert or consenting targets" but also "elements of its articulation" or vehicles of power (PK, 98). This description of the dual function of the individual's relation to power seems perfectly accurate and acceptable; the problem, however, remains with the ambiguity regarding the simultaneity of the individual functioning as a "target" and a "vehicle." What, more precisely, is the nature of the relation between the individual as the object of power and its simultaneous subject? Through what mechanisms are given discursive formations able to function the individual simultaneously as object and subject? It seems to me that the Marxian distinctions between use value and exchange value as well as those between the cost of labor-power and the value extracted from that labor can clarify the economy that simultaneously functions the subject in two forms. Accordingly, from a structural viewpoint, discursive practices can be seen as forming or constructing individuals as their objects within a given regime of truth and thereby deriving "use value" from their formation, or, rather, from functioning them in the "form" of use value. However, these processes of formation also empower them as subjects, as agents of action or as vehicles of a further turn in the circuit of exchange, thereby functioning them in the form of exchange value in the same regime of truth. From the individual subject's viewpoint, a discursive formation "permits" him/her to function in the form of exchange value in the external moment of exchange in return for his/her "willingness" to function in the form of use value in the internal moment. This formulation, however, immediately demands a dual qualification. First, value/power can be possessed, and paradoxically even accumulated, within this system only in the form of exchangeability. Second, as both Marx and Foucault would agree in their different ways, neither the intentionalities of the ideogical or discursive systems nor those of the individual or collective subjects need manifest themselves as conscious or contractual agreements. What can be mapped *ex post facto* as "contractual agreements" are in fact part of the structural constitution of the subject in the capitalist/modern regime of truth.

The clearest example of such a relation within Marxian analysis is the one that he deliberately privileges: that between capital and labor. In exchange for the cost of his labor-power, a laborer sells his labor for its use value to the owner of capital, who then transforms the value of the product of that labor into exchange value; then from the differential between the cost of that labor-power and the value of the product he extracts surplus value, which then gets reinvested via capital. From the viewpoint of the laborer, the wages s/he receives for her/his "use" value must be immediately utilized for their "exchange" value, which then permits her/him to acquire commodities for their use value. The dual functioning of the individual as object and subject operates simultaneously by "negatively" limiting him/her, that is, by the particular way in which it forms and "uses" him/her, and positively empowering him/her, that is, opening up a diverse field of possibilities, a field of exchange, for the subject. Within the utopian Marxian-Hegelian vision, this field of possibilities is formulated as the assurance that the laborer-slave shall inherit the earth, with all the plenitude implied therein, and which in turn is reformulated in the Nietzschean-Foucaultian vision as an element in a discursive formation designed to redefine the circuit of power.

V

Of the many consequences of the above remarks on the isomorphism of value and power as well as of my attempt to combine the two, I can take up only two significant moments: one that marks a conjunction in need of further articulation and another that marks a disjunction produced precisely from an unwillingness to articulate the conjunction.

As Spivak notes in her article on value, the moment in which capital fully develops "entails the *historical* possibility of the definitive predication of the subject as labor-power. Indeed, it is possible to suggest that the 'freeing' of labor-power may be a description of the social possibility of this predication. Here the subject is predicated as structurally superadequate to itself, definitively productive of surplus-labor over necessary labor" (Spivak, p. 161). This moment coincides with the emergence of what Foucault defines as the disciplinary mode of power, a mode that is also implicitly predicated on the superadequation of the subject as a source of power. The system of value and that of power both constitute transformative matrices capable of generating and deploying enormous quantities of value/power. It is inadequate to articulate the historical emergence of these systems either in terms of a temporal "coincidence" or even in terms of related but temporally discontinuous series of epistemic ruptures. The effectivities that link the emergence of capital with that of the disciplinary mode of power within an overall structural totality need further definition. The above remarks on value and power constitute a small contribution to an articulation of this conjunction.

Foucault's flirtation with and refusal to elaborate the conjunction and the structural relations between value and power, which must be treated here as symptomatic, then constitute the moment of disjunction. This moment, too, cannot be considered here in great detail. However, I would like to end with a few remarks on Foucault's disavowal. In the first place, a romantic, individualistic reading of this disavowal as an Oedipal drama between Foucault and Marx is not likely to be productive in the long run. It is not Foucault's anxiety about acknowledging the influence of Marx that is of interest, though it must be noted that the official Marx may have been so contaminated for Foucault by the PCF and the Lysenko affair that he had to distance himself from all of that in order not to be swallowed by a metaphysical Marxist model that posits a privileged access to truth.

It is far more interesting to read Foucault's disavowal as a symptom of a *political* unconscious formation, that is, as a signifier of a "culturalist" tendency in Western progressive thinking. Such culturalism—of which Foucault's disavowal is a product that then becomes a source further augmenting it—functions by simultaneously acknowledging the determining power of political economy and refusing its efficacy by postponing it. The disavowal typical of such culturalism operates by a mechanism that, ostensibly temporary but in effect permanent, consigns the force of political economy to the category of "determinant in the last instance." However, unlike the Althusserian model, which requires that the determining relations be mapped in terms of complex structural effectivity, in the culturalist model "last" ends up being read in terms of an infinite temporal postponement or deferral. This mechanism then permits, according to the economy of disavowal, the determining intensity of the economic to be displaced onto the efficacy of cultural determination. As Fredric Jameson has argued, for Marxism "the categories of power are not the ultimate ones, and the trajectory of contemporary social theory (from Weber to Foucault) suggests that the appeal to it is often strategic and involves a systematic displacement of the Marxian problematic."[24] Within such a process of displacement structure, Foucault's disavowal takes the form of an unconscious acceptance of Marx's work, which is then masked by a conscious denial. And the conscious denial then prevents him from explicitly linking power and value. His avoidance of the materialist predication of the subject leads to a rather vague theory of power, against which one must insist, as Jameson puts it, that "the ultimate form of the 'nightmare of history' [is not the deployment of power but] rather the fact of labor itself, and the intolerable spectacle of the backbreaking millennial toil of millions of people from the earliest moment of human history."[25]

notes

I would like to thank Mitch Breitweiser, Fred Dolan, Jim Merod, and Paul Thomas for their comments on earlier drafts of this essay. Their suggestions have been most helpful. As usual, all inadequacies are mine. I would also like to thank Alisa Colloms, Yufi Hauswald, Jenny Kim, and Jin Park for their research assistance.

1. A more dramatic instance of Foucault's hesitation and anxiety in coming to terms with Marxian thought is evident in "The Eye of Power," where he avoids direct engagement with questions about "labor" and "production." Michel Foucault, *Power/Knowledge* (NY: Random House, 1980) See particularly pp. 160–61. Further references to this work appear in the text as "PK."

2. The tension between the thought of Marx and Foucault has been the object of abundant critical commentary, which cannot be evaluated here. Suffice it to mention the most notable instances: Mark Poster's sympathetic and cogent *Foucault, Marxism and History* (Cambridge: Polity Press, 1984); and Etienne Balibar's dramatic claims about the progressive influence of Marx on Foucault's entire *oeuvre*, "Foucault and Marx: The Question of Nominalism," in *Michel Foucault: Philosopher*, ed. Timothy Armstrong (New York: Routledge, 1992), pp. 38–57).

3. In the strongest of such claims about Marx's influence on Foucault, Balibar hypothesizes that "in ways that were constantly changing, the whole of Foucault's work can be seen in terms of a genuine struggle with Marx, and that this can be viewed as one of the driving forces of his productiveness." Based on his analysis of the Marxian influence on *History of Sexuality*, Balibar argues that Marx's influence accounts for the unity of Foucault's research and for the "strategic complexity" in the relationship according to which "a movement is made (in Foucault's work) from a *break* to a tactical *alliance*, the first involving a

global *critique* of Marxism as a theory; the second a partial *usage* of Marxist tenets or affirmations compatible with Marxism. One might suggest that the latter becomes at the same time more and more limited and more and more specifically Marxist. Thus, in contradictory fashion, the opposition to Marxist 'theory' grows deeper and deeper while the convergence of the analyses and concepts taken from Marx become more and more significant." Balibar, "Foucault and Marx," pp. 39 and 53.

Balibar's suggestion that Marx's influence on Foucault be investigated in the diachronic structure of the latter's work may well yield fascinating results. However, this chapter is less concerned with developmental issues than with a synchronic cross-reading.

4. Poster, however, is inclined to ascribe the discontinuities in Foucault's historical works to a Nietzschean influence. See particularly *Foucault, Marxism and History*, pp. 70–94 and 148.

5. Foucault's selective use of phenomenological method and his complex and ambiguous relation to the work of Husserl, particularly to the supposedly humanistic teleology of the latter, demands an entirely different and separate study.

6. See Balibar, "Foucault and Marx," and Gayatri Chakravorty Spivak, "More on Power/Knowledge," *Rethinking Power*, ed. Thomas E. Wartenberg (Albany: SUNY Press, 1992), pp. 149–73. See Louis Althusser and Etienne Balibar, *Reading Capital* (London: Verso, 1979) for Althusser's analysis of the link between the nominalism and the epistemological break that characterize various linked concepts that Marx uses to define value.

7. See, for instance, Jeffrey C. Issac, *Power and Marxist Theory: A Realist View* (Ithaca: Cornell University Press, 1987); and Nicos Poulantzas, *Political Power and Social Classes* (London: New Left Books, 1973) and *Class and Class Structure* (London: New Left Books, 1975).

8. Indeed, it seems to me that Althusser's articulation of the Marxian concepts of "structural totality" and "structural causality" may well have had a salient influence on Foucault's definition of discursive formation. In terms of structuring metaphors, Althusser's emphasis on Marx's attack on a pre-Marxian "anthropological" analysis of political economy is reproduced almost exactly in the Foucaultian opposition between "anthropology" and "archaeology." For the Marxian/Althusserian critique of anthropology, see Althusser and Balibar, *Reading Capital*.

9. Karl Marx, Capital, 3 vols. (Moscow: Foreign Language Press, n.d.), vol. I, p. 178. Further references to this work appear in the text as "C" followed by volume number.

10. While it is not possible to elaborate here the complex interdependence of the moments of "production" and "exchange" or of their "constitutive" and "expressive" functions in Marx's analysis, I would maintain that for him "production" and "exchange" are not fixed binary opposites in their capacity to constitute value. It is quite consistent to argue, within the Marxian framework, that the moment of production is itself constituted by processes of consumption and exchange, for instance between the capitalist and laborer, and that therefore capitalist production itself cannot exist outside the circuits of exchange. To be sure, production does at times seem to enjoy a privileged rhetorical and perhaps even an unexamined metaphysical status in Marx, but this must be distinguished, via an analysis of the structural totality of the production-distribution-consumption process, from the more rigorous interdependence of production and exchange that is imminent in the labor theory of value. I do briefly examine later the closely related issue of the simultaneous constitution of value by labor and exchange.

An interesting example of the attempt to privilege production over consumption and distribution can be found in the logical fiat through which this is declared to be the case in chapter 8 of Althusser and Balibar's *Reading Capital*, which examines the interdependence of these three major "regions of the economic space." See particularly p. 168. It may be plausible to argue, in an Althusserian fashion, that production does determine consumption and distribution, but "only in the last instance."

11. Bob Fine, "Struggle Against Discipline: The Theory and Politics of Michel Foucault," in *Capital & Class*, 9 (Autumn 1979), pp. 75–96. Further references to this work appear in the text as "Fine."

12. Foucault is careful to avoid an essentialist notion of freedom, but in its place he simply posits "the recalcitrance of the will and the intransigence of freedoms" without defining them in any detail (Dreyfus and Rabinow, 221–22). Foucault goes on to say, "Rather than speaking of an essential freedom, it would be better to speak of an 'agonism'—of a relationship which is at the same time reciprocal incitation and struggle; less of a face-to-face confrontation which paralyzes both sides than a permanent provocation."

13. In his discussion of consent Foucault seems to be responding to Antonio

Gramsci's distinction between dominant and hegemonic relations, though without explicit reference to Gramsci it seems to me that Foucault's theorization of
the relations between consent and power (i.e., hegemony in Gramscian terms)
does not improve on that of Gramsci. Foucault's critique is confined to consent
as a deliberate, rational, quasi-contractual agreement. However, in Gramsci
consent operates more as an acceptance, conscious or otherwise, of the prevailing discursive structures.

14. Michel Foucault, "Nietzsche, Freud, Marx," *Critical Texts*, 3, 2 (Winter 1986),
pp. 1–5.

15. For an analysis of the relations of power and interests, contractual or otherwise,
see Barry Hindess, "Power, Interests, and the Outcome of Struggles," *Sociology*
16, 4 (November 1982), pp. 498–511.

16. "Sexuality on/of the Racial Border: Foucault, Wright and the Articulation of
Racial Sexuality," in *Discourses of Sexuality From Aristotle to Aids*, ed. Donna
Stanton (Ann Arbor: University of Michigan Press, 1992), pp 94–116.

17. Throughout this essay the attention paid to "use value" has been minimal. This
is so partly because that concept does not demand attention within the logic of
this essay, but partly because the concept of use value seems to include a series
of teleological assumptions that still remain to be theorized. In his most naive
formulation, Marx simply asserts that "the use-value of objects is *realised without exchange by means of a direct relation between the objects and man*, while, on the
other hand, their value is realised only by exchange, that is, by means of a social
process" (*Capital*, vol. I, p. 83.) The problem, quite briefly, is that the moment
one steps beyond apodictic bodily needs a host of culturally determined intentionalities must come into play in the definition of use value, and these intentionalities, as already determined by ideological apparatuses or discursive
formations, must then be seen as already saturated by exchange value, or, as
Baudrillard would have it, by an entire signifying code that structures and functions capitalism. It would seem, then, that within use value as such we must at
least distinguish between the moment of "use" and the moment of "exchange."
For a somewhat different problematization of use value, see Gayatri C. Spivak,
"Scattered Speculations on the Question of Value," *In Other Worlds: Essays in
Cultural Politics* (New York: Methuen, 1987), pp. 154–75. Further references to
this work appear in the text as "Spivak."

18. See particularly chapter 12, Content and Form of Value," of I. I. Rubin, *Essays
on Marx's Theory of Value* (Detroit: Black and Red Press, 1972), pp. 107–124.

Further references to this work appear in the text as "Rubin." While Rubin's analysis goes a long way toward clarifying Marx's theory of value, the controversy surrounding that concept still continues. See, for instance, Diane Elson, ed., *Value: The Representation of Labor in Capitalism* (Atlantic Highlands: Humanities Press, 1979); and Ian Steedman, Paul Sweezy, et al., *The Value Controversy* (London: Verso, 1981).

19. This particular formulation is cited by Rubin from the 1867 edition (*Kapital*, I, p. 6, emphasis in the original): "Now we know the *substance* of value. It is labor. We know the *measure of its magnitude*. It is *labor-time*. What still remains is its *form*, which transforms *value* into *exchange-value*." It is perhaps important to distinguish here, as Rubin does, that by "value" Marx does not mean the various "forms of value" (such as equivalent, accidental, expanded, etc.) but "value as form," that is, value as the *social form* of the product of labor. See Rubin, "Essays," p. 112.

20. As Rubin notes ("Essays," p. 116), while Marxian analysis is unequivocal about defining labor as the content of value, it is ambivalent about what kind of labor constitutes this content. At times Marx articulates abstract labor and at times socially equalized labor as the content of value. Rubin eventually supports the former interpretation; however, as noted before, the controversy over Marx's theory of value continues.

21. In an extended consideration of this suture, "value" would have to be defined not only in its Marxian form but also in its Nietzschean form.

22. Foucault's acknowledgments of the isomorphism between capitalist political economy and disciplinary forms of power remain ambivalent and contradictory. Thus in "The Eye of Power" he strenuously avoids questions about "labor" and "production" designed to explore the isomorphism, whereas in *Discipline and Punish* the linkage is very strong. In the first place, he argues, the "accumulation of men" and the "accumulation of capital" are interdependent and mutually reinforcing, "each (making) the other possible and necessary; each (providing) a model for the other"; in the second place, his claims that "massive projection of military methods onto industrial organization" as an example of the disciplinary modeling of the division of labor recalls Marx's language about the military regimes of factory organization; and finally, but most importantly, Foucault seems to admit that the disciplinary mode of power is in fact developed by capitalist organization, thus implicitly accepting Marx's description of the microstructure of that political economy: "Let us say that discipline is the uni-

tary technique by which the body is reduced as a 'political' force at the least cost and maximized as a useful force. The growth of a capitalist economy gave rise to the specific modality of disciplinary power, whose general formulas, techniques of submitting forces and bodies, in short, 'political anatomy,' could be operated in the most diverse political regimes, apparatuses or institutions. (*Discipline and Punish*, 220–21).

23. Spivak's "Scattered Speculations on the Question of Value," p. 157 (emphasis added).

24. Fredric Jameson, "Marxism and History," *The Ideologies of Theory: Essays*, vol. 2 (Minneapolis: University of Minnesota Press, 1988), p. 162.

25. Jameson, "Marxism and History," p. 162.

ZHANG LONGXI

marxism: from scientific to utopian

> The left cannot renounce utopia; it cannot give up goals that
> are, for the time being, unattainable, but that impart meaning
> to social changes.
>
> —Leszek Kolakowski, *Toward a Marxist Humanism*

Perhaps anyone moderately familiar with the literature of
Marxism could recognize in the title of this essay a reversal of the title of a
famous book by Friedrich Engels, *Die Entwicklung des Sozialismus von der Utopie
zur Wissenschaft* (1880). Melvin Lasky has commented on a peculiar change
in the title of this work in most of its European translations—*Socialisme utopique
et socialisme scientifique; Socialism: Utopian and Scientific; Il Socialismo utopico ed il
Socialismo scientifico*. By changing the noun into the adjective, Lasky argues,
the translation looses (and loses) the rigidity of a closed system. "Loyalty to
the adjective (*scientific*) tended to make for flexibility and open-mindedness;
loyalty to the noun (*science*), for ponderous orthodoxy."[1] That may be so, but
Lasky does not sound very convincing, to me at least, when he remarks that

Engels, in choosing to use the noun and not the adjective, "appeared to be less concerned with the scientific qualities of method than with the systematic character of socialist philosophy."[2] Surely for Engels, the superiority of Marxism over what he calls utopian socialism lies precisely in its claim to scientific qualities. If the utopian socialists, Claude Henri de Saint-Simon, Charles Fourier, Robert Owen and their followers, could only paint what Marx and Engels call "fantastic pictures of future society" and build "castles in the air," it was not because their philosophy was any less systematic than Marxism but simply because their time was not ripe; because at their historical moment, again according to Marx and Engels, "the proletariat, as yet in its infancy, offers to them the spectacle of a class without any historical initiative or any independent political movement."[3] It is only time or history—history understood as the temporal unfolding of the course of events according to the relentless laws of historical necessity— that gives full force to the word *Entwicklung* (development) and its end product *Wissenschaft* (science) in Engels's original title. Over empty utopian fantasies Marxism now triumphs as a science, that is, as both a systematic philosophy (historical materialism) *and* an effective methodology (that of a political movement and proletarian revolution). It is a science made available by the very process of historical evolution.

My complaint about the translation of Engels's title concerns not so much the change of nouns into adjectives as the omission of the emphatic sense of progress in time. It seems to me that the juxtaposition of the two adjectives, *utopian* and *scientific*, misses the whole point of historical teleology implied in the German title, namely, the idea that not only does Marxism as the theory of scientific socialism grow out of and supersede all other types of socialism as utopian thinking, but that socialism as a science promises to realize the very telos of history, the perfect human society in the future.[4] In the book itself, Engels first acknowledges the utopian thinkers as precursors of modern socialism and then credits the Hegelian dialectics with the achievement of providing rational ways to see human history "as the process of evolution of man himself," rather than a chaotic mass of isolated facts and events, and "to trace out the inner law running through all its apparently accidental phenomena."[5] Hegel's conception of history, however, is idealistic in that it is seen as part of the evolvement of the absolute Idea, whereas for the utopian thinkers, according to Engels, "socialism is the expression of absolute truth, reason and justice" and as such is not unlike the Hegelian Idea, namely, an abstract notion "independent of time, space, and of the historical development of man."[6] The time has come, so Engels believes, to stop dreaming about the perfect society and theorizing about it on a purely abstract basis and instead to give scientific accounts of historical development and change existing social order into a new order. "To make a science of socialism," says Engels, "it had first to be placed upon a real basis." And that basis, he argues, has already been found by Karl Marx in his discovery of a materialist conception of history—which stands Hegel, so to speak, on his head—and his discovery of surplus value as the key to understanding the capitalist mode of production. "With these discoveries socialism became a science," Engels declares. "The next thing was to work out all its details and relations."[7]

The third and the longest part of Engels's book aims precisely to work out the details and relations of the theory of scientific socialism, the Marxist theory of historical evolution as a process of precarious balance and incessant strife between the productive forces and the economic and political structure of a certain society. In Engels's metanarrative of historical development, the productive forces are identified as the revolutionary drive for progress and freedom that constantly pushes the social structure as a whole toward the telos of history. A social structure or mode of production is legitimate to the extent that it frees the productive forces and allows them further development, but it loses legitimacy and must be replaced by a new social order as soon as it outlives its useful function and turns into a hindrance to the forward movement of the forces of production. Following the logic of this metanarrative, the socialist revolution is bound to happen not because it is demanded by "absolute truth, reason and justice" but because the capitalist mode of production has become obsolete and unable to further promote the very forces that it has set free in the industrial revolution, the transformation of labor from the medieval individual mode to the modern socialized means of production. The freeing of the productive forces obstructed by the capitalist system is thus demanded by history, and history itself has prepared the agency for fulfilling this task because the bourgeoisie, in the process of concentrating the means of production, has also created its opposite, the proletariat, "to accomplish this revolution."[8] Conceived as a historical mission, as a consequence of the conflict between modern productive forces and the capitalist social structure, the proletarian revolution is thus not a matter of theory or philosophical con-

templations but the necessary outgrowth of historical development, something made ripe by time or the zeitgeist, something not "engendered in the
mind of man" but existing "objectively, outside us, independently of the will
and actions even of the men that have brought it on."[9]

The impersonal tone and the belief in the true objectivity of a theoretical
proposition are typical of the scientism at the time, which led Engels to identify the exact place where the "final causes" of all social changes and political
revolutions are to be found. They are to be sought, says Engels, "not in men's
brains, not in men's better insight into eternal truth and justice, but in changes
in the modes of production and exchange. They are to be sought not in the
philosophy, but in the *economics* of each particular epoch.[10] The claim to scientific truth is thus firmly lodged in a confident grasp of the material reality,
especially the economic basis of the social structure, as well as the laws that
govern the change and progress of history. Socialism as a science is clearly
modeled on what the nineteenth century knew of natural science. "Active
social forces," says Engels in a typical tone of scientific determinism, "work
exactly like natural forces: blindly, forcibly, destructively, so long as we do not
understand, and reckon with, them." But just as natural science can force
nature to surrender its secrets and can harness natural forces, scientific socialism will likewise control the social forces and finally be able to make history
freely, according to human intention and rational planning. And that, Engels
declares, is "the ascent of man from the kingdom of necessity to the kingdom
of freedom."[11]

The unabashed scientism in Engels's book, the confidence in the objective
laws of nature and society, the teleology of history as the unfolding of historical necessity beyond human will and consciousness, all these become highly
suspect in a world of post-Hegelian philosophy and post-World War II politics. For many late-twentieth-century Marxists outside the Soviet Union, for
"humanist" and "critical" Marxists, scientism in social theory can be an embarrassment, and so they "join non-Marxist philosophers in rejecting the claims of
Marxists to be scientific."[12] A convenient way to clear Marxism internally of
that embarrassing Hegelian and positivist scientism is to blame it on Engels,
but that seems to me an act of expediency rather than an argument of principle and good reasoning. Darko Suvin's essay, "'Utopian' and 'Scientific': Two
Attributes for Socialism from Engels," which offers a strong critique of Engels
from the Left, can be seen as an example of such expedient criticism. Although

he rejects "the total opposition of a bad, 'positivistic' Engels and a good, 'structuralist' Marx," Suvin nevertheless proceeds to suggest that Marx in his thinking about socialism kept a "precise distance from Engels."[13] That suggestion, however, fails to persuade, because Marx showed as little patience with the utopian socialists as Engels did. Just to quote one of a number of such critical comments, Marx once wrote in a letter to Friedrich Sorge: "Naturally utopianism, which *before* the time of materialistic-critical socialism concealed the germs of the latter within itself, coming now *after* the event can only be silly—silly, stale and basically reactionary."[14] Here Marx clearly speaks of utopian socialism as an early and imperfect form now outgrown and superseded by scientific socialism. In fact, the famous eleventh thesis on Feuerbach reads in this context as much as a critique of utopianism as of Hegelianism: "The philosophers have only *interpreted* the world, in various ways; the point, however, is to *change* it."[15] According to Engels, it is Marx's discovery of the objective and scientific laws of social development—the materialist concept of history and the theory of surplus value—that made Marxism a guide to praxis, a theory of revolution capable of changing the world, rather than a mere utopian dream about "absolute truth, reason, and justice." If much of this notion seems now vitiated by its unwarranted scientism, we should remember that scientism, or the belief in objective and deterministic "laws" of nature, was powerfully influential in Marx's time as part of the intellectual milieu.

Despite Marx's and Engel's confidence in an imminent proletarian revolution, dictated by the inner laws of history, in the most advanced industrial countries in Europe and North America, the course of history has turned out to be more erratic than they predicted. The debate on the truth-value of Marxism has of course marked the history of Marxism itself. In the late 1960s, some leading Marxists were already trying to reckon with the vexed question of the relevance of Marxism to modern Western society. In an article provocatively entitled "Is Marx Obsolete?" Theodor Adorno, though he definitely meant to give a negative answer to the title question, had to concede that "capitalism had discovered resources within itself which enabled the collapse to be relegated to the Greek kalends," and that "the relations of production proved to be more elastic, in the face of this technological development, than Marx credited them with being."[16] If the theory of the relations of production forms the cornerstone of Marx's materialist conception of history and differentiates Marxism from utopian socialism, the failure of the course of history to bear out that theory must inevitably cast doubt on Marxism's claim to scientific truth. "It was far too optimistic on Marx's part," Adorno admits, "to expect that the primacy of the forces of production would inevitably arrive and necessarily explode the relations of production." In this respect, he goes on to say, "Marx, the sworn enemy of German idealism, remain[ed] true to its affirmative construction of history."[17] Ironically, it is classical Marxist political economics which precisely makes the so-called scientific socialism "scientific," that has proved to be essentially Hegelian and idealistic, far from being the sure grasp of historical and economic reality that it once claimed to be.

When an elaborate prophecy falls through, the credibility of the prophet is called into question. Indeed, what was presented with assurance by Engels as science, that is, the account of "the mechanisms and dynamism of history," as Krishan Kumar remarks, "seems most dubious" and "has no more hold on the future than any other theory, utopian or otherwise. Its certainty that capitalism will give rise to socialism is a matter of desire and hope, not of 'science'."[18] But if capitalism in the West has not given rise to socialism as Marx and Engels predicted, the vision of the final end of capitalism may still be entertained; the eschatological vision, like the idea of the millennium and the Second Coming, though not yet realized, may still be postponed to a later date and thus leave the faith of true believers unscathed.[19] In the East, in Russia and China, much greater damage has been done to the credibility of Marxism by the very reality of socialism, which materialized under the auspices of Marxism only to mock Marx's vision and turn it into a nightmare.

It is not surprising that the claim to scientific truth was much emphasized by the orthodox "scientific Marxists" in the former Soviet Union. They could state, in the influential *History of the Communist Party of the Soviet Union (Bolsheviks)* that "the science of the history of society, despite all the complexity of the phenomena of social life, can become as precise a science as, let us say, biology, and capable of making use of the laws of development of society for practical purposes."[20] Once the party, or more precisely its leader, claims to have mastered the science of social development, the party and the leader become infallible and unchallengeable as the incarnation of truth, which demands absolute obedience. It is certainly not accidental that the cult of the individual, theoretically so alien to Marx's vision of communism, became a common phenomenon in communist countries, notably in Stalin's Russia and Mao's China. Although Stalinism had, by the 1960s, lost credibility among

Leftist intellectuals in the West, Maoism was still widely held as another haven of hope. Many Western Marxists and Leftist intellectuals saw Mao's China as taking a different route from the orthodox Soviet line and, in the words of one commentator still feeling inspired by the Chinese Cultural Revolution in 1977, "struggling to deepen the revolution and carry it forward from one stage to the next, always in the direction of greater equality and fuller participation by the masses in controlling and managing their own lives."[21] In the late 1960s, it was still possible for Adorno to dismiss utopia as the opposite of Marxism in the context of the international political confrontations between the East and the West;[22] and it was still possible for Herbert Marcuse, when he tried to redefine the concept of revolution and socialism, to salvage the Marxist concept of "an authentic and accurate *Aufhebung*" and to see the Marxist vision alive and working wonders in "the Third World, where it provides the popular support for the national liberation fronts" and "in Cuba, in China's cultural revolution; and, last but not least, in the more or less 'peaceful' coexistence with the Soviet Union."[23]

Again, the course of history has mercilessly frustrated even these readjusted hopes and expectations. The Chinese Cultural Revolution, which had inspired many Western Marxists and Leftist intellectuals in the late 1960s, among them Marcuse and especially Louis Althusser, was proclaimed a failure and disaster by the Chinese communists themselves in the late 1970s. Post-Mao China, which was officially declared to be on the brink of a complete economic breakdown, was forced to take care of its belly before its head, that is, national economy before Marxist ideology, and quickly embarked on a free-market-oriented road of economic reform that violently clashed with the political structure of the regime and led to ugly bloodshed in Tiananmen Square in 1989. In the meantime, democratic insurgencies exploded Eastern Europe and the Soviet Union, where the ruling communist parties were ousted and even proclaimed illegal. When the Berlin Wall came down, communism also collapsed. The Soviet Union was disbanded, and the horrible war raging over Bosnia and Herzegovina has made any hope for revolution transferred to Third World nationalism seem absurd and irresponsible. In the last decade of the twentieth century, the questions Adorno and others faced in the late 1960s have reemerged with much greater urgency and seriousness: Is Marx obsolete? Have we reached "the end of history," as Francis Fukuyama declares? Has the collapse of communism also spelled the death of Marxism, of the vision and beliefs of Marx as a revolutionary thinker?

Facing such difficult questions, committed Marxists are understandably upset and depressed; some Western intellectuals on the Left would rather see things in a different light and wish that what we see in global politics were not real, that the course of history could be rolled back; some would even blame the Chinese, the Russians and the East Europeans for abandoning a revolutionary ideal and a nobler way of life to embrace a Western-style democracy and capitalism.[24] But whatever our political sympathies and responses, the fact is that communism is dead, that is, communism as we know it, communism not as a theory or vision in Marx's writings but as historical reality, as the political power that established itself in the East. Communism or the so-called scientific socialism has failed, and it has failed not because its capitalist enemies say so but because the people who have lived under it have rejected it as both repressive and repulsive. As a Marxist interpretation informed by historical materialism would tell us, the collapse of communism in the East can be the only outcome of the internal contradictions in their systems, the necessary consequence of the economic and political crises in the socialist countries, rather than the workings of external forces. But how does that interpretation relate to Marxism in the West? When one considers that the Russian revolution, according to Vladimir Lenin and Joseph Stalin, happened in the weakest link of the chain of imperialism; that the Chinese revolution, according to Mao, took place in a semifeudal and semicolonial country, and that Cuba and the other socialist countries have never been advanced industrial countries with a large working-class population, one may argue that the socialism that materialized in the world is not the socialism Marx and Engels envisioned in the first place. In other words, there are ways in which one may see Marx's prophecy as yet unrealized and may still detach the Marxist vision from the reality of socialism, or Marxism from failed communism. That does not mean, however, that Western Marxists and Leftist intellectuals should quickly wash their hands of any relationship and attachment, political, emotional or otherwise, to socialism in the East. That kind of response to the collapse of communism may be an expedient way to keep their ideological moorings unperturbed, but it is not a healthy attitude because it fails to face reality squarely. If Marxism is to have any real force in the future of humanity, all Marxists, in the West as well as in the East, must take into consideration the serious question of how to understand the failure of socialism and how to deal with that failure and its implications for Marxism as a whole.

If socialism as reality in the East is dead, socialism as a vision, that is, Marxism as a theory and Weltanschauung, is, by contrast, very much alive and constitutes a formidable intellectual force in the West, especially in the academic environment of the university. Western Marxism has its own tradition in radical social and political thinking, and it has always been strong not as a real political force but as a philosophical orientation. From the Frankfurt School to the present-day critical theories and cultural critiques, the influence of Marxism has been a powerful presence, and it is powerful partly because it has never been an official ideology or a predominant orthodoxy in the society at large. That is to say, its power consists precisely in its being an oppositional discourse and ideology. It has succeeded in the academic world, and rightly so, because the university, ever since its inception in late medieval times, has always been the *antitopia* of the world, the oasis of free and independent thinking in a vast desert of social and political conformity. Marcuse has put it very well: "The *character of the opposition* in the center of corporate capitalism is concentrated in the two opposite poles of the society: in the ghetto population (itself not homogeneous), and in the middle-class intelligentsia, especially among the students."[25] In a way, opposition has always tended to unite precisely the heterogeneous ghetto population and the middle-class intelligentsia. As long as corporate capitalism dominates the material and social life in the West, Marxism as an oppositional ideology will always have an invigorating influence among students and the intelligentsia. As a philosophical orientation rather than the ideology of a revolutionary party, however, an essentially intellectual Marxism must at the same time forfeit its claim to scientific qualities, especially the kind of scientism in politico-economic terms that informed Engels's critique of utopian socialism.

Ever since the rediscovery of the young Marx's *Economic and Philosophical Manuscripts* of 1844, a whole new dimension of Marx's thinking, a humanist and utopian dimension, has radically changed the meaning of Marxism. The enthusiasm about the *Manuscripts* in intellectual circles is by no means accidental, for this early work by Marx legitimizes the effort to differentiate Marxism from the kind of communism we saw in the Soviet Union and China. "To Marx," Robert Tucker declares on the authority of the *Manuscripts*, "communism did not mean a new economic system. It meant the end of economics in a society where man, liberated from labor, would realize his creative nature in a life of leisure."[26] That is to say, communism as Marx himself understood it is the perfect future society at the end of history, a posthistorical utopia of the most daring kind. In what Krishan Kumar calls "the most breathtakingly utopian of all Marx's comments on the future society," [27] Marx portrays his dazzlingly idealistic vision of the future in unmistakably Hegelian terms:

> *Communism* is the *positive* abolition of *private property*, of *human self-alienation*, and thus the real *appropriation* of *human* nature through and for man. It is, therefore, the return of man himself as a *social*, i.e. really human being, a complete and conscious return which assimilates all the wealth of previous development. Communism as a fully developed naturalism is humanism and as a fully developed humanism is naturalism. It is the *definite* resolution of the antagonism between man and nature, and between man and man. It is the true solution of the conflict between existence and essence, between objectification and self-affirmation, between freedom and necessity, between individual and species. It is the solution of the riddle of history and knows itself to be this solution.[28]

Though the *Manuscripts* remained unpublished during Marx's lifetime, the vision portrayed here does not vanish in his later works that advocate class struggle and proletarian revolution; rather, class struggle and revolution can be seen as the means to the final realization of this grand vision. In a world of very different political and economic conditions and with the failure of the Marxist experiment in the East, much of what Marx said about the means has lost its relevance, but the end he envisioned, his utopian vision of the future society, may still inform and encourage our effort to fight for a better future of humanity. "The aspect of Marx with the greatest enduring significance and relevance for our time," as Tucker argues, "is the Utopian aspect, the part that we today might call his 'futurology.'"[29] As Fredric Jameson observes in commenting on a statement made by Georg Lukács about Fourier and Marx, one can detect "a deficiency in Utopian thinking" in the socialist countries, while in Western Marxism, especially in the works of Herbert Marcuse and Ernst Bloch, there is a "revival of Utopian thinking."[30] This revival is also evident in Jameson's own works as well as those of many others who are less dogmatic but more dynamic than the old-time orthodox Marxists. In fact, in socialist countries, Marx's *Manuscripts* gave as much inspiration and encouragement to intellectual opposition as it did in the West. Indeed, when communism has

collapsed in the East, when what went on in the name of Marx and his political theory has proved to be disastrous and repressive, it is the utopian vision,
the desire and hope for a more authentically human society, more than any
"scientific" approach designed to reach that land of prophecy through class
struggle and the dictatorship of the proletariat, that may yet sustain our interest in Marxism and command our respect for Karl Marx as one of the great
visionaries of human history.

notes

1. Melvin J. Lasky, *Utopia and Revolution* (Chicago: University of Chicago Press,
   1976), p. 100.

2. Ibid., p. 99.

3. Karl Marx and Friedrich Engels, *Manifesto of the Communist Party*, in *Selected Works
   in One Volume (hereafter SW)* (New York International Publishers, 1968), pp. 60,
   61.

4. In *Utopianism and Marxism* (London: Methuen, 1987), Vincent Geoghegan notes
   that Marx and Engels saw their dispute with the utopians as a methodological
   issue: "The utopian socialist vision is at best a subjective imaginative abstraction
   from the division of class society, whilst the communist vision, by contrast, is
   the objective *telos* capitalist society creates as it negates itself" (p. 29).
   Geoghegan also thinks the contrast between the German title of Engels's book
   and its English title significant: "the former suggesting Marx and Engels' historical materialist analysis of utopianism, whereas the latter implies a sharp dual-
   ism of world-views; one true, one false" (p. 30).

5. Friedrich Engels, *Socialism: Utopian and Scientific*, SW, pp. 413, 414.

6. Ibid., p. 409.

7. Ibid., pp. 410, 416.

8. Ibid., p. 429. See also Marx and Engels, *Manifesto of the Communist Party:* "The
   advance of industry, whose involuntary promoter is the bourgeoisie, replaces
   the isolation of the laborers, due to competition, by their revolutionary combination, due to association. The development of Modern Industry, therefore, cuts
   from under its feet the very foundation on which the bourgeoisie produces and
   appropriates products. What the bourgeoisie, therefore, produces, above all, is
   its own gravediggers. Its fall and the victory of the proletariat are equally

inevitable" (*SW*, p. 46).

9. Engels, *Socialism: Utopian and Scientific, SW*, p. 418.

10. Ibid., p. 417. See also Marx, "Preface to *A Contribution to the Critique of Political Economy*": "The mode of production of material life conditions the social, political and intellectual life process in general. It is not the consciousness of men that determines their being, but, on the contrary, their social being that determines their consciousness" (*SW*, p. 182).

11. Engels, *Socialism: Utopian and Scientific, SW*, p. 432.

12. John P. Burke, Lawrence Crocker and Lyman H. Legters, introduction to Burkes, Crocker and Legters (eds.) *Marxism and the Good Society*, (Cambridge: Cambridge University Press, 1981), p. 18. Burke, Crocker and Legters identify three main groups of contemporary Marxists: the "scientific Marxists," who follow the orthodox Soviet line of Marxism-Leninism and emphasize the scientific laws of social development to legitimize the Soviet society as the good society; the "humanist Marxists" in Eastern Europe, who dissent from the Soviet doctrine to interpret Marx primarily in terms of the positive aspects of his vision of a future communist society; and the "critical Marxists" in Western Europe, who are primarily interested in Marx's negative critique and his attacks on the status quo (see pp. 17–18).

13. Darko Suvin, "'Utopian' and 'Scientific': Two Attributes for Socialism from Engels," *Minnesota Review* 6 (Spring 1976): 69 (n.1), 67.

14. Marx to Sorge, October, 19, 1877, in Karl Marx and Friedrich Engels, *Selected Correspondence: 1846–1895*, trans. Dona Torr (New York International Publishers, 1942), p. 350.

15. Karl Marx, "Theses on Feuerbach," *SW*, p. 30.

16. Theodor W. Adorno, "Is Marx Obsolete?" trans. Nicolas Slater, *Diogenes* 64 (Winter 1968): 2.

17. Ibid., p. 9.

18. Krishan Kumar, *Utopia and Anti-Utopia in Modern Times* (Oxford: Basil Blackwell, 1987), p. 53.

19. For an extremely interesting discussion of the endless postponing of the eschatological end, or the "indifference to disconfirmation," see Frank Kermode, *The Sense of an Ending: Studies in the Theory of Fiction* (Oxford: Oxford University Press, 1966). Citing the work of sociologist Leon Festinger, Kermode notes how disconfirmation of a prophecy can always be "quickly followed by the invention of new end-fictions and new calculations.... Men in the middest make consider-

able imaginative investments in coherent patterns which, by the provision of an end, make possible a satisfying consonance with the origins and with the middle. That is why the image of the end can never be *permanently* falsified" (p. 17).

20. *History of the Communist Party of the Soviet Union (Bolsheviks)* (Moscow: Foreign Languages Publishing House, 1939), p. 114; quoted in Geoghegan, *Utopianism and Marxism*, p. 76.

21. Paul M. Sweezy, "Theory and Practice in the Mao Period," in Burke et al. (eds.), *Marxism and the Good Society*, p. 220. This essay was first published in February 1977 in *Monthly Review* 28, no. 9.

22. See Adorno, "Is Marx Obsolete?" pp. 8–9.

23. Herbert Marcuse, "Re-examination of the Concept of Revolution," *Diogenes* 64 (Winter 1968): 22, 25.

24. For a critique of such leftist idealism and armchair radicalism, see Zhang Longxi, "Western Theory and Chinese Reality," *Critical Inquiry* 19 (Autumn 1992): 105–130.

25. Marcuse, "Re-examination of the Concept of Revolution," p. 20.

26. Robert C. Tucker, "Marx and the End of History," *Diogenes* 64 (Winter 1968): 167.

27. Kumar, *Utopia and Anti-Utopia*, p. 62.

28. Karl Marx, *Economic and Philosophical Manuscripts*, in *Early Writings*, trans. and ed. T. B. Bottomore (New York: McGraw-Hill, 1964), p. 155.

29. Tucker, "Marx and the End of History," p. 167.

30. Fredric Jameson, "Introduction/Prospectus: To Reconsider the Relationship of Marxism to Utopian Thought," *The Minnesota Review* 6 (Spring 1976): 54.

ANDREI MARGA

the modern world and the individual

from the metamorphosis of eastern
european marxism to marx's errors

After the collapse of "real socialism" by the end of the 1980s, Marxism is no longer a topic of debate or, at best, if considered, seems to have become a passed issue. But the question arises, can a world outlook which had such a strong impact upon history leave the scene all of a sudden? In Eastern Europe, at least, Marxism, although avoided in public debate, still survives in mentalities and motivates decisions. Moreover, in the spectrum of political life in several eastern European countries, against the background of the difficulties brought about by reform, there are political parties that can hardly hide their Marxist inspiration. Therefore, neither approaching nor breaking with Marxism is possible in the absence of its thoroughgoing analysis. With this in view, this essay is an attempt to critically analyze

Marxism and its perspectives.

EASTERN MARXISM

The collapse of "real socialism" rescued the eastern part of Europe from an oppressive, inefficient, and essentially totalitarian social system and raised, once more, the question concerning the character of the ideology that legitimized it and of the philosophy that grounded it. After the publication of the *Economico-Philosophical Manuscripts* and in connection with the antidogmatic trend of the "Prague Spring" and of Eurocommunism, there were still voices claiming that eastern socialism, which was in a permanent state of crisis, did not exhaust the practical possibilities of Marxism and that the alternative of "socialism with a human face" still existed. *Solidarnost* in Poland represented a thoroughgoing turning point, in this respect, because it focused awareness of the fact that socialism in general was not a solution to the crisis in Eastern Europe. The political and social movements that swept away eastern socialism had an antisocialist character. In their view, no Marxism, not even the one of Marx, represented a reference point any more. In this way Marxism entered a new stage, which I call an abandonment, a situation that allows and requires a new reflection upon history and, of course, a new reflection upon Marxism.

One cannot speak of Marxism today without first stating which of its complicated historical ramifications one has in mind. A discussion of Marxism runs the risk of being irrelevant if it does not distinguish among the concretization of the Marxist inheritance relative to each communist regime in Eastern Europe; communism as a political movement, which, after World War II, seized power in this part of the world; Eastern Marxism as a body of general, philosophical options that shaped this movement ideologically; Marxism as a posthumous systematization of the theses that Marx and Engels had never presented in a coherent and ultimate form; and Marx's philosophy strictly speaking.

Starting from these distinctions, I would like to sum up the attitude towards Marxism in Eastern Europe, after the collapse, illustrating my statements with the example of Romania where, it is well-known, the final stage of "real socialism" was a dramatic one.

The most conspicuous characteristic of the present situation of Marxism in Eastern Europe is its abandonment, namely, the situation in which it is neither assumed nor considered, even critically, in an explicit and systematic way. After holding a monopoly on intellectual life, being for many years a compulsory subject in universities, and being spread through official propaganda, Marxism is buried in oblivion and, actually, dispatched to the museum. The immense frustrations experienced by the majority of the population under "real socialism" correlated with the saturation caused by the previous monopoly has resulted in the present disregard of the doctrine. This abandonment, however, is not a simple parting with Marxism. In fact, an ideological critique has been vigorously carried on in Eastern Europe since 1989. It is based on the lived realities of former "real socialism," starting with the terror launched in its early years, moving to the repression and the constant control of the intellectual and political life, and finishing with a widespread penury. This critique was addressed, first, to the concretizations of the Marxist heritage relative to each communist regime in Eastern Europe, and took specific, contextual accents. In Romania, for instance, where the communist regime took the caricatured form of a family dictatorship with feudal ornaments, the critique has been sharper in all respects. But all over Eastern Europe this critique has developed beyond the above-mentioned concretizations into a critique of communism and of the socializing forms of life. Viewed by its critics as more than the different political figures and trends, communism in the first place is considered responsible for all the drawbacks of life in Eastern Europe, since it "developed our non-liberty and our ignorance."[1] The critique of communism started with a critique of Stalinism, which soon turned into the critique of Leninism and, thus, even if not in a systematic way, developed into a critique of Eastern Marxism. Some prominent intellectuals have thought of "bringing forward the problem of communism through its most important representative, Lenin."[2] Others consider the difference between the dogmatists (Lenin's followers) and the rest of the Marxists to be irrelevant at this point, claiming that the antidogmatists are, in their turn, no more than "moderate dogmatists," also outrun by history.[3] Therefore, Marxism itself appears to be responsible, like other theories in the history of philosophy, for having produced oppressive "utopias.[4]

Scarcely begun, the debate concerning the "guilt" of Marxism has degenerated into superficial recriminations in which passion often replaces arguments. Consequently, there are voices that draw attention to the need to avoid confusing the different components in the historical movement of Marxism and to replacing pamphleteering with analysis.[5] It has become obvious that "Marxism also had grown out of an effort of understanding, and that its accomplishments are more than exceptions," but it has become equally evident that, in eastern history, what counted were not its positive sides, but rather the appalling social costs called forth by putting it into effect.[6] And these costs induce us to look for their sources, which necessarily bring forward not only Eastern Marxism, but also Marxism itself.[7] The dramatic experience under Eastern socialism cause one to question Marxism as a whole and not only one or another of its "concretizations."[8]

Marxism cannot be transcended without first being critically analyzed, but so far little has been done in this direction. Consequently, the critique of communism itself runs the risk of being hasty, of obsessively resuming—but only at a journalistic level—important themes, and in spite of the new possibilities of the time, of causing, in its turn, another saturation. It is very clear that "Marxism is not only a sum of mistakes. But, at the moment, history constrains us to insist upon its errors."[9]

Critical analysis is called for not only by those preoccupied with reconstructing philosophy after the collapse of Eastern socialism. Objectively speaking, it should be undertaken as an antidote against naiveté and against a new dogmatism. There are solid arguments in favor of the thesis concerning the inner differentiation of the Marxist movement according to which Marx is distinct from Marxism, Marxism from Eastern Marxism, and the latter from the individualized communist regimes. However, the statement that "dialectical materialism had nothing to do with Marx's philosophy"[10] is contrary to fact. And it is equally untrue that "it is only the analytical philosophy of Marx that can be used to clear up what its so-called eastern followers had entangled so badly," partly because some of its initial premises had been either erroneous or chimerical.[11] And this is so because the very "guilty premises" pass sentence on the method. It is also important to consider the interested dogmatism of the restorative tendencies launched with increased insistence in the East by the radical and dogmatic wings of the former communist parties that struggle to come back to power, putting forward an image of Marxism, be it theory or method, unaltered by the recent eastern history.

Both the mere abandonment and the dogmatic rehabilitation of Marxism block the necessary clarification of the present situation in Eastern Europe. The first approach does not lead to an understanding of what Marxism was all about. Yet without this understanding, it is not possible to build up a different

world. This trend allows the disorderly persistence of the remnants of an ideology that once had dramatic effects. The second approach restates, as an
ideological instrument, an outlook that is not at all immune to the danger of
being put into operation in order to legitimize domination. Therefore, it is of
the utmost importance to Marxism that it be critically analyzed, i.e., to confront its theoretical society and humanitarian project with what had actually
come out of it, and to draw theoretical conclusions so that Marxism might be
unbiasedly reconstructed.

The critique of communism rightly concerned its experienced reality, taking in its different aspects as a totalitarian system. But so long as the scrutiny
does not go back to the theoretical premises of "real socialism," it is an incomplete critique. Although put aside in practice, communism survives in
mentalities. The greater the difficulties of the transition, the more it tries once
again to ascend to power in the East. Therefore, a genuine critique would ask
for research into the theoretical basis of "real socialism" which, directly, was
neither Marx, nor Marxism, but Eastern Marxism as such.

The delimitation of Eastern Marxism can be traced back to Rosa
Luxemburg's famous rejection of the incipient Leninist tactics of opposing
the "dictatorship of the proletariat" to democracy and of dispatching the latter
to an indefinite future. "Jawohl: Diktatur! Aber diese Diktatur besteht in der
Art der Verwendung der Demokratie, nicht in ihrer Abschaffung, in energis-
chen, entschlossenen Eingriffen in die wohlerworbenen Rechte und
wirtschaftlichen Verhältnisse der bürgerlichen Gesellschaft, ohne Welche sich
die sozialistische Umwälzung nicht verwirklichen lässt."[12] Lenin's option to
win and keep power by using every possible means was counteracted by Rosa
Luxemburg's view of Marxism which considered the deepening of the bourgeois democracy to be the main practical problem of Marxism. Thus, on the
political level, Marxism split up into "Eastern Marxism" and "Western
Marxism."

In what follows, I will not insist upon the historical aspects of this distinction, but rather concentrate my analysis on the metamorphoses of Eastern
Marxism. This form of Marxism had to face not only the difficult problems of
east European history, but also its own limitations.

From its early days, Eastern Marxism had taken over the life problems of
the individuals living under these regimes in a superficial and distorted way.
This led to difficulties it tried to overcome, and in so doing it was compelled

to undergo metamorphoses. Nevertheless, it still fell apart because of the
errors of its construction.

Through Leninism initially, Eastern Marxism had incorporated, besides
the vision of an egalitarian utopia, the disagreement, inherent in the October
Revolution, between the proclamation of radical emancipation on the one
side, and its standard bearers, who had not reached the modern liberal men-
tality on the other. Being applied in a historical situation which lagged behind
its generalizations, Marxism was converted from a theory that had aimed at
assuming and then critically and emancipatively analyzing human experience, into an ideology legitimizing the power of those who claimed to be its
standard bearers. It was used to answer the need of "den revolutionären
Legitimationsbedarf einer nachrevolutionären Gesamtgesellschaft."[13]

Stalin had granted Eastern Marxism a durable form by postulating in its
premises the split of the world into USSR and the "capitalist world." The
strategy of "socialism in one country" brought about not only the conversion
of Marxism into a legitimizing ideology, but also its concentration on a non-
specific objective, i.e., the social disciplination with the view of increasing
production. "Die Paradoxie, in welche die Marxsche Theorie durch ihre sov-
jetische Umformung gerät, besteht darin, dass eine im Kern historische
Theorie aussergeschichtlicher Legitimationsgründe und rituellen
Neutralisierung ihres revolutionär praktischen Gehalts bedarf, um im
Interesse ihrer historischen Wirksamkeit auf ein rückständiges Land und eine
rückständige Bewölkerung anwendbar sein zu können."[14]

Stalin legitimized the discretionary power of the communist leaders and
justified the subordination of the individuals to socialist production,[15] deriving
from the improvisations of Leninism the theses of a philosophy in which individuals, deprived of initiative, were asked to prove faith and submission:
dialectics is the method describing the evolution of nature through the mechanisms of contradiction; matter is the substance of reality; there is an objective
reality, outside and independent of consciousness; knowledge is the reflection of reality; society is an extension of the matter and of its evolutionary
mechanisms; the production forces make up the decisive factor in the social
dynamics, etc..[16] No other philosophy of the period claimed its adherence to
the actual historical conditions of the lives of individuals, and so insistently.
And no other dealt with them in a more simplified manner: by subordinating
them to power.

The serious shortcomings of the Marxist system had been noticed from within, but they were constantly minimized as "das ungenügende Begreiffen der Grundlangen des Marxismus-Leninismus und die noch vorhandenen Einflüsse der bürgerlichen Ideologie."[17] Eastern Marxism was to remain Stalinism, and, therefore, an absurd "logic of power" even when the crimes of the gulag were laid open. After 1959, it detached itself from the "personality cult" and the ideological tricks that had served Stalin's power, but not from its Weltanschauung—"dialectical and historical materialism." This continued to be influential as the official philosophy of Eastern Marxism until late in the 1980s. And against the current perception, it would consider "real socialism" to be "a superior kind of global determinism and a superior type of liberty." In its view, the subject of change was not represented by living human beings, with their needs, their interests, and their ideals, but by the abstract and impersonal "material world."[18] The late phase of Stalinism felt the necessity of having a closer contact with the problems of human experience, but it altered them, from the very beginning, using the abstract cover of "major problems which are specific to the period," or reducing them to the rational use of resources, demographic control, the elimination of economic discrepancies, etc.

Under the impact of dissatisfactions and protests in eastern Europe, Eastern Marxism was constrained to undergo changes. Moreover, as a consequence of the assimilation of the writings of the "younger Marx" within Marxism, the latter could no longer avoid the alienation problem without running the risk of being accused of irrelevancy. Eastern Marxism could not elude the "humanist" trend which developed in post-war Marxism. But, even when it tried to assume the new series of problems, it could not go beyond its limitations. Consequently, it took the shape of a Marxism suffering from an inferiority complex, proclaiming its "opening" towards human experience under circumstances in which it constantly asked for "consistency," i.e., the dogmatic claim of the "scientific character," derived from the postulate of "materialism in its dialectical phase." This Marxism had in view to secure the "humanism" valence by using the theoretical means of a hidden Stalinism, concentrated in the thesis according to which "historical materialism should be conceived as an organic part of dialectical materialism, that is, it should be deducible from dialectical materialism,"[19] which, actually, betrayed it from the beginning.

Being reduced to a legitimizing ideology, as well as being pressured by

Eurocommunism forced Eastern Marxism to reexamine its foundations. Consequently, the 1970s brought about the reactivation of Marxism as a philosophy of praxis. The initiators of this trend hoped to put an end to communist dictatorships by returning to the "authentic Marx" and regaining the perspective of praxis as an alternative to the discredited metaphysics of Leninism. But when the problem of praxis was brought forward, they again did not make the differentiations; they could not grasp the actual experience of individuals, and, therefore, they produced vague generalizations, tributaries to this metaphysics, such as "praxis is nothing else but the ensemble of the forms of human activity, determined on each step of history, through which society reproduces its existence."[20] They realized that the "historical necessity" called upon by Marxism whenever the establishment of the strategy of action was at stake included not only "material conditions," but also the "collective determination of individuals." However, they could not express the real will of these individuals since they constantly remained the prisoners of the formal abstraction of the "interdependence between the basis and the superstructure."

The incapacity to solve the problems of the life of the people and the lasting crisis within "real socialism" compelled the communist regimes to look for a new legitimation. And this was found in nationalism, which was to represent the last phase of Eastern Marxism.

Nationalism was brought forward in eastern Europe against the background of the split between Moscow and Beijing, which permitted the reconsideration of Soviet Marxism by some communist regimes. Theses legitimizing communist domination were preserved, but this domination was no longer subordinated to Moscow, which appeared to be the source of evil. Generalizations such as the "universal laws of dialectics" came to be regarded, in their practical significance, as the ideology of Soviet domination, and were abandoned in favor of the so-called "creative development of Marxism according to the actual historical conditions." This approach appeared to be legitimate since Marxism was reduced to a "guide of action."[21] The idea of nation as the fundamental factor of development became central.[22] The vague elements and remains of a Marxism which had practically ceased to exist were now organized around it. The new eastern ideology included aspirations towards national emancipation and manipulated these aspirations in the form of the theory of a specific national character, or even of a specific view of the world. This culminated in the primitive ontology of a supposed "nature of the people" which would not be interested in a genuine democracy. Consequently, late communism transformed national aspirations into instruments of isolation. Nationalism was to surpass "real socialism" and was to become a trend of reference in the post-communism eastern Europe.

"Soviet Marxism" met with reluctance from mainstream Marxism in the 1950s, and after the experience of Stalinism, its philosophy had to face the political action it had engendered.[23] Today, when the experience of "real socialism" is over, we can look back to Eastern Marxism through the prism of its collapse. How can it be explained now, against the background of its failure?

One way it can be explained is by analyzing its conditions, such as historical conditions (the inadequacy of a program of post-bourgeois emancipation in a context which had not taken advantage of the traditions of bourgeois emancipation), the economic conditions (the inconsistency of the planned economy), the technical and scientific conditions (the incapacity of the bureaucracy to keep pace with the revolutions in science and technology), the military conditions (the new level of discouragement reached in technology). Without diminishing the importance of these conditions, I should like to dwell upon the type of thinking incorporated in Eastern Marxism, which particularized it along its existence and prevented it from adhering to the actual experience of man. One cannot explain the history of Eastern Marxism and, especially, its surprisingly sudden breakdown without considering this type of thinking. Moving away from the temptation to abandon Eastern Marxism, it as something past and gone, and from the dominant approach today which analyzes only its effects without examining it as such, it is time to elaborate on the philosophical errors of Eastern Marxism, at least for throwing light on the past and present situation in eastern Europe.

In the post-World War II period, the structural errors of Eastern Marxism—resuming a mechanistic and metaphysical (in a pejorative sense) concept of reality; the noncritical use of the idea of universal legislation; the subjection to a schematic economic determinism; the confusion between the state and society, to name a few—were repeatedly drawn attention to. Instead of discussing all these problems again, they can be considered after the collapse, from a new perspective. My opinion is that the errors perceived at different levels of the theoretical construction of Eastern Marxism were the surface effects of a fundamental and typical error, namely, the conception of the concrete as something composed of heterogeneous—informal and formal, perceptible and intellectual, contingent and necessary—elements, so that this conception could never offer sure and, in a certain sense, binding landmarks; therefore, it was liable to be manipulated by any force in power under "real socialism." This error can have various effects in different philosophies, but it has tremendous weight when a philosophy encloses the principle of its transposition into social organizations.

In what follows, I will illustrate this point going through some philosophical options of Eastern Marxism. *First*, the view of reality with which its philosophy usually started: This reality had been taken out of what people effectively experienced in their everyday life and had been placed beyond what was accessible to action. The concept of the "reality that is independent of our will and consciousness" structured an outlook of the world in which reality included some elements of the current experience, besides strongly formal assumptions, so that men's experience had no place in it. Eastern Marxism proclaimed the pre-eminence of revolutionary action in the genesis of social reality, but, having previously postulated a legislation competing with the objectivity of natural laws, it necessarily converted actions into submission.

The problem of action was much talked about in Eastern Marxism, but even some of its adherents shared the acute feeling that its philosophical generalizations could not describe a single action. They were also aware of the deep gap between the description produced by this Marxism that was at best conceptual and a genuine description of situations, which contradicted it. But neither were they able to conceive of action beyond its formal level, because, besides some empirical elements, they only took into consideration the formal conditions of its efficiency. The result of action mattered more than the way in which it had been obtained, since Eastern Marxism constantly avoided paying attention to what was present in any action, i.e., the reciprocity of behaviors. In this way, instrumentality annulled normativity within Eastern Marxism.

Second, the outlook on human existence was a permanent source of tension. It took over, in its turn, the problem of alienation, but only at the empirical level of the loss of the product of work through change in the market. This was quickly absorbed into a concept of alienation impervious to the current frustrations of human existence. Therefore it blocked the ability to approach, in a critical way, social interactions and, in general, peoples' lives. Its critique fell into ideology and there it remained. Its "humanism" was only propaganda, because its strategy of analysis tacitly—and from the beginning—stood upon the premise of the "end of the individual." This led to the impossibility of realizing, for instance, that the efficacy of actions no longer depended on the mere expense of energy, but also on other factors, which were apparently only of secondary importance, such as communication and motivation. Therefore, it was unable to adjust to a world in which the main adaptive *démarche* was creation.

Third, being extremely concerned to take over and "go beyond" the central concepts of the modern world, Eastern Marxism had grasped the importance of "liberty." But it constantly defined it by giving a metaphysical dimension to an empirical element—the assumption of necessity—so that, under the very abstract determination of liberty as the understanding of necessity, human necessities themselves were excluded. Consequently, the concept of liberty was compatible from its early days with the most tenacious dictatorship.

Fourth, another error pertaining to Eastern Marxism resides in the relationship between theory and praxis. As is well known, Eastern Marxism was very concerned about this relation and would constantly ask for an exemplary approach to the matter. However, in spite of the formal guarantees, it conceived of theory as mere empirical generalizations and praxis as labor. In fact the two terms were modified according to the difficulties resulting from the holding out of power. But, besides this aspect, the connection between theory and praxis was conceptualized in Eastern Marxism by giving the breadth of universal "truths" to some empirical statements: the theory-praxis connection implies a "transfer" of theoretical knowledge into organizing measures which are asked for by a theoretically informed praxis. This conceptualization still eluded the fact that in the connection between theory and praxis there are several phases to take in consideration—the elaboration of theory, spreading theoretical knowledge, the organization of action—each of which has specific achievements: true propositions, authentic beliefs, adequate decisions. Due to its constant state of uncertainty, Eastern Marxism approached the theory-praxis connection from the narrow perspective of the immediate action, which it applied to both the spreading of theoretical knowledge and the elaboration of theory. The consequence of this perspective was that the establishment of authentic beliefs was replaced by the propagandistic remaking of ideas, and the elaboration of true propositions, by the miming of texts considered to be sacrosanct. Adequate decisions were replaced by conformism and blind submission.

Examples of the faulty conception of the concrete within Eastern Marxism could go on. It took, as a starting point of its generalizations, the date of the experience, but its assessment was partial and arbitrary. It worked out ambitious and totalizing extrapolations, giving the impression of a high rank generalization theory. The first result of this approach was the incapacity, of a methodological nature, to establish the state of facts in an accurate way and, as a necessary consequence, the incapacity to formulate realistic prognoses. As a matter of fact, the history of Eastern Marxism is a history of miscarried prognoses. Another result was the real difficulty in criticizing this Marxism which nourished two illusions: the illusion of the adherence to the data of experience and the illusion of a thought which totalizes experience as a condition for the promotion of human identity. The intellectual community was late in realizing that between the contingent empiricism of Eastern Marxism and its formal rationalism, it was precisely the actual experience of man that could not be grasped. This fact was to become obvious only when its praxis started to be examined.

MARXISM "IN QUESTION"

"Real socialism" revealed some essential truths. Some examples of these truths are that the emphasis upon the role of the economy coupled with overlooking political and cultural emancipation could not provide for the economic development (it is known that even in its most promising moments, "real socialism" was not able to go beyond the level of the industrial development reached by the western European countries in the fifties, moreover it brought about a vast pauperization; an exclusively economic development (i.e. without change of institutions) cannot lead to the "post-industrial economy;" democracies are unbeatable in the field of economic development; the philosophies of "objective dialectics" are, by their nature, ideologies of totalitarianism and only the concept of history as a "struggle for recognition" is capable of endorsing democracy. However, all these truths were disclosed indirectly. What "real socialism" actually meant was a totalitarian society that aggravated not just alienation against the product of labour (thus generalizing frustrations), but also against one's own activity (destroying motivation) and against the generic human being (turning the specific attributes of the man acquainted with culture into a means of securing survival). This terrifying reality invalidated the claims of Eastern Marxism and compromised it definitively. Nevertheless, Eastern Marxism was, besides its self-understanding, an historical expression of Marxism. Does its failure question Marxism as a whole? My argument here is that beyond the assimilation of Marxism in Eastern Europe (which presented distortions), beyond the typical errors of Eastern Marxism (having to do with its very bases), there are errors pertaining to Marxism as such, which should be taken into consideration at this point.

"Real socialism," an instance where Eastern Marxism was actually put into effect, brought about discontents and protests and generated hard questions concerning its relevance as a test of Marxism itself, and even of Marx's theses. In the last analysis, are consequences not a decisive test for a theory? If this is the case, the answers, although very different, fall under some headings.

The followers of Marx, affected by the human tragedies generated by "real socialism" and by the stagnation of Marxism in the West, produced the thesis that Marx has not been understood so far. He remains "profound and subtle (and still uncomprehended)."[24] In virtue of the unusual complexity of his outlook, the problem of testing it should not be raised yet. In any case, "real socialism" is not a relevant test. However, this argument is practically impossible to defend, not only because it means abdication from responsibility, but also because of the agnosticism involved in it, which contradicts the theory itself. "Rather like Kierkegaard's existentialist God, whom we know only because he is unknowable, Marx's superiority arises from the fact that nobody can really understand him!"[25] That is why most of those who are faithful to Marx unreservedly consider Marxism to be innocent and the mistaken way it has been put into effect should be blamed for the course taken by "real socialism." Marx's adherents turned Marxism into an instrument of propaganda, against the background of the absence of the bourgeois-democratic traditions in eastern Europe.[26]

Nevertheless, the distinction between Marxism (which would be, strictly speaking, without essential shortcomings) and its putting into effect (which is responsible for its distortions) does not succeed if we take into consideration the fact that each transposition into "real life" brought about the same results: economical, social, political and moral crises. Their scope and frequency questions the outlook, in addition to its enactments. "More fundamental still were the philosophical roots of the failure. In the final analysis, Marxist-Leninist policies emerged from a basic misjudgment of history and from a fatal misconception of human nature. Ultimately, communism's failure is thus intellectual."[27] The failure being the failure of Marxism-Leninism, the question concerning the value of Marxism as such remains unanswered.

It is hard to leave out Marxism when we embark upon analyzing Eastern Marxism and "real socialism," since, historically speaking, the former was their premise (although it was assumed in a distorted way). Further, Marx was a continuation of humanism in modern times, and his work is the proof of an "undeniable humanist inspiration." This is betrayed, however, by Marx's strategy of analysis: in spite of being a materialist, he was not enough of a materialist. "Il faut renoncer au dogme selon lequel le pouvoir économique est à l'origine de tous les maux, admettre les dangers de toute forme de pouvoir incontrolé, et, adoptant un point de vue plus matérialiste encore que celui de Marx, nous rendre compte que le problème politique essentiel est d'empêcher d'abord toute violence physique, c'est-à-dire d'assurer la liberté dite formelle."[28] But Marx's strategy of analysis cannot be adequately characterized by opposing it to modern liberties since, on the one side, its original sense was to serve these liberties, and, on the other, an approach focused on the impact of the economy upon social life cannot be completely disqualified only because of its misuse. Therefore, I consider that, having in view the attachment of Marxism to modern humanism, but also its responsibility for what happened under "real socialism," the deepest source of shortcomings with Marxism should be looked for at the level of its strategy of analysis, which even within its lasting sides contains the premise of inadmissible compromises.

But, after all, what do we understand by Marxism? A philosophical work may quite commonly undergo variation and changes. However, an "-ism" attached to a work nails it in history. It implies the articulation of a univocal body of problems, ideas and theses. In the case of Marxism we could sum them up as follows: (a) The modern world has pointed out that man creates himself, but, at the same time, after having emancipated himself religiously (through the separation of the state from religion) and politically (by recognizing the fundamental rights and liberties of the individual granted constitutionally) he did not succeed in bringing to an end this emancipation, reaching a human emancipation (i.e., an agreement between existence and the free, the rational and the creative human essence). His existence is an alienated existence and the source of all his alienation is the alienation in the process of work under the conditions of private property; (b) knowledge of modern society includes a view of transcending alienation and implies a theory with a high degree of generalization and reflection; (c) the history of humanity is a progress, through alienations, towards the suppression of alienation; (d) this suppression supposes a practical approach; (e) praxis offers the general horizon of knowledge and of the understanding of reality; (f) communism is the social form without alienation, which brings about, at the same time, the transposition of philosophy into real life and the agreement between man's existence and his essence—it is also the framework in which the individual can freely express his creative capacities; (g) the social agent that is associated with the achievement of communism is the proletariat; (h) the revolution is the condition of the passage to communism.

This corpus of problems, ideas and theses is to be found in all the early and late analyses Marx and Engels produced. The changes that occurred in their outlook did not alter the main body of thought. The actual differences between Marx and Engels are concerned with their interpretations of the relation between action and reality. While Marx cultivated historicism as a philosophy of praxis, Engels was an adherent of a naturalism, concentrating on the idea of general laws of nature, society and thinking. Eastern Marxism was to take the latter as its basis. It viewed the "materialist conception of history" as a *Weltanschauung*, and knowledge as a "reflection of reality;" it also made use of the idea of the "dialectics of nature," and interpreted the "end of philosophy" as a development of the "positive science of nature," etc. But the ascending line in Eastern Marxism does not lead only to Engels, since the latter formulated concepts which essentially agreed with those of Marx. And if, later, there were differences to be seen, one may say that Engels took it upon himself to explain what was not very clear in Marx. For instance, Engels claimed that the origin of historical materialism consisted of the passage from the cult of the abstract man to real people, considered in their concrete historical action.[29] But "concrete historical action" takes place in the field of "objective reality," which constantly glides from the status of reality mediated by praxis (which it most often does in Marx), to the status of metaphysical reality, which prescribes norms for action that Marx did not preclude. With Marx under pressure from the philosophy of romanticism, there appeared to be, besides the program of approaching reality as something concrete and historical, a slide towards the assumption of the facts of experience associated with the formal premise which alters them in the framework of an obsolete metaphysics.

The slide from a concrete historical analysis of reality to a processing conditioned by preliminary formal assumptions was not a benign tendency but a fact in Marxist writings. Consequently, from the very beginning, the terms in which Marxism took over the reality of the facts of experience were, of course, not only important but mainly insufficient and, in the end, the prognoses based on them were not confirmed. The history of Marxism was, therefore, coextensive with a failed struggle for adequately representing human experience. In what follows, I would like to illustrate this idea by examining the fundamental anthropological concepts of Marxism.

Originally, Marxism was an anthropocentric philosophy, and given the way in which it approached human essence, Engels was right, of course, to particularize Marxism by showing its interest in "real people and their actual historical action." In the sphere of "actual historical action" Marx noticed the important position held by work, but he assumed it—being conditioned by the tradition of modern philosophical monism—as a sort of "substance" of human reality. In spite of the formal guarantees that their view would remain faithful to the "real premise" and was thus placed, without deviations, in the field of history, beyond the distinctions made, for instance, in *German Ideology*, Marx and Engels bestowed a privileged status on "work," to the detriment of other components of "actual historical action." The latter, even if registered, was lost under the weight of the metaphysics of "work." In his strong, but very popular wording, Engels considered "work" to be the "key for the understanding of society," and the only distinctive character between "human society" and a "flock of monkeys."[30] Evidently enough, Marx's inspired remark concerning the importance of work in human ontology was inadequately made use of through a generalization contrary to concrete history and liable to be misread.

Why is it that thoroughgoing remarks were inadequately made use of in Marxism? I would say that, in order to answer this question, we should take into consideration the characteristics required for a philosophy that contains the principle necessary to induce social change, as compared to a philosophy that confines itself to produce reflection. In the first category we have a philosophy which eludes the complexity of reality since it derives almost everything from a prime factor. And Marx followed that way when he stated the relation between "basis" and "superstructure," or the "technology in production" and the fundamental social relation. This philosophy becomes an Ursprungsphilosophie.[31]

The approaching of the states of facts through observation, mediated by a philosophy which constantly recognizes a prime factor (that determines or generates all the other factors), is to be found as a prototheoretical structure in Marxism. My opinion is that the presence of this structure is due to the alignment of Marx and Marxism to a philosophical tradition which may give results so long as it only promotes reflection, but which risks enormously when it embarks upon reorganizing society. The above-mentioned structure had an impact, first of all, upon the concept of the modern world with which, Marx operated, a restrictive concept from the outset. As everywhere else, Marx and Marxism proclaimed the rule of concrete analysis and, as a preliminary step, the rule of an analysis anchored in the "real premises" of the people's life; however, these premises quickly vanished within a "dialectics" that constantly abandoned the facts and even defied them.

I would like to illustrate this point by examining the connotation of the concept of modern society as it appears in *The Manifesto of the Communist Party* (1848), *Anti-Dühring* (1878), *Capital* (1867). In these works, Marx and Engels specified the idea of modern society at four levels. On the economic one, there is the replacement of "manufacturers" by "large industry," and of the "division in the means of production" by their "centralization," there is the permanent "revolutionizing" of the means of production, and the "cosmopolitan" character of production and consumption. On the social level, there is the triumph of "modern bourgeois property," social polarization and the appearance of a "new class antagonism," the replacement of the "industrial middle class" by the "modern bourgeoisie," the increasing "proletarization," losing the independent character of work, the transformation of the worker into an appendage of the machine, the replacement of "local insolation" by "multilateral exchange," and the manifold interdependence among nations. On the political and administrative level, there is "political emancipation," and the state as the "formal administration" (the power of which is limited by "civil society") controlled by the holders of the economic power who promote their interest within the parliamentary representatives. Finally, on the cultural level, there is the spread of the Enlightenment, the expansion of nomological knowledge of nature and society, on an experimental basis, the building up of "world literature," and the transformation of science into a factor for the development of technology and production. The description of many levels of modern society is full of piercing remarks and it is impressive in its scope.[32] However, this description is constantly employed under the control of a restrictive interpretation, which reduces modern society to a hypostatic objectivation of production. Beyond all its variants, Marxism never gave up the hypostatization of production, and the famous introduction to the *Critique of Political Economy* clearly expressed its paradigm.

POST-COMMUNISIM AND MARXISM

In the early 1980s it had become clear that no attempt to reform "real socialism" could give any beneficial results and that the idea of "socialism with a human face" had no chance of survival. Therefore, socialism itself had to be questioned and, with it, of course, its philosophical basis, i.e. Marxism. The aggravation of the economic, political, cultural and moral crisis brought about the collapse of socialism and of Eastern Marxism. The champions of change as well as the masses who lived to experience the satisfaction of getting rid of the nightmare of communism did not need Marxism any more and did not want to have anything to do with it, even if there had been times when they had embraced Marx's turning against dictatorship. The classical philosophies of liberty were presently taken up instead. The legislation of totalitarian coercion fell apart once the citizens could exercise their liberties. The building up of a new internal and international political order, based on the proclamation of the fundamental rights and liberties of the individual and on the state of justice, has started.

However, the establishment of the new political order is neither simple, nor guaranteed, as it was hoped in the quasi general post-1989 enthusiasm. Quite to the contrary, in spite of the proclaimed liberties, there is constantly the risk of stopping half-way or even of falling back. I would like to consider two of these major risks, which are evident at the present moment.

The concept of society produced by "real socialism" supposed a large enterprise, the rationalization of which consisted in its organization and disciplining by a single centre of command. This view of society and its rationalization generated deep crises whenever it had been put into practice, such as economic crises and crises of legitimation, of motivation and of creativity. The market economy proved to be once again superior and it definitively eluded an ideological interpretation being in agreement with human nature, modern society, science and advanced technology. In the first analysis, society can only be conceived, from now on, as a huge market with protagonists exchanging performances. The policies implemented in eastern Europe after 1989 have enforced the need to conceive society starting from the market economy, yet they have restrained society to a market. They have been persuaded that the natural movement of the market forces would generate a new society. Today it is very clear that these policies represent procedures of change, which are no doubt necessary, but they do not contain procedures of changing society, which are also necessary. We cannot speak of a society in the real sense of the word where the functioning is not grounded on a sufficient normative basis. If we see the facts from this point of view, we can say, then, that in eastern Europe we do not have enough structured societies based on liberties guaranteed by norms, but, for the time being, have only a social libertinism which, in its turn, perpetuates old crises. It is here that "se developpe ce que les Américains ont appelé le libéralisme libertaire. Mais comment oublier que cette société, réduite à son instrumentalité, à son changement et à la stratégie de ses dirigeants, est aussi une société, réduite à son instrumentalité, à son changement et à la stratégie de ses dirigeants, est aussi une société sauvage où les laissés-pour-compte ont de moins de chances de rentrer dans la course, où les inégalités sociales augmentent, bien que ne cesse de croître la classe moyenne, et dont ne se tiennent éloignées que les adeptes des cultures minoritaires qui entretiennent avec la culture majoritaire des relation inégalitaires de disglossie."[33] And against this background, there appears the major risk, in some at least of the east European countries, that the line of thought of those who had endorsed "real socialism" might have a short term success among some poorly informed people that continue to be the victims of the confusion between order and the totalitarian "order."

This success is not so improbable as it seems at first sight since the ideology of "real socialism" has meanwhile acquired a false consciousness—with a strong impact in east European cultures where the traditions of the Enlightenment were awakened by totalitarian domination—i.e., nationalism. Under the circumstances of the wearing out and the impairment of the social ideals of Marxism (equality, freedom from exploitation, emancipation, etc.) the former adherents of "real socialism" proclaimed the defense of the nation—postulated as being in permanent danger—in order to obtain a new totalitarian mobilization of the people. The xenophobic nationalism, often disposing of the still undemolished "network" of the old regime propaganda, tries to install itself as a new dominant ideology.

The lasting crises in eastern Europe cannot be solved by the ideology, however changed, of "real socialism." Reorganized, this can hamper and delay the solution to the problems, which requires the passage to an enlightened liberalism. The situation in this part of Europe clearly shows that the time of socialism and of the social libertinism is past, and that only by joining a constitutional liberalism, with a legislation capable of endorsing the social equilibrium without setting limits to natural liberties is it possible to open the true way out of the structural crises that threaten to become chronic. On the other hand, it might be that the "new alliance" between liberalism and social reformism is not only the problem that now challenges those who live in eastern Europe, but is also a general European problem, one especially pertaining to the united Europe.[34] Whatever the situation after the collapse, we are not at the "end of history," but rather at the beginning of a history which has to be conscientiously edified as a history of liberty. In order that the history we are building up be a history of liberty, a critical consciousness and, as a matter of fact, a critical theory of society, is needed. Reluctant, in principle, to the market economy and to the modern doctrine of the natural rights and liberties of the individual, Marxism, however detached from the eastern totalitarian experience, cannot play the role of this theory. At a broader level, one needs to accept the fact that society has enormously changed, and, thus, Marxist theorems require a critique of themselves. Marx was right from a very important point of view: under the circumstances of advanced modernity, it is only through "solidarity" that men can live in a *richtige Gesellschaft*. But this is another kind of solidarity than the limiting one, the one liable to generate the totalitarian regimes of the proletariat or of other particular groups: "die Solidarität der Menschen als endlicher, von Leiden und Tod bedrohten Wesen, die schöner, helter und länger leben wollen, eine Solidarität die schliesslich auf die Kreatur schlechthin sich erstreken könnte."[35]

Although oriented towards the "real premises" of life, Marxism did not consider the natural bent of the individual to assume himself as a finite being. Moreover, Marxism was not concerned, in a systematic way, with the fact that the modern world had brought about an increase in reflexivity (which it actually encouraged) so that here individuality may constitute itself on a deeper

level. The individual mediates the reality of the world through his own experience; it is on this basis that his socialization takes place. Marxism did not
perceive the complexity of the mediation of socialization in modern society by
the processes of reflective individualization and, consequently, came to conceive of socialization as being separated from the lived reality of human life.
Therefore, in order to adjust the theory to this reality, Marxism (as in Engels'
case) was bound to resort to supplementary hypotheses taken from an evolutionary metaphysics of which it soon became compromised.

On the historical level, Marxism is now defeated by the enlightened liberalism initiated by Locke, Montesquieu and Jefferson. This defeat is not the
fallacious appearance of an actual victory,[36] even if the economic dynamics
of the West cannot be fully separated from the pressures exercised by the
working movement. Despite the movement's goals of diminishing the frustrations of and eliminating alienation from modern society, its program of
achieving this goal failed, despite the initial declared intentions and promises,
to their aggravation. This is not to be explained by the common difference
between a theory and putting that theory into effect, but rather by the fact
that the theory itself contains shortcomings liable to betray its objectives. Most
recently, the unexpectedly rapid disintegration of "real socialism" and the
sudden abandonment of Marxism in eastern Europe in favor of liberalism
proves the inadequacy of Marxism, as a theory and practice, to the real needs
of the individual.

After "real socialism" has become, like fascism, merely a chapter in history,
and liberal democracy is embraced more and more, it is tempting to consider
the latter as being triumphant on a large scale. The political fights seem to
take place on its ground now. History, in the traditional sense, the political
confrontation between mutually exclusive alternatives, seems to have come
to an end. Francis Fukuyama argues that, if we look upon "history" in a
Hegelian way, as an "oriented development," and if we take into consideration the fact that liberal democracy, which disposes of two solid
principles—equality and liberty—favors the solution of major social conflicts, one can now speak of the "end of history."[37] But his line of argument
involves certain essential elements: that there has been a general assimilation
of the advantages of the liberal society; that liberalism does not nourish antagonistic directions which might endanger it; and that liberal democracy is
constantly triumphant. But reality offers us another picture. The critique of

liberalism—and not only the critique that blames the weakening of the community, insufficient opportunities for the democratic participation, and the stimulation of egoism, for liberalism's woes (i.e, a critique that can be absorbed by liberalism itself), but also the critique from the standpoint of the national-communism, which excludes liberalism—has not ceased, in spite of its important victory in eastern Europe. Its strategy has become, however, more reflective and it actually resumes the antiliberal attack of the thirties in Europe. The liberal democracy, based on the market economy, the state of justice, natural rights and the liberties of the individual has proved to be once again superior. Its abandonment always had painful consequences. But even the history we have to run through in Eastern Europe compels us not to consider the history of the fight for recognition, and, in fact, for liberty, as being a closed one, in other words, for "history" as such, in the traditional sense.

Marxism was a catalyst in the reflection attached to the idea of the transformation of history into a history of liberty. A large part of the last century's philosophy, sociology, politics and culture, in general, cannot be understood without its suppositions. As a philosophy containing the principle of its transposition into social praxis, it has registered a defeat: the market economy proved to be the economic framework of civilization and not a form condemned by history; the insistence upon work to the detriment of the other components of human ontology proved to be a way of pauperization; the proletariat is not the bearer of a new society, but a social group that struggles for a better life; the autolimitation of liberty does not prepare a new liberty, but the destruction of all liberty; the placement of the mechanisms deciding the direction of evolution of society outside the individual praxis creates an objectivism that legitimates dictatorship. etc. The collapse of "real socialism" determined the withdrawal of Marxism from actual life, although, at least not all over eastern Europe, social reality has not taken a univocal direction yet. There are no factual arguments in favor of an alternative to the liberal society, but a liberalism that contains nothing else besides a mere confidence in its principles and institutions promotes, as some countries of the region illustrate already, the national-communism and, with it, the self-destruction of liberalism. Therefore, the only solution now is a liberalism aware of the conditions of its possibility, i.e., a substantive liberalism.

The future of Marxism can be estimated by taking into consideration the practical need of this substantive liberalism. The essential question is whether

Marx's theoretical work offers the intellectual instruments that could serve this liberalism. It is known that for quite a long time, Marxism had taken up the project of a new cultural harmony, which expressed itself in the "normative totality" of the theory.[38] The project proved to be utopian and the "normative totality" turned out to be a speculative product. The history of Marxism is a progressive reduction of its normative claims and of its normative totality, in consequence of which Marxism revealed itself to be a critique of the social reality nourished by the phenomenon of alienation in modern times. Since it failed, this critique determined an aggravation of alienation. After the collapse of "real socialism" we should raise not only the somewhat trivial problem of the causes of this failure, but rather we should go through the inner shortcomings of Marxism which made the reality of Marxism contradict its theory.

This approach is not altogether new. It has been thought for quite some time now that the Marxist theory conceptualizes important components of experienced reality, such as the production component, but the inevitable components, such as the normativity of social interactions and reflexivity, are dealt with incompletely or even avoided, so that the result of its objectivation differs, necessarily, from what it had promised in theory. Many intellectuals who embraced Marxism were ready to examine the theory itself from a critical standpoint. They took up important initiatives: the re-establishment of "human nature" against its dissolution in social relations (Adorno); the strengthening of "structure" as an ontic reality against its dissolution in psychological praxis (Althusser); the recovery of nature, in general, against subjectivism (Eberman); the ruling out of the reduction of the cultural reproduction of the species to the production of goods (feminism); the recovery of democracy as such, against its instrumentalization (Castoriadis), to name a few. But, these initiatives, however salutary, are mere adjustments within a theory which needs to be questioned as a whole.

This questioning can approach Marxism from two points of view which should be clearly distinguished: first, Marx's work as a theory concerning the dynamics of modern society and Marx's work as a theory and project of transcending alienation in a practical way. These two sides are usually not well-differentiated in the analysis of Marxism and, therefore, it very often happens that either the theory concerning the dynamics of modern society is denounced in the name of the failure of the project or that the theory and the project are defended in the name of some hypotheses relative to modern society. Nowadays, in eastern Europe even qualified intellectuals consider the theory as something passed and gone, since they take into consideration the failure of the project.

Marx's work remains a work of historical importance to research to modern society. The most recent phase of the Marx-Weber debate pointed out, for instance, that "the Marx-Weber discussion" is a theoretically fruitful encounter, both sides having resources the other can use, so that there is a visible and justified tendency towards a "continuous interaction" of the two outlooks, which can be considered as "complementary." "However, if convergence is construed to mean no more than complementary, then some justification for the assertion exists. Even such a diminished claim should not be mistaken for one of parity: Marxism can stand alone without Weber's theory, but without the base of Marxist conceptualizations, Weberian class theory lacks even an agenda." [39] There are also the comprehensive analyses of the "great failure," that explain the phenomenology of "real socialism" through the characteristics of the Marxist-Leninist ideology, but distinguish this aspect, related to the Marxist theory and project, from Marx's hypotheses and theorems concerning modern society.

But if we start from the *Theses on Feuerbach* it is clear that a Marxism regarded as a theory of modern society, competing with Max Weber, or Durkheim, or another complementary thinker, is only half-Marxism. One can assume that the half-Marxism is still Marxism. However, Marxism as a whole is, by its nature, an approach to social reality from the standpoint of its practical change with the view to eliminating alienation, and is, therefore, both a theory and a project, or, in a word, a project-theory. What can be said about it now? Is it valid and does it have any future?

Marxism is organized around the problem of alienation in modern society consisting of an attempt to articulate the theory that assumes the human specific character, and formulating practical solutions in given contexts. Marxism, with its anthropocentric purport, is based on anthropological concepts. These communicate, of course, with the economic, sociological and historical concepts. However, they remain fundamental and they condition the whole organization of the theory. But the theory is, at least in principle, like any other theory of an emancipatory kind, reflective, i.e., it includes the knowledge of the conditions of its possibility (genesis and application). When these conditions change, the theory should be reformulated.

Now, the conditions of application have changed to such an extent that, for a long time, the problem with Marxism has been not only the need to reformulate the theory, but also to reconstruct it. This means not just a reformulation of the theses which leaves the bases unchanged, but a resettlement of the bases themselves. *"Rekonstruktion* bedeutet in unserem Zusammenhang, dass man eine Theorie auseinandernimmt und in neuer Form wieder zusammensetzt, um das Ziel, das sie sich gesetzt hat, besser zu erreichen: das ist der normale (ich meine: auch für Marxisten normale) Umgang mit einer Theorie die Revision bedarf, dessen Anregungspotential aber noch (immer) nicht ausgeschöpft ist."[40]

The need for reconstruction was not brought forward by the collapse of "real socialism." It was felt as early as the end of the last century, when it had become obvious that the prognoses concerning the fatal crisis of the market economy was erroneous, and that the theory endorsing it was wrong. Later, it was constantly evident as modern society was achieving (of course, not without crises), instead of the foreseen crash, technical, scientific, cultural, economic and historical progress. And the need for reconstruction was also acute when it had become clear that the society resulting from the application of the strategies inspired by Marxism not only failed to bring about the promised leap into the "empire of liberty," but, quite on the on the contrary, caused the aggravation of man's dependencies. However, the collapse of "real socialism" strongly pointed out that this reconstruction was not an option between alternatives, but the only chance left for Marxism to play a significant part as an emancipatory theory.

Habermas took up the reconstruction of Marxism by adequately choosing the plan of the anthropological concepts as a starting point and by answering the question concerning the necessary and sufficient concepts in order to seize the specific human characteristics in a theory of social evolution. He realized that "das Marxsche Konzept der gesellschaftlichen Arbeit eignet sich mithin zur Abgrenzung der Lebenweise der Hominiden gegenüber der Primaten; aber es trifft nicht die spezifisch menschliche Reproduktion des Lebens."[41] Habermas suggested that "work" and the "communicatively mediated interaction" should be included among the anthropological concepts of Marxism. He found the way in which the necessary reconstruction could be accomplished; the extension of the list of anthropological concepts which cannot be derived one from the other. His suggestion—justifiable by the material taken into consideration (studies of interactions guided by norms) and the theoretical context (marked by the variants of technocratism)—should be, however, widened by taking into consideration new data (studies of human nature and behaviors) in a new theoretical context (in which we should be cautious as far as the programs of extended socialization of life are concerned). And this is because an anthropology grounded on the concepts of "work" and "communicatively mediated interaction" cannot sufficiently account for the constant values of human nature and misses, in its turn, the "concrete analysis of the concrete historical situation." The new ethnology and, in general, the anthropological and psychological study of man, as well as the defeat of "real socialism," whatever circumstances we could take into consideration, force us to rethink the weight of human nature within human experience. Habermas would be right, and his list of anthropological concepts would be applicable, if the subject-object relation and the communicatively mediated interaction could "absorb" the other determinations of the human specific character. But these cannot be approached either as extensions of the process (since they do not wholly depend on it) or as interactively or communicatively mediated phenomena, since they are individualized by their nature.

Without entering into details of the list of anthropological concepts, I should only point out that Marx's work could not face this problem even if in *The German Ideology*, for instance, he extended the list to include, besides work, communicative interactions and consciousness. Although extended, the list did not account for the situation that apart from the function "circle" of work, language and consciousness, man is, "by nature," endowed with some needs, namely, he has the capacity to choose, he is reflective and he strives for liberty. All these needs are present not in the facts of human experience, but only in the "media" created by production and the social interactions. Nevertheless, they do not let themselves melt in these media for the simple reason that they precede them in some respects.

From what I have said, if we reconstruct anthropology as the basis of social evolution so as to seize in concepts the human specific character and account for the natural components of human actions—then we should admit that: (a) the list of concepts cannot be restricted to work, language, or communication, since it should also include human needs; the capacity to choose, to work, the communicatively mediated interaction, reflectivity, liberty; (b) none of these determinations can be derived from one another, as a mere effect, or can be interpreted, without remainder as the mere "superstructure" of another. A reconstructed Marxism should assume, in its turn, the following two truths: an extended list of anthropological concepts and the failure of monism. However, one may raise the question of whether the result of this reconstruction is not something else from what Marxism used to be: a theory that appeared as a result of Romanticism which brought to light the "continent" of social interactions, revealing deep insights, which later turned into concepts under an enormous unifying pressure, imposing formal conditions to the approach to the status of fact, continuing the line of metaphysical monism. Rather, a Marxism reconstructed at the level of present experience would be a distant follower of Marx, the result of complicated marriages, which could no longer justify the name of Marxism.

notes

1. Gabriel Liiceanu, "Intre chilie si agosa," in *22*, nr. 6, 1990, p. 12.

2. Alexandru Zub, "Pentru a stapini prezentul puterea ne-a furat trecutual," in *22*, nr. 7, 1991, p. 10.

3. Sorin Vieru, "Ginduri despre filozofie," in *22*, nr. 4, 1990, p. 22.

4. Grin Antonescu, "Despre 'intelectualii' de servicin," in *22*, nr. 19, 1991, p. 11.

5. Ihor Lemnij, "Piata—un calculator bine temperat," in *22*, nr. 11, 1990, p. 9.

6. Gabriel Andreescu, "Din nou despre Marxism," in *22*, nr. 31, 1990, p. 13.

7. Henri Wald, "Marx, azi," in *22*, nr. 21. 1991, p. 14.

8. Andrei Marga, *Introducere in metodologia si argumentarea filozofica* (Cluj-Napoca: Dacia, 1992), p. 32-33.

9. Gabriel Andreescu, p. 15.

10. Adrian Miroiu, "Dincolo de diletantism," in *22*, nr. 5, 1990.

11. Silvin Brucan, "Socialismul mondial la rascruce," in *22*, nr. 1, 1990, p. 4.

12. Rosa Luxemburg, "Die russische Revolution (1918), in Rosa Luxemburg, *Schriften zur Theorie der Spontaneität* (Reinbek bei Hamburg; Rowohlt, 1970) p. 191.

13. Oskar Negt, "Marxismus als Legitimationswissenschaft Zur Genese der stalinistischen Philosophie," in *Kontroversen über dialektischen und mechanistischen Materialismus*, ed. Nikolai Bucharin, Abram Deborin (Frankfurt am Main: Suhrkamp, 1974) p. 15.

14. Ibid., p. 21.

15. M. Mitin, "Über die Ergebnisse der philosophischen Diskussion," in Bucharin, Deborin, p. 345.

16. I.V. Stalin, "Über dialektischen und historischen Materialismus," in Hans-Joachim Lieber, Karl-Heinz Ruffmann (Hrsg.), *Der Sowjetkommunismus Dokumente.* Band 1, Die politische-ideologischen Konzeptionen (Köln, Berlin: Kiepenhen & Witsch,1963) p. 393-400.

17. A. A. Shdanow, "Kritische Bemerkungen," in Lieber, Ruffmann, p. 407-413.

18. Vezi Calina Mare, *Introducere in ontologia generala,* (Bucuresti: Albatros, 1980) p. 45.

19. Ioan Ianosi, *Umanismul: viziune si intruchipare,* (Bucuresti: Eminescu, 1978), p. 40.

20. Radu Florian, *Antonio Gramsci, Un Marxist contemporan* (Bucuresti: Editura Politica, 1982), p. 69.

21. Dumitru Ghise, *Dimensiuni umane,* (Bucuresti: Editura Eminescu, 1979), p. 5–64.

22. Angela Botez, "Cultura si creatia—permanente tematice ale culturii românesti," in Dumitru Ghise, Angela Botez (coord.) *Cultura, creatia, valoarea—motive dominante ale filozofiei românesti,* (Bucuresti: Editura Eminescu, 1983), p. 13-23.

23. Jürgen Habermas, "Literaturbericht zur philosophischen Diskussion um Marx und den Marxismus," in *Theorie und Praxis,* (Frankfurt am Main: Suhrkamp, 1974), p. 387-463.

24. S.Timpanaro, *On Materialism,* (London: New Left Books, 1975), p. 74.

25. John Hoffman, *The Gramscian Challenge, Coercion and Consent in Marxist Political Theory,* (Oxford: Basil Blackwell, 1984), p. 8.

26. Bloch, p. 165–166.

27. Zbigniew Brzezinski, *The Grand Failure, The Birth and Death of Communism in the Twentieth Century,* (London: Macdonald & Co., 1989) p. 242.

28. Karl Popper, *La société ouverte et ses ennemis,* Tame 2, *Hegel et Marx,* (Paris: Edition due Senie, 1979), p. 41.

29. Engels, "Ludwig Feuerbach si sfirsitul filozofiei clasice germane," in Marx, Engels, *Opera alese,*(Bucuresti: Editura Politica, 1965), vol. II, p. 356–357.

30. Marx, Engels, *Opere,* (Bucuresti: Editura Politica, 1964), vol. 20, p. 473.

31. Theodor W. Adorno, *Zur Metakritik der Erkenntnistheorie, Studien über Husserl and die phänomenologischen Antinomien,* (Stuttgart, 1956), p. 15–16.

32. Andrei Marga, *Rationalizare, comunicare, argumentare,* (Cluj: Dacia, 1991), p. 19–20.

33. Alain Touraine, *Critique de la modernité,* Paris: Fayard, 1992), p. 211–212.

34. Ralf Dahrendorf, *Reflexions sur la révolution en Europe 1989–1990,* (Paris: Senil,

1991), p. 88.

35. Max Horkheimer, "Marx heute (1968)," in *Gesellschaft im Übergang*, (Frankfurt am Main: Athenäum Fischer Taschenbuch Verlag, 1972), p. 160.

36. August del Noce, "Le marxisme meurt a l'est parce qu'il s'est realisé a l'ouest," *Krisis*, Paris, nr. 6, 1990, p. 125.

37. Francis Fukuyama, "The End of History?" in *The National Interest*, 1989. See Francis Fukuyama, *The End of History and the Last Man*, (New York: The Free Press, 1992).

38. Martin Jay, *Fin-de-Siècle Socialism and Other Essays*, (New York, London: Routledge, 1988), p. 2.

39. Morton G. Wenger, "Class Closure and the Historical/Structural Limits of the Marx-Weber Convergence," in *The Marx-Weber Debate*, Norbert Wiley, ed. (Newburg Park, Beverly Hills, London, Delhi: Sage Publications, 1987), p. 63.

40. Jürgen Habermas, *Zur Rekonstruktion des Historischen Materialismus,* (Frankfurt am Main: Suhrkamp, 1976), p. 9.

41. Ibid., p. 149.

GAYATRI CHAKRAVORTY SPIVAK

supplementing marxism

I will make six points telegraphically. First: Early and late, Marx painstakingly established a definition for the term "social" which involved a rationalization of the merely individual. To grasp this rationalization is class-consciousness. To be able to use it is the Enlightenment project of the public use of reason, but with the proletarian rather than a bourgeois subject. When, however, Marx used the word social or society to project or describe the goal of such a public use of reason he seemed to be relying on an unresearched, incoherent, humanist notion. In the gap between these two uses of the "social," systemic Marxisms bloom, fester and fail. Any reformist critique of Marxism which further rationalizes the social ignores and runs the same risk.[1]

Second: The strongest humanist support of Marxism is the critique of the reification of labor. This implicit critique, sometimes unrecognizable as such, and sometimes surrounded by more spectacular arguments, runs like a red thread from great national liberation movements all the way to romantic anti-capitalism. In its vaguest yet most robust articulation it asserts that labor itself must not be commodified and is grounded in a binary opposition between labor and commodity.[2] Marx's notion of the use of reason as class consciousness in a socialized society, however, was the recognition that labor as a particularization of labor power was a commodity, although of a special kind. In Marx's view, it is only with this understanding that the agents of production, the workers, can move to become the agents of the social. Indeed, Marx describes the common double nature of commodity and work as "the pivot [*der Springpunkt*] around which the understanding of political economy revolves [*dreht um*]."[3] It is because of this pivotal concept that he recommends the explanation of the circuit of capitals spelled out in terms of the commodity as the most serviceable for class-conscious workers bent upon change, upon appropriating the surplus for redistribution. Without work on the second use of "social," which I believe is insufficiently thought through in Marx, neither the possibility nor the impossibility of such moves can be grasped (see note 1).

Third: If the Marxian project of class-consciousness were not anchored in a fully saturated, rationalized class subject and secured by the assurance of a certain end, it could serve to give shape to a persistent critique of capitalism; to combat the humanist critique of reification which can be and is co-opted and modernized to recode unreconstructed global capitalism as democracy. A brief presentation permits telegraphic sketches, therefore let me say that this persistence may juggle to an uneven three-step where communism is a figuration of the impossible which Derrida's work allows us to call spectrality: Communism is a figuration of the impossible in view of which capitalism and socialism can be perceived with some effort as each other's *différance*.

Jacques Derrida has recently shown some appropriate irritation with the harnessing of deconstruction by "a community of well-meaning deconstructionists reassured and reconciled with the world in ethical certainty, good conscience, satisfaction of service rendered and the consciousness of duty accomplished, or more heroically still, yet to be accomplished."[4] I hope therefore that he will not be dismayed if I say that in this sketching of the three-step where communism is a figuration of the impossible in view of which capitalism can be effortfully perceived as socialism's *différance*, I have brutally reduced his work to formulas. For the first part, the figuration of the impossible, I quote, "the law is the element of calculation and it is just that there be law. But justice is incalculable. It requires us to calculate with the incalculable."[5]

Let us reduce further. Socialism is in the element of calculation and it is just that there be socialism, but communism is incalculable. It requires us to calculate with the incalculable, precisely what Marx left dangerously uncalculated. I owe another formula to my friend Theodor Shanin: socialism is about justice, not primarily about development. For the second part of my sketched three-step where capitalism and socialism can be effortfully perceived as each other's *différance*, I have walked back to a much earlier remark of Derrida's and reductively treated it as a formula:

> The same, precisely, is *différance*...as the displaced and equivocal passage of one different thing to another, from one term of an opposition [here capitalism and socialism] to the other. Thus one could reconsider all the pairs of opposites...on which our discourse lives, not in order to see opposition [between capitalism and socialism] be erased but to see what indicates that each of the terms *must* appear as the *différance* of the other, as the different and deferred within the systematic ordering of the same.[6]

Please note that I have not said that this transformation or the rational calculation will take place or even will have taken place. I have not even said may take place, but merely can take place. The *savoir* may be here but the *pouvoir* is elsewhere. A conference can only ask a question, whither Marxism, remembering that a blueprint of this *différance* is teleologically given in the final pages of the third volume of *Capital*.[7]

Fourth: What role can my group play? Again, a telegraphic definition. "My group." The middle class professional migrants who entered the United States after Lyndon Johnson relaxed quotas in 1965, leading to a 500% increase in Asian immigration, otherwise called the brain-drain, disguising the poaching it sometimes was. More important, I am speaking of their children, Americans psychologically integrated into the expectation of civil agency here.[8] I am speaking of, and indeed for this group because when we talk about Marxism at academic conferences in the U. S. we so often lay out grand plans whose agents, if they exist, never come to these conferences. Or we lay plans which presuppose incredible systemic changes. What I am going to suggest will no doubt make no more than a minute contribution to the great collective persistent critique that I sketched in point three, but it is something we can do tomorrow, or in fact, today.

Of the earlier generation of these migrants I speak only of those not directly involved in the financialization of the globe, *rentiers* of the New World Order, so to speak. Indirectly, the entire group, having migrated, has a stake in dominant global capital; leaving post-colonial problems, leaving the failure of decolonization, coming with the hope of justice under capitalism. This fact, which recodes itself as the often unacknowledged unease of having left, appears as various sorts of psychic phenomena which, in another code, may perhaps be called "reaction-formations." (Please remember, I am not speaking of refugees and exiles, or of the underclass, but rather of economic migrants after 1965, relatively well-placed new immigrants, model minorities. We have to take into account that, even within this group, women are most often exilic, since they seldom have a "real choice" in the decision, and are often obliged to act out a custodianship of "culture"—in food habits, dress habits, sexual codes and the like—in migrancy).

The most noticeable of these "reaction formations" in the current conjuncture is an unexamined culturalism, which in turn allows the recoding of capitalism as democracy. Of course matters are rather more indeterminate if one pauses to ponder, but my register allows the abstract, telegraphic, rational-expectations language with which we make sense of our lives.

Unexamined culturalism. The telegraphic mode welcomes dictionary entries and accordingly I offer one on reaction-formation: "Psychological attitude or habitus diametrically opposed to a repressed wish, and constituted as a reaction against it…. In [psychic] economic terms, reaction-formation is the counter-cathexis of a conscious element: equal in its strength to the unconscious cathexis, it works in the contrary direction."[9] This precarious pathology—the American dream cooked in an hallucinatory culturalism—makes the place of nationality or nationalism willy-nilly negotiable for my group. The energy of that negotiation can be more productively channelled into the area where responsibility has an unavoidable bond with freedom of subjective consciousness or purity of intentionality. If we as a group are in the grip of a dream of reparation by our culturalism, our negotiable nationality can, through teaching and learning of rational transnational awareness, come to realize that in the current post-Soviet conjuncture, to work at the *différance* of capitalism and socialism in the heart of dominant capitalism may be more reparatory towards the places we left behind than the culturalism that feeds, financially and otherwise, the various fanaticisms that lodge in the fault line between nation and state opened up by that very conjuncture. This last sentence is not only telegraphic but telescopic. Believe me, I unpack every phrase and clause of it daily in areas and arenas where I have more time and greater responsibility. Here I must acknowledge again that I have, without offense, I hope, made use of a bit of Derrida in my reductive way: "One can doubtless decenter the subject, as is easily said, without challenging anew the bond between, on the one hand, responsibility, and, on the other, freedom of subjective consciousness or purity of intentionality."[10] Giving shape without end to what I have telescoped in a sentence is, I hope, one small way of accepting that challenge.

Fifth: A word now about another way of working with the rational kernel of Marx's rational thought in the context of a more diversified struggle in which some of us also take part. To tabulate: feminism, anti-racism, anti-colonialism. Here I will repeat a conviction that has been growing over the last few years. In this context the nascent crisis theory implicit in much of Marx, especially in some sections of the third volume of *Capital*, has to be added to that kernel forever split on the track of *différance*. What I have continued to say is that these movements, the three that I have mentioned, should swallow and digest these dynamic materials rather than seek to correctly fit the authoritative label "Marxist." If I may once again analogize, somewhat fancifully, from individual pathology to the history of the present, I would say that today it is a necessarily incomplete incorporation. Incorporation seems a particularly productive act of semi-mourning for the perpetually deferred death of an insufficiently rationalized systemic vision.

Sixth: If we think transnationally, rather than only in the Group of Seven theatre, we cannot emphasize the role of the state centrally. In order for the machinery of the state to participate in persistent socialism as the difference and deferment of capitalism, we need the great globe-girdling movements of resistance to Development, capital "D." Let us set out the improbability of setting the socialist calculus in motion by way of a telegraphic account of what it looks like from the perspective of the global other side, including those ex-communist countries attempting to be satisfied with the promises of an underdeveloped capitalism. For it is impossible to escape the orthodox con-straints of a neo-liberal world economic system which in the name of Development (capital D) and now sustainable development removes all bar-riers between itself and fragile national economies, so that any possibility of social redistribution is severely damaged. Further, the people who have politi-co-economic power or consumerist ambitions in much of the old third world share a common interest in and therefore often welcome subordination (invariably represented as aid or collaboration) by dominant global capital. In this situation of increasingly lost hope, confusion and the failure of decol-onization, the always dubious hyphen between nation and state is violently renegotiated by dystopic fanatics in the old third world as well as in the newly defined second in the name of a once glorious and pure nation. Enthusiastic movements have always known that the best chance for action or a feeling of agency is to guarantee a cure that will bring about the return of the glorious repressed of history—"we were powerful once"—as its cathartic end. The script is violence in the name of the nation. Caught between the specters of development and nation, the state is not the prime mover of the affirmative calculus of difference. The globe-girdling movements of resistance to devel-opment have a critical relationship to the state. Much of the strength of that critical relationship comes from that culture's active and interminable diges-tion of the pulverized and augmented rational kernel of Marx's thought. These movements are obviously better networked in the old third world, and among those activists in the first world who attempt to decolonize their sense of resis-tance. These specific networking lines are hard to lay down in the newly defined second world, and it is still hard to swallow a culture as medicine that has so lately been a poison.

The two movements I speak of are the two I know best: the non-eurocentric ecological movement, and the non-eurocentric movement against reproduc-tive and genetic engineering, the latter relating to so-called "population control" imposed upon the North by the South. I call them globe-girdling, rather than international because, (a) of their critical relationship to the many so-called nation-states they encompass, and (b) because they try to learn from subalternity and womanspace, areas that have not been considered as central resources for the conceptualization of the modern state.

(Subalternity is the name I borrow for the space out of any serious touch with the logic of capitalism or socialism, the differential logic I have touched on earlier. Please do not confuse it with unorganized labor, women as such, the proletarian, the colonized, the object of ethnography, migrant labor, political refugees, etc. Nothing useful comes out of this confusion. The word becomes useless then, not that a useless word is necessarily a bad thing when we pause to ponder.)

Elsewhere I have argued that these non-eurocentric, globe-girdling movements or surges are not interested in state power on the model of some eurocentric older "New Social Movements." Here let me say just a few words about the area of the uncalculable that must be risked by these movements. Alas, in such brief compass—one minute—and in such a frame, the audience in front, and me speaking at a microphone, these words will sound bizarre, romantic, exoticizing, and will take us clear out of philosophical speculation and political realism. It pains me, but it cannot be helped.

A.

The traffic with the incalculable in the non-eurocentric ecological movement: It is a dream driven by the conviction that change is hardly ever possible on grounds of reason alone. In order to mobilize for non-violence, for example, one relies, however remotely, on incanting the sacredness of human life. "Sacred" here need not have a religious sanction but simply a sanction that cannot be contained within the principle of reason alone. In this sense, nature is no longer sacred for civilizations based on the control of nature. The result is global devastation due to a failure of ecology. It is noticeable that less advanced groups in the fourth world still retain this sense as a matter of their cultural conformity. I am not exoticising or romanticizing the aboriginal, they are not all "radicals." It is a matter of their cultural conformity, if only because they are still subaltern. What we are dreaming of here is not how to keep the aboriginal in a state of excluded cultural conformity, but how to learn and construct a sense of sacred nature by attending to them—which can help mobilize and drive a globe-girdling ecological mind-set beyond the reasonable and self-interested terms of long term global survival. We want to open our minds to being haunted by the aboriginal. We want the spectral to haunt the calculus.

If this seems impractical we should perhaps look at the other side, the World Bank's environmental report for the fiscal year 1992:

> The world's remaining indigenous peoples—estimated to number more than 250 million in seventy countries—possess knowledge fundamental to the sustainable management of resources in these regions. In cooperation with the Center for Indigenous Knowledge, the Environmental Department prepared a bank discussion paper entitled *Using Indigenous Knowledge in Agricultural Development* (Warren 1991). Region-specific technical papers are being prepared to support the implementation of the directive.[11]

World Bank assistance comes at the request of states. I have spoken of the state and I have spoken of the state of states. I need not belabor the point.

B.

Non-eurocentric movement against reproductive and genetic engineering: Just as on the differential calculus between capitalism and socialism, the ecological movement takes on the World Bank, this movement confronts the multinational pharmaceuticals and their conglomerative associates. (These are movements that have eaten and daily chew—actively ruminate upon, as Nietzsche would say—the hard nut of Marxist economic theory; and they daily half-mourn the differential tug of capitalism, even in their own resistance. But half-mourning is also half-jubilation.) Here I speak of that calculus. I speak of their traffic with the indefinite margin of the incalculable in a helplessly programmatic way. In the absence of globality in the as yet beleaguered Queer Theory, and in the absence of serious consideration of Queer Theory in Marxist or anti-Marxist talk, I cannot hope to be understood. Not because this is difficult, but because, to quote Freud on the occasion of the fiction of the uncanny, it is "something that cannot come forth under the conditions of [the] experience [*unter dem Bedingungen des Erlebnis nicht vorkommt*]" that can be structurally assumed as common to us here, at an academic conference.[12] You have to take it on trust that I understand what I am saying, and here it comes:

All initiatives of population control or genetic engineering are cruelly unmindful of the dignity of reproductive responsibility. The imperative collective calculus for winning the right to sexual preference and pleasure, to equitable work outside and in the home, and the right to equality in education must be supplemented by the memory that to be human is always and already inserted into a structure of responsibility. To distinguish this strictly from heterosexual communitarianism, we must connect with the subaltern pre-supposition where heterosexual reproduction is a moment in the general normativity of a homosexuality for which the sexual encounter itself is a case of the caress.[13] And this difference between homo- and heterosexuality is as unrecognized as it is underived in that theatre.

I have spoken, then, of: (1) the difference between the two "social"-s in Marx; (2) class-consciousness as critique of reification theory; (3) socialism as capitalism's *différance* in view of the spectrality of communism; (4) the role of the new immigrant; (5) eating Marxism; (6) globe-girdling movements. Supplementing Marxism is my title. Supplementing here does not only mean stuffing the holes in Marxism as Marxism stuffs our holes. As my intractable ending shows, I have not forgotten Derrida re-citing Rousseau: the supplement is dangerous because it opens us to the incalculable.[14]

notes

1. This assumes purity of motive in leaders, of course. I have developed the difference between the two "social"-s in "Limits and Openings of Marx in Derrida," *Outside in the Teaching Machine* (New York: Routledge, 1993), p. 107–110. Even if an entire society were composed of what Marx called "the agents of production," the positive use of class-consciousness by every member of that society would need something other than reason, something that would have rendered into "habit" (as Gramsci would say) the conviction that the other (or society as a big Other) was more important than the self, relearning class-consciousness as the lesson of responsibility. Even apart from the fact that no society is composed thus, the human mental theatre cannot learn responsibility fully. "Ethical teaching" whittles away at the impossibility. As for the risks mentioned in my text, let me offer two examples from the Armenian post-Soviet case: "[Harnush] HACOPIAN [one of eight women in the 260-member Armenian parliament]: Only if there is a strong economy, a good standard of living. Only after these are secured can people pay attention to the humanitarian

and benevolent goals ...[Rouben] SHOUGARIAN [Assistant to the President for Foreign Affairs]: ...I guess first we look to the West for technical assistance, to the civilized world and then to Oriental countries," (Michael M. J. Fischer and Stella Grigorian, "Six to Eight Characters in Search of Armenian Civil Society Amidst the Carnivalization of History," in *Perilous States*, ed. George Marcus (Chicago: Univ. of Chicago Press, 1994), p. 95, 116. And Armenia is not representative of capitalism and socialism (wedded in a "mixed economy" in the post-Soviet context), repeating the mistake of ignoring the prior importance of the lesson of responsibility. We will no doubt hear differently from the Tatars, the Bashkirs, the Kazakhs, and the other members of the Commonwealth of Independent States and the Russian Federation. Stalin is an example of a rational analysis run to the extreme consequences of the ignoring of responsibility, the body politic hacked to pieces to fit the "rational" diagram. We must remember that a Western European rememoration of Marx, however important, is a comparatively minor episode.

2. For "pure" formulations of this, see Harry Braverman, *Labor and Monopoly Capitalism: The Degradation of Work in the Twentieth Century* (New York: Monthly Review, 1975), and Harry Cleaver, *Reading Capital Politically* (Austin: Univ. of Texas Press, 1979).

3. Karl Marx, *Capital: A Critique of Political Economy* trans. Ben Fowkes (New York: Vintage, 1976), vol. 1, p. 132; translation modified.

4. Jacques Derrida, "Passions," in *Derrida: A Critical Reader*, ed. David Wood (Cambridge: Blackwell, 1992), p. 15.

5. Derrida, "Force of Law: The 'Mystical Foundation of Authority'," *Cardozo Law Review* 11.5–5 July/Aug 1990), p. 947.

6. Derrida, "Différance," in *Margins of Philosophy*. trans. Allan Bass (Chicago: Univ. of Chicago Press, 1982), p. 17.

7. Marx, *Capital*, trans. David Fernbach (New York: Vintage, 1981), vol. 3, pp. 1015–1016. All thought of capitalism and/or socialism is inaugurated in difference, the most obvious being lodged in the notion of life as the pursuit of the happiness of me and mine as opposed to others, on the one hand; and as responsibility towards others, on the other. It is dependent, in other words, on the general law of *différance* (which is not *a* law, being itself grounded in splitting). But, and perhaps more important, the relationship between capitalism and socialism is also susceptible to the passage on *différance* quoted in my text, roughly as follows: As the passage referred to in *Capital* volume 3 would show, socialism is not

in opposition to the form of the capitalist mode of production. It is rather a constant pushing away—a differing and a deferral—of the *capital*-ist harnessing of
the *social* productivity of capital. Because of the impossibility of the fully ethical, the calculations toward this *différance* get constantly jerked around the other
way, the movement as much like a hardly-arrested vibration in everyday decisions as like the broad-stroke swings between the public and the private sectors
charted in Stephen Resnick and Richard Wolff's essay in this volume. It scares
me to think of the risks of attempting, in more than merely an academic way,
the double-sided program laid out in the early Derridian project in the passage
quoted in the text, in terms of capitalism and socialism; yet it is the substance of
organized and unorganized economic resistance. If conceived as end rather than
figured as *différance* we arrive at the Marxian description referred to in the text.

8. Please note that I am not speaking of "cultural" assimilation. I have written
   more extensively on the question of multiculturalism and civil society in
   "Multiculturalism," in *Cultural Diversity*, ed. Thomas W. Keen (forthcoming).

9. J. Laplanche and J.-B. Pontalis, *The Language of Psychoanalysis*. trans. Donald
   Nicholson-Smith (New York: Norton, 1973), p. 376. I have discussed this in
   greater detail in "Psychoanalysis in Left Field; and Field Working: Examples to
   Fit the Title," in *Speculations After Freud*, Michael Munchow and Sonu
   Shamdasani, eds. (London: Routledge, 1994).

10. Derrida, "Mochlos; or, the Conflict of the Faculties," in *Logomachia: The Conflict of
    the Faculties*, Richard Rand and Amy Wygant, eds. (Lincoln: Univ. of Nebraska
    Press, 1992), p. 11.

11. *The World Bank and the Environment* (Washington: The World Bank, 1992), pp.
    106, 107.

12. Sigmund Freud, "The Uncanny," in *The Complete Psycho-Analytic Works* trans.
    James Strachey, *et al* (New York: Norton, 1961), vol. 17, p. 249; translation mod-
    ified.

13. I use "caress" here in the philosophical sense given to it by Luce Irigaray in
    "The Fecundity of the Caress: A Reading of Levinas', *Totality and Infinity* sec-
    tion IV, B, 'The Phenomenology of Eros'," in *Face to Face With Levinas*, ed.
    Richard Cohen (Albany: SUNY Press, 1986), p. 231–256. I have discussed this
    essay at greater length in Spivak, *Outside*, pp. 163–171.

14. Derrida, *Of Grammatology*, trans. Spivak (Baltimore: Johns Hopkins Univ. Press,
    1976), pp. 141–164.

PART TWO

transition to/from socialism

CARLOS VILAS

forward back

capitalist restructuring, the state and the working class in latin america

THE INTERNATIONAL REARTICULATION OF
THE LATIN AMERICAN ECONOMIES

Delinking was the almost unanimous reaction of Latin American governments to the 1929–1930 debt crisis. Default enabled several of these governments to push forward processes of extensive capital accumulation oriented
toward domestic markets, which in turn bolstered economic and social differentiation and contributed to the establishment of national-popular, developmentalist regimes. However, during the 1980s every Latin American
government resorted to international financial rearticulation in order to manage the new debt crisis. Particularly relevant was the leverage this decision
got both from U.S. government agencies and from multilateral organizations

(the International Monetary Fund [IMF], World Bank), which combined political pressure and financial resources to prevent the repetition of the historical precedent and the building of any type of debtors' cartel.

As a consequence, during the 1980s Latin America devoted almost U.S. $224 billion to foreign debt payments (i.e., 67 percent of the original 1982 debt which amounted to U.S. $332.4 billion), although by 1992 the Latin American combined debt amounted to U.S. $451 billion, that is, a 32 percent increase; the debtors' attempts to conduct multilateral negotiations were easily neutralized. Furthermore, creditor banks forced Latin American governments to nationalize the private foreign debt—that is, to convert it into public debt, although the banks had previously charged the private borrowers a risk rate—which contributed to accrued fiscal deficits. The arithmetic of Fidel Castro, which in the mid-1980s had argued that no Latin American country could ever afford to pay its debt and that the more they payed the more they were going to be indebted, proved to be correct. However, the underlying economic supposition went astray: from the creditors' perspective, the key issue was not so much to obtain full cancelation of debts as to discipline the debtors and keep them within the boundaries of the international financial system, even through modest or symbolic debt payments.

As figures show, debt payments were more than just symbolic; a huge transference of financial resources from Latin America to the international market took place. Since no further loans were granted to the region, Latin American governments had to rely on export earnings and on sharp cuts in public spending to pay the debts. Because the 1980s were negative years for most of Latin America's exports due to falls in international prices, export efforts were additionally painful. A widespread and very fast reorientation of productive and financial resources took place in order to propel exports. This reorientation was achieved through the implementation of a range of specific state public policies: massive devaluations, shifts in relative prices, drastic cuts in credit policies and subsidies and in public investments, removal of tariffs protecting manufacturing and so on. In the absence of new financial inflows easing shifts in surplus, income and employment among economic sectors and social groups, the initial recessive impact of policy changes was harder and lasted longer.

This impact was not a thunderclap in the open skies. The domestic market, which from the late 1940s on had fueled capital accumulation for both the Latin American bourgeoisie and foreign-owned subsidiaries, had been losing leverage as the engine of capital accumulation since the late 1960s and early 1970s. However, the overflow of international liquid assets as a consequence of the first oil boom provided both the inward-oriented fractions of the Latin American bourgeoisie and several military governments with additional resources either to insist on an increasingly exhausting economic scheme or to expand military budgets, fuel political clientelism and prompt capital flight—or a combination of all.

On the very eve of the debt crisis, multilateral agencies, which shortly thereafter would turn into the most severe advocates of financial stringency, saluted heavy indebtedness as a proof of economic wisdom (e.g., World Bank 1981). In countries like Chile and Argentina, indebtedness was promoted by crass military regimes waving the banner of neoliberal economics and resorting to balance-of-payments policies to deal with domestic inflation. The interplay of trade restrictions and wide financial international opening accelerated the crisis and made its impact stronger when the lending banks decided to increase interest rates and to abruptly stop further lending.

Following the 1982 crisis, exports rapidly replaced the domestic market as the locus of capital accumulation, which in turn led to profound changes in income distribution and political power-sharing among both capitalist fractions and social classes and between domestic and international markets. Commodities based on advanced technologies increased their share in Latin America's exports, although this shift did not prevent further international marginalization: Latin America's share in world trade, which had reached 8 percent in 1960, then fallen to 6 percent in 1980, was additionally reduced to 3.3 percent by 1990.

The reorientation of investment, production and foreign trade policies had mixed results. Latin America's gross domestic product (GDP) registered an accumulated growth of 18 percent (1982–1990), although the quality of life deteriorated for scores of the Latin American population: during the same period per capita GDP experienced a drop of more than 7 percent and even more in countries such as Argentina (24 percent), Venezuela (20 percent) and Bolivia (23 percent) (CEPAL 1992a). Massive devaluations and a huge fiscal deficit due to the already mentioned nationalization of foreign debt triggered inflation at a three-digit yearly rate in several countries—and even at a four-digit rate in some of them. Shattered by currency devaluations, balance-of-payments antiinflationary policies and credit shortages, industrial production stagnated; value added by manufacturing moved from a 6.1 percent average annual growth rate in 1971–1980 to a symbolic 0.4 percent in 1981–1990 (IDB 1992a). Living standards plummeted. The population below the poverty line grew by 44 percent between 1980 (135.9 million or about 40 percent of the entire Latin American population) and 1990 (196 million or 46 percent of the total population) (CEPAL 1992b).

An export-led strategy is also an import-oriented one. Investment and consumption related to the domestic market are no longer considered to be relevant inputs for growth, as had been the case in the previous economic scheme. As the realization of surplus value tends to lose ties to the domestic market, working and middle-class wages are no longer approached as tools for capital accumulation but as expenses to be saved in order to enhance international competition and accumulation. Domestic demand for investment and consumption tends to be met increasingly through imports, involving a redefinition of the domestic market in terms of higher levels of income and purchasing power and, subsequently, in terms of different social groups—a smaller although more affluent domestic market. Higher reliance on imports bolsters political tensions with regard to the exchange rate—that is, the financial link of a national economy to the international one. Under explicit or implicit approval from both the IMF and the World Bank, Latin American governments have recently tended to resort to different levels of exchange overvaluation as a tool of anti-inflationary policy and debt payments—that is, the two prioritized goals of postcrisis economic performance. An overvalued exchange rate implies stronger efforts to sustain export growth unless access to foreign currency is secured, which tends to be a difficult task due both to the very overvaluation of the exchange rate and to restrictions in the international capital markets, which only very recently started to recede.[1]

To a certain extent the outward economic shift looks like a retreat to the traditional Latin American linkage to the international market between the 1870s and 1930. Nevertheless, it is just a formal resemblance, and it would be misleading to push it too far. Today's external articulation through trade lacks the complement of the huge financial inflows of the past and is basically processed through commodities frequently produced in smaller plants articulated to a transnational network combining high-tech and relatively unskilled labor. Export-led growth is now as much a matter of trade as a matter of a new type of industrialization, of a sophisticated service sector and of highly efficient and modern economic and social infrastructure. Export-oriented manufacturing combines high-tech with deskilling of complex operations, the latter being transformed into simpler ones conducted in assembly plants deployed in countries where extremely cheap labor and weak union organizing are available. This transformation also applies to agro-exports, which for the last decade and a half have been experiencing dramatic changes linked to the development of new staples (such as flowers, fruits and vegetables). These changed include heavy reliance on chemicals and other industrial inputs, mechanical irrigation, automated packing and the like, which have introduced profound changes in both land-use patterns and the rural labor market as well as in production schedules. Full employment and growth in mass consumption are no longer policy goals; collective labor contracting is bypassed through individual dealings and subcontracting. In all, economic transformations make up for the Latin American version of "post-Fordism."[2]

Economic reorientation was supported by, and in turn pushed for a power shift from, fractions of the Latin American bourgeoisie having their surplus value realized through the domestic market to the benefit of traditional and modern export-oriented fractions of the bourgeoisie. The very notion of a domestic market as distinct from the international one has been losing heuristic potential as the transnationalization of Latin American economies advanced in past decades. However, the distinction between a receding inward-oriented bourgeoisie and an expanding export-oriented one mirrors the structural changes going on in the economy as well as in society. It is useful to understand power shifts and policy reorientations, particularly at the lower and middle echelons of the Latin American bourgeoisie, where this distinction is still sharp.

A NEW PATTERN OF STATE–MARKET–CLASS RELATIONS

Latin American states played active roles in managing the economic crisis and in the subsequent international rearticulation as well as in the distribution of profits and failures among social groups and classes. The already mentioned economic policy tools were important for reaching economic outward reorientation, which, in turn, built up preferential conditions for accumulation for specific business groups, marginalized others and contributed to the rapid impoverishment of scores of the labor population. This junction of structural

and policy ingredients favored a strong and protracted pumping of income
from the wage earners to capitalists and rentiers (see Table 1) and from Latin
America to the international creditors. From 1983 to 1992 the Latin American
current account balance accumulated a U.S. $116.8 billion deficit.

Table 1

Share of Wages in GDP in Several Latin American Countries (%)

	1970	1980	1985	1989	1990
Argentina	40.9	31.5	31.9	24.9	—
Bolivia	36.8	39.6	26.9[a]	—	—
Brazil	34.2	35.1	36.3	—	—
Colombia	42.1	46.2	45.3	42.6[b]	41.8
Costa Rica	52.7	56.1	53.9	56.7	57.8
Chile	47.7	43.4	37.8	—	—
Ecuador	34.4	34.8	23.6	16.0	15.8
Guatemala	32.3	33.6	30.8	30.6	—
México	37.5	39.0	31.6	28.4	27.3
Panamá	54.5	48.8	53.8	53.4	50.0
Paraguay	37.1	37.1	32.5	29.4	25.8
Perú	40.0	32.8	30.5	25.5	16.8[c]
Uruguay	52.9	35.7	36.3	39.7	48.4
Venezuela	40.3	42.7	37.6	34.6	31.1

a. 1986
b. 1988
c. 1991
Source: CEPAL, *Anuario Estadístico de América Latina,* several years

As shown in Table 1, transitions from military regimes to elected civilian
governments did not have any relevant impact on either the magnitude or the
class direction of these transferences. Despite their decisive role in people's
and citizens' mobilizations to oust military regimes in Argentina, Bolivia,
Brazil, Chile or Uruguay, the working class and lower-income strata, who for
more than a decade paid the price of dictatorship and repression, as well as
several segments of the middle classes, were now forced to carry the costs of
economic crisis and capitalist restructuring. Neither does institutional stabil-

ity have an apparent impact, as shown when comparing Costa Rica—where the wage share increased after a mild fall in 1980–1985—to México, Venezuela or Ecuador, where the wage share shrank throughout the 1980s.

Export efforts were not enough to fulfill creditors' demands. After the rapid exhaustion of several attempts at debt swaps, governments resorted to privatization. Despite current allegations regarding its impact on economic modernization, privatization has been faced as a chapter of the overall strategy to come to terms with creditors' demands and to achieve institutional and financial support from multilateral agencies. Although the proceeds of every privatization are not devoted to foreign debt payment, privatization as a whole is linked to foreign debt dealings inasmuch as it is an ingredient of debt-related restructuring of the Latin American economies. It also meets one of the creditors' basic conditions by granting the Latin American governments access to partial debt reductions.

This apparently technical decision has had deep and pervasive consequences all over the region. Its most obvious effect is the sharp reduction in state intervention in society and the economy. State agencies are getting rid of the public sector through the wholesale of business enterprises, factories and ports and by relinquishing their previous power of regulation over market relations. The state retreats, and private corporations fill the vacuum at such a rapid pace that it has even been suggested that Latin America is entering something like a poststate stage of history (Cavarozzi 1992). According to this perspective, the state, which up to the 1980s was the dynamic axis of Latin American socioeconomic life because of its extensive ownership of assets in production, trade and transports; its social and economic infrastructure; and its capabilities of price-fixing and other market regulations is now moving toward a progressive self-dismantling, to the benefit of marketplace and society: a neoliberal post-Marxist version of the "withering away of the state."

The quantitative approach to state-market relations underlying this perspective points to a set of quite obvious facts. The state has given up a broad scope of micro and macro interventions, both direct and indirect, in economic affairs; at present Latin America has a slimmer public sector than existed in previous decades. But as important as this quantitative dimension is the network of state-market relations making up the new institutional and socioeconomic setting. From this perspective, the relevant point is not just "how much" state or "how much" market but the arrangements between state and market and their impact on specific social classes and economic interests. The shifting mode of state-market relations in contemporary Latin America is not just an effect of the slimming of the state and the subsequent strengthening of market relations—as in a zero-sum game. It is most of all an outcome of international rearticulation and subsequent economic restructuring and of specific "market actors" and the interests being bolstered or hindered by those actors.

The major shortcoming of a quantitative approach to state-market relations is that it fails to capture the link being forged between public policies and social actors as well as their impact on politics and society. The notion that civil society advances and the marketplace expands as state draws back conceals the fact that not everyone within civil society or the marketplace is making his or her way to progress or well-being, and that certain social groups and classes are increasing their share in power, wealth and the good life while others have been forced to accept downgraded income and living standards or are pushed out of the labor market and below the poverty line. Privatization of public services, together with cut-downs in subsidies, social public outlays and welfare, leads to a profound redistribution of income from families to the state. This redistribution mostly affects lower- and middle- income families, thus aggravating the impact of income redistribution caused by shifts in the labor market such as rising unemployment, fall in real wages and expansion of the informal economy. Since state reform up to now has not included any relevant tax reform, the traditionally regressive Latin American tax structure has been preserved, with indirect taxes making up for a larger proportion of tax revenues than taxes on income and property. Indirect taxes are linked to the consumption of goods and services with a low income-elasticity of demand. The lower a family's income is, the larger the proportion of its "consumption basket" made up by indirect taxes. Subsequently, lower- and middle-income families are forced to pay comparatively more for a state that spends comparatively less for their needs.

The pervasive economic degradation of the working population and the increasing inability of unions to keep a voice in policy-making and to shape the labor market are in sharp contrast to the ability of business associations— or even particular corporations—linked to the globalization of the Latin American economies to upgrade themselves via the close links being built between them and state agencies. Business organizations have never been alien to economic policymaking in Latin America, but in the past corporate involvement in government decisions was articulated through corporatist institutions formally parallel to those articulating unions' participation. In addition to unions' retreat, we are now witnessing a more direct insertion of big business in government agencies and public policies.[3]

PRIVATIZATION OF STATE-OWNED ASSETS

Privatization is a pertinent illustration of this involvement. According to studies and evaluations of several countries' experiences, privatization has been accomplished through a complex, informal network of implicit state subsidies to private investors who are usually related in one way or another to government officials. It is the state, much more than the marketplace, that in the last analysis sets the terms of each specific case of privatization, with regard both to financial and administrative matters and to the specific participating investors. The overall process is carried out through administrative procedures with no parliamentary accountability. Those with particular concerns in government's participation have discriminated against some would-be investors and favored others. It is not an easy task to assess how much room for competition has been left after the active involvement of state agencies and officers. Furthermore, state agencies usually absorb the debts of firms in the process of privatization; undervalue assets to be privatized, fixing somewhat arbitrary low prices; fight workers in order to reduce the payroll of firms to be privatized and absorb workers' compensation; and grant price and tariff increases. In all, these procedures contribute to the reproduction of the traditional rentier behavior of Latin American business elites (Bienen y Waterbury 1991; Vilas 1992). It must also be pointed out that while government actions tend to secure the profitability of public enterprises that are to be privatized and to make them attractive for would-be investors, they also show that state-owned firms may be perfectly efficient as long as there is political interest in achieving efficiency.

At the macroeconomic level, state manipulation of privatization has tended to create, or consolidate, monopolistic or oligopolistic settings, granting captive markets to investors as in México, Chile and Argentina (Bouin and Michalet 1991; Pozas). An assessment of the financial costs of privatization as compared to the effective inflow of private capital is a particularly difficult task. Figures disclosed by several Latin American governments for the net amount of financial resources resulting from privatization do not permit an assessment of what the financial alternatives could have been in the absence of the already mentioned state subsidies. This point is particularly relevant because arguments for privatization stress its impact both on the public sector's finances and on scaling back state subsidies.

As a result, the process of privatization has been conducted as "a very private affair."[4] It is worthwhile to point out that even in countries such as Argentina, Brazil or México, where full-fledged stock markets exist, governments have tended to bypass them as a way to conduct most privatizations. The lack of openness of most cases of privatization and their exclusive management by administrative agencies free from parliamentary accountability afford opportunities for bribery and corruption at every level of the government agencies involved in them (Verbitsky 1991; Little 1992). At the least, these transactions have led to citizens' distrust of the entire process. In addition to state subsidies to investors, these factors tend to endow most of Latin America's privatization and state deinvestment experiences with a heavy resemblance to primitive accumulation and white-gloves privateering at the expense of state-owned capital. The Uruguayan plebiscite of December 13, 1992, forcing the government to stop and review ongoing privatizations, may be interpreted as a rejection of both privatization of public services and government's mismanagement of the specific case under citizens' scrutiny.

This discussion should not be interpreted as endorsing an across-the-board defense of state ownership of corporations. Unquestionably, many state-owned firms were inefficient, their operations frequently subordinated to political patronage, masking private interest under the nation's flag. The assessment that past instances of state intervention and public-sector expansion were devoted to "supporting the poor," to income redistribution to wage earners or to feeding unions' "corporatism"—as recent revisionist approaches to Latin American populism suggest (Dornbush y Edwards 1990; Cardoso and Helwege 1991)—is not supported by data (see Vilas 1992–1993). Then, as now, state agencies and policies were arenas for competition among various political groups and social classes as well as being active participants in this competition. The novelty of Latin America's contemporary political economy is not just the society or the marketplace substituting for the state but the pattern of state-market-society relations bolstering specific segments of the capitalist classes, hindering the development of others, downgrading large fractions of the middle sectors and setting the conditions for new, or renewed, downgrading and marginalization of the working population.

Foreign support for privatization is not enough reason for its overwhelming acceptance by Latin American governments, though pressures coming from multilateral and foreign governments' agencies have been persistent, as was the promotion of neoliberal economics and ideology during the Thatcher-Reagan-Bush years. Privatization and state deregulation were long-time ingredients in the ideology of fractions of the Latin American bourgeoisie related to foreign trade. Arguments questioning state intervention go back to the 1920s and 1930s. However, the way Latin American capitalism paved its own way to development tended to marginalize such arguments as much as mass-based populist and developmentalist regimes marginalized neoliberal supporters in the electoral arena. Advocates for neoliberal economics showed up time and again to advance their prescriptions to military governments but were forced to step aside each time electoral politics resumed. These advocates were brought back to the center of the economic debate in the early 1980s, and the international rearticulation of Latin American economies gave leverage to their recommendations of a free market, export-led growth, fiscal stringency, financial deregulation and, above all, labor discipline. Their ideology presented as a virtue what was really a necessity stemming from the crisis and from previous governmental handling of it. When a particular policy was presented as a necessity, class interests bolstered by that policy were advanced under the guise of national goals.

AN ILLUSTRATION: THE CASE OF MÉXICO

The slimming of role of the the state at the micro, entrepreneurial level has been coupled with increased regulation of market relations through macroeconomic policies. Contemporary México provides a vivid illustration. Appealing to traditional policy tools, the Mexican government is pushing forward its own version of capitalist modernization and international articulation, combining the most important process of privatization and a near command economy. Overvaluation of the exchange rate affords cheaper foreign currency to keep up debt payments and, together with lowered restrictions on imports, maintains control over domestic inflation.[5] Increased import expenses and relative discrimination against exports lead to persistent trade imbalances and eventually to balance-of-payments deficits (see Table 2).

Table 2

México: International Accounts, 1988-1992 (U.S. $ millions)

	Trade balance (goods)	Balance of Current Account	Balance of Capital Account	Global Balance	Total Foreign Debt	Exchange Rate[a]
1988	1,668	-2,613	-4,025	-6,638	100,900	-17.3
1989	645	-4,111	4,289	178	95,100	-9.1
1990	-4,433	-8,413	10,716	2,303	90,700	-3.3
1991	-11,063	-13,469	21,461	7,992	105,800	-3.0
1992[b]	-18,830	-20,750	23,250	2,500	106,000	—

a. Change in real exchange rate, %

b. Preliminary estimates

Source: Economic Commission for Latin America and the Caribbean, International Development Bank

Table 3

México: Growth in Wages, Prices, Employment and Gross Product

	Real Wages[a] (%)	Consumer Prices[b] (%)	Urban Unemployment (%)	Growth in GDP (%)	Growth in GDP per capita[c] (%)
1988	-1.3	51.7	3.5	1.2	-0.1
1989	9.0	19.7	2.9	3.3	1.0
1990	2.9	29.9	2.9	4.4	2.2
1991	2.4	18.8	2.7	3.6	1.4
1992[d]	2.4	12.9	3.2	2.5	0.6

a. Growth in wages, salaries and benefits in manufacturing

b. December/December

c. Real values

d. Preliminary estimates

Source: Economic Commission for Latin America and the Caribbean, International Development Bank

In order to bypass the negative impact of the overvalued exchange rate on inflows of the foreign liquid resources needed to make up the deficit, domestic interest rates are held positive with regard to domestic inflation rates and to the programmed evolution of the exchange rate, which, in turn, makes foreign financial investment much more attractive than productive investment: between 1991 and 1992 foreign investment in the Mexican stock exchange soared from U.S. $4.2 billion to U.S. $27 billion. But high real interest rates deal a strong blow to domestic investors and industrialists, whom the official rhetoric blames as inefficient and doomed to bankruptcy. As the strategy advances, financial compromises impinge upon production goals as official concerns for economic development and growth recede (Table 3).

As an unintended but graphic illustration of prevailing concerns, the 1992 renewal of the government-supported wage-price agreement (Pacto de Estabilidad, Crecimiento y Empleo [PECE], or Agreement for Stabilization, Growth and Employment) substituted "competition" for "growth" in the official name of the agreement: it now reads "Agreement for Stabilization, Competition and Employment"—the question being how to preserve employment if growth is no longer a central concern.[6] In all, the current México strategy involves a shift back to the much-criticized pre-1982 "debt-induced development": from 1989 to 1992 México's foreign debt increased by U.S. $10.9 billion, or 11.4 percent, after being cut down by U.S. $7.3 billion in 1987–1989, though facing a decreasing GDP growth rate.

According to government officials, México's economy demands an estimated inflow of U.S. $150 billion throughout the next decade in order to consolidate ongoing reforms.[7] Here is where the North American Free Trade Agreement (NAFTA) fits in: it is much more a matter of investment than trade because México already devotes almost three-fourths of her foreign trade to North American partners and is well advanced in removing tariff protection. Because the average wage differential in México's export manufacturing sector amounts to 1:6 or even 1:8 at productivity levels similar to those in U.S.-based firms, cheap labor and high interest rates are considered two important incentives for U.S. and Canadian firms and capitals to move south of the Rio Grande, fueling the current México government's macroeconomic scheme.

By establishing conditions for business efficiency and competition through specific public policies, the government's economic strategy strengthens the upper segments of the México financial bourgeoisie while reinforcing their role as privileged partners of foreign investors. Government-supported segments of the México business elite own the recently reprivatized banking sector and command 25 huge holdings, which account for 47 percent of the Méxican GDP (Grinspun and Cameron 1993). Just five such groups control 75 percent of the banking and credit markets as well as 66 percent of investment partnerships (Acosta 1993a).[8]

The regulation of financial markets is matched by solid state intervention in fixing wages and keeping them at a low level with regard to both productivity and prices. Although reduced labor costs through tight wage controls might lead to a stronger market position for small and medium-size industrialists, the impact tends to be neutralized because of such firms' prevalent orientation toward the domestic market, where labor accounts for a relevant proportion of direct and indirect demand. This is not the case for the above mentioned outward-directed fractions of the financial and industrial bourgeoisie. Nor is it the case for foreign, above all U.S., investors, who benefit from huge real wage differentials in similar occupations and at productivity levels similar to those in their countries of origin when operating south of the Méxican border. The final result is an increased oligopolistic market, not a more competitive one, and a precarious equilibrium for wages and employment.

At present, when the Latin American state is so actively involved in the promotion of specific private class interests, as in the Méxican case (Pozas; Rodriguez Castaneda 1992, 1993; see also *El Dia*, February 23, 1992, p. 5); or wages for ministers of economy are directly paid by private business, as in the case of Argentina's current minister (*La Jornada*, November 12 and 16, 1992), the notion of state autonomy should be submitted to close scrutiny. What emerges out of ongoing patterns of state-market relations is the reduction of the state and of state agencies to captive tools not just of the business class but of sometimes extremely particular segments of that class.

What we are witnessing is more than just the privatization of public assets and services: it is the privatization of state policymaking and policymakers on behalf of specific private interests—the privatization of the government of a country on behalf of the "owners" of the country. It is then appropriate, in late-twentieth-century Latin American post-Fordism, to recall Adam Smith's eighteenth-century conception of government as a private affair of the propertied classes: "Civil government, so far it is instituted for the security of property, is in reality instituted for the defense of the rich against the poor, or of those who have some property against those who have none at all" (Smith 1776:674).

STATE AND MARKET RE-ARRANGEMENTS AND THE WORKING CLASS

The interplay of postcrisis external rearticulation, structural changes and state policies has propelled severe changes in the working population—as in society as a whole:

1. As shown in Table 1, a sharp retreat of wages' as a proportion of national income has been experienced, dropping from an average of almost 42 percent in 1980 to less than 35 percent in 1989. In 1989 real wages were 76 percent of their 1980s level, 63 percent in 1992 (CEPAL 1992a).

2. The sociodemographic dimensions of the working class have been redefined by the relative reduction of the formal labor market and subsequent growth of the urban informal sector (UIS), occasional employment and self-employment, together with increasing diffusion of individual labor contracts. Throughout the 1980s growth in informal employment more than doubled that in the formal private sector (70 percent and 29 percent, respectively). In cities such as Lima, Managua and Guatemala City the informal economy accounts for two-thirds of the urban active population. Within the formal sector, the labor force is being transferred from the larger to the smaller firms, where working conditions tend to be harsh; during the 1980s employment in small firms almost doubled, while it virtually stagnated in large and middle-sized firms (Infante y Klein 1991).

3. The inability of unions to deal with gender- and ethnic-differentiated constituencies, as well as governments and business manipulation, has led women and Indians to avoid involvement in formal labor relations, increasing labor market fragmentation. The rate of unionization of the female labor force is lower than that of male workers; increases in women's labor participation through the 1970s and 1980s did not produce equivalent changes in union structures in order to adapt traditional organizational criteria to the new gender composition of the rank and file. Discrimination against the female labor force is particularly strong among the self-employed and in the UIS. The probability of joining the UIS labor force is higher for women (as well as children), than for men, as is their concentration in lower-paid occupations such as "maquilas," furrow labor in agroexports or personal services (Arriagada 1990; Carton de Grammont 1992). Ethnic and gender hierarchization of both the social and the political systems make their imprint on progressive political parties too. Even today most parties reproduce the andro/ethnocentric make-up of the political system, preventing a more active involvement in party and

electoral politics by those segments of the subordinated classes identifying themselves more through gender or ethnicity than through socioeconomic issues.

4. Organizational dimensions as well as institutional projections of class identity have become feebler, particularly those dealing with the labor market. Issues such as the increasing fragmentation of labor markets, the explosion of the UIS, the expansion of individual contracts at the expense of collective union-led bargaining or the shrinking in government social spending reduce the room for labor activism and progressively dilute the organizational dimensions of working-class identity.

This process takes place as poverty grows at an extremely fast pace: 44 percent between 1980 and 1990, or an increase of 60 million Latin American poor. Widespread growth in poverty has gone hand in hand with increased social inequality as a vivid illustration of uneven social distribution of gains and losses. Income polarization is greater in Latin America than in southern Europe or southeast Asia, traditional comparative parameters to Latin American countries (Table 4). The relation between neoliberal macroeconomics and increasing mass poverty is an indisputable aggravation to already existing income inequalities.

Extreme levels of income polarization make for a sharper fragmentation of Latin American societies. What is there in common for any of the six million Brazilian families earning an average income of U.S. $240 a month and those earning an average of U.S. $6,300 a month, or even a monthly average of U.S. $9,200—as the families of the top 10 percent do? This is no longer a matter of mere income differentials but of people living in two different dimensions of life. However, both dimensions are closely intertwined and mutually interdependent, and all the fences and electronic devices surrounding rich neighborhoods and villas are not able to turn them into a separate world.

Rapid deterioration of working-class neighborhoods; growth of the populations of old and new slums; downgrading of such basic public services as health care and elementary education; a four-year-old continent-wide cholera epidemic; several hundreds of thousands of people surviving on remittances from their relatives who have migrated to the U.S. (CEPAL 1991); food riots in Brazil and—believe it or not—Argentina; increasing numbers of retired elders taking their own lives; frightening crime statistics; growing involvement in drug trafficking (Giusti 1991); violence against chil-

Table 4

Comparative Distribution of Household Income[a]

Country	(1) Lowest 20%	(2) Middle 60%	(3) Highest 20%	(4) 3:1
Brazil (1983)	2.4	35.0	62.6	26.1
Colombia (1988)	4.0	43.0	53.0	13.2
Costa Rica (1986)	3.3	42.2	54.5	16.5
Guatemala (1979–1981)	5.5	39.0	55.5	10.1
Jamaica (1988)	5.4	45.4	49.2	9.1
Perú (1985–1986)	4.4	43.7	51.9	11.8
Venezuela (1987)	4.7	44.7	50.6	10.8
Italy (1986)	6.8	52.2	41.0	6.0
Spain (1982–1983)	6.9	53.0	40.1	5.8
Hong-Kong (1980)	5.4	47.6	47.0	8.7

a. Percentage of national income appropriated by the poorest 20 percent, middle 60 percent and the richest 20 percent of households. Countries included sum up to 56 percent of the Latin American population.

Source: World Bank, 1992

dren (Amnistía Internacional 1990; Dimeinstein 1991), which includes more than 20,000 children kidnapped and sold every year to U.S. and European customers for purposes of prostitution, adoption or organ transplants (Mergier 1992; Piñeiro 1992): all of these facts are evidence of an ongoing process of production of poverty, inequality and social degradation paralleling the process of production of incredible wealth, state policies having in each movement as strong a role as the marketplace. Increased mass poverty— through lower wages, higher unemployment, welfare crisis and the like—may well be interpreted as a counterpart of, and even as a condition for, the reconstitution of the profit rate. While the ideology of the ruling class reinvigorates itself by going back to its Smithian foundations, the Latin American people are forced to a massive retreat to the Hobbesian state of nature; where there is "no Society, and what is worst of all, continued feare, and danger of violent death; and the life of man, solitary, poore, nasty, brutish, and short" (Hobbes 1651:65).

THE SEARCH FOR ALTERNATIVES

INITIATIVES FROM BELOW

An extensive literature on Latin American social movements considers them as would-be substitutes for more traditional organizations such as political parties and unions.[9] These organizations are said to subordinate true people's initiatives to political designs that only express the goals of party and union bureaucracies and their inevitable compromises with the political system, the state and the ruling class. Moreover, parties and unions are considered to tend to suppress the cultural diversity of movements via class or state reductionist approaches. This suppression prevents them from endorsing people's initiatives and from expressing true grassroots dynamism. In contrast, because they are the product of the autonomy and the diversity of the people, social movements provide personal support and rehabilitation as much as they contribute to strengthening cultural identities.

As a matter of fact, "social movements" is a rather loose term pointing to a broad variety of predominantly urban organizations. They include neighborhood and community organizations dealing with poor settlements and housing, basic education and health services—for example, literacy and vaccination campaigns—as well as communal kitchens, human and civic rights, counterculture and environmental issues, the term "social" reflecting a nonpartisan recruitment as much as a nonclass appeal. However, the predominant enrollment comes from both the working-class and the lower-middle-class strata; social movements are not working-class organizations, but they are not alien to the world of labor and poverty. Women's involvement has been particularly important in the neighborhood movements as well as in those organized primarily to denounce the most outrageous aspects of political repression. Social movements stress self-reliance not just as a way to get things done but also as a method of self-training and grassroots empowerment and of strengthening people's identities, issues that more traditional or conventional organizations—such as parties and unions—have problems addressing.

I will not discuss here the literature on social movements or the criticism to which it has been subjected. Certainly social movements have been active participants in both social and political struggles in recent decades, particularly in countries experiencing harsh authoritarian regimes. Social movements were prominent not just in advancing microcentered demands—such as neighborhood or community actions—but also in gathering support for broad national issues, such as mobilization for democracy or against human rights abuses, as well as increasing social concern for environmental issues. They have also been active in advancing gender and ethnic or race issues. Although autonomy vis-à-vis political parties and unions has frequently been overstated, social movements' ability to advance their specific demands relied to a certain extent on the loose ties they were able to keep with regard to traditional organizations, particularly when the movements were the targets of political repression. Nevertheless, overemphasis on autonomy clouds the involvement of party and union organizers in the makeup of social movements in a number of countries.[10] In several cases, autonomy from parties and unions has been greater than autonomy from church agencies and from foreign-based non-governmental organizations (NGOs).

Although they are still rather active in countries such as Perú, Brazil or México, social movements knew their heyday in the late 1970s and early 1980s. Their leading role was related as much to their own dynamism and creativity as to their ability to fill the empty space left by parties and unions that were being repressed by dictatorial regimes. The debt crisis, the advent of postmilitary regimes and capitalist restructuring changed the scenario and the scope of their struggles. Long-lasting literary enthusiasm notwithstanding, today they show a much lower profile and appear to be an ingredient of the popular sectors' overall social and political predicament as much as a way out. Let me deal in a very brief manner with two aspects of this new setting.

First, electoral politics places political parties once again at the center of the institutional arena and forces them, as well as social movements, to look for ways of working together. In addition to the new institutional setting, as long as social movements intend to move from a microcentered concern to a regional or national one, they have to reach some kind of political articulation. This necessity has led to mixed experiences. Either parties tend to subsume social movements to their own agenda, schedule and strategies and the movements lose identity and autonomy, or movements have isolated themselves from politics and lost efficacy and frequently membership. Usually party affiliations cut across social movements' constituencies, thus introducing party competition within them. This division does not necessarily lead to fragmentation, but reaching a compromise is not an easy matter: it demands energy, time and political abilities. In other cases the movements have contributed to building new political parties, as with the Brazilian Partido dos

Trabalhadores (PT, or Worker's Party) and, to a certain extent, México's Partido de la Revolución Democrática (PRD, or Party for Democratic Revolution).

Second, a number of social movements' demands have state and government agencies as their direct or indirect targets. This is the case, for example, in squatters' demands for street lights, sewage, health centers and the like. People can manage to build a community health or day-care center, but they have to rely on government support to keep it working. They may conduct a vaccination campaign, but they have to have the vaccines. Even the most reluctant of social organizations has to involve itself in some type of political action to have access to resources. They may do it either by appealing to some type of clientelistic strategy, or by behaving as what was once called "pressure groups," or in other ways, but they have no alternative to dealing with politicians or, at least, with government or party bureaucrats. This is particularly so when local or microcentered gains depend on macro public policies—as the everyday working of a school depends on the state's educational and financial policies. As government social spending slows down because of public policy shifts related to economic restructuring, people face increasing difficulties in keeping these basic achievements working in a decent way, or working at all. Certainly this fact is quite obvious for social movements engaged in environmental or human rights issues: in order to be effective, they have to produce results at the national, and even international, level.

In addition, it must be pointed out that the consolidation of grassroots improvements is in one way or another dependent on state policies— such as health and educational policies—whose formulation falls out of the reach of social movements. Moreover, the failure of social movements to have an impact on economic policies or on market relations directly linked to their agenda and to the daily concerns of their members—for example, by organizing mass rallies to oppose consumer-price policies and rising cost of living—suggests that there is no substitute for political action when shifts in general policies are involved.

For several years government or state hostility or indifference was compensated for by NGO support. Both churches and foreign NGOs have been strategic in supplying social movements with technical and financial resources, supporting their confrontations with government agencies and even contributing to developing specific agendas. But as military regimes receded and NGO headquarters in Europe, Canada or the U.S. develop an increasing concern for efficient use of resources (Kruijt 1992), social movements face a problematic horizon.

In all, prospects for social movements to reduce the impact of current economic restructuring and increasing poverty look feeble, to say the least. As we know them, social movements were not devised to deal with the kind of social environment set forth by increasing mass marginalization. For one thing, their reach is extremely reduced when compared to the rapid increase of poverty in Latin American societies. To many people, the search for individual alternatives, or for alternatives that may afford more immediate outcomes, seems to be more promising. Even the contribution of social movements to the strengthening of social identities is now experiencing the impact of the new setting. Identities as a dimension of culture are not independent from access to economic resources and to political institutions. Gender, ethnic, generational, class or any other identity is reinforced as collective participation leads to some kind of tangible reward: be it legal rights, social prestige, economic improvements, symbolic issues or any other. When, on the contrary, people wander from failure to defeat, the organizations they join no longer work to strengthen social identities, or, if they do, they build people's identities in close association to subordination and defeat.

The preceding discussion does not ignore the contribution social movements have made to the democratization of Latin America and to opening up the democratic agenda to issues marginalized by such traditional collective actors as public bureaucracies, political parties and unions. But the present setting is quite a different one. However important past experience may be in addressing current problems, it is not enough. Some type of strategic articulation with unions and political parties must be reached. Due to the already mentioned limits of both, this is not an easy task. But unless it is faced, it is hard to see a way out "from below." On the contrary, emphasis on a romantic concept of autonomy and the alleged purity of social movements confronting the intrinsic corruption and authoritarianism of parties and unions leads to no more than a reinforcement of the fragmentation of popular struggles, and thus to a strengthening of the prospects for failure.

INITIATIVES "FROM ABOVE"

In recent years a number of Latin American governments as well as several

multilateral agencies have sponsored emergency social programs affording
temporary employment and low-income alternatives for segments of the
unemployed active population in projects aimed at building or repairing economic and social infrastructures. Supported by foreign funding from agencies
such as the Interamerican Development Bank (IDB) or World Bank, these
initiatives rely on hiring unskilled, mostly male labor for short periods of time
to build or repair roads, bridges, ports and the like. Salaries are low, not infre-
quently falling below the legal minimum, and the workers lack access to
welfare benefits. The rationale of these programs, as stated by funding agencies, is twofold: (1) to address development of infrastructure, a much-delayed
dimension in Latin America's economic development over the past decades;
(2) to effect a cheap reabsorption of workers previously expelled from the
labor market, through programs being addressed to people "willing to accept
low wages" (IDB 1992b:9). To put it in crass terms: workers are expelled from
previous formal occupations, then reemployed at downgraded, lower-paid
working conditions. We are apparently witnessing the development of a new
labor market going beyond the traditional formal/informal sectors differentiation and combining ingredients from both: state and international agencies
together with capitalist corporations (i.e., formal sector) relying on labor
employment according to informal standards; no minimum wages, no access
to welfare, no unions, no legal protection, no job stability.

By their very nature most of these programs have but a limited impact on
selected target populations. When properly designed and administered they
may address particular cases of extreme poverty. However, once this low
threshold is reached, their ability to move toward higher levels is question-
able. Moreover, because they are able to deal only with small segments of the
population, these approaches usually reinforce people's fragmentation as
much as they foment renewed clientelistic and corporatist practices. Access to
a temporary job in a road-building project, or to material resources to build
the neighborhood's day-care center, may be not so much a question of fitting
into an official, statistical definition of poverty as much as a matter of knowing
someone at the mayor's office or at the governing party's *delegación*. Because
such programs are administered by government agencies, usually people and
community organizations have no alternative but to get involved in a sharp
competition to get favors—that is, resources—from bureaucrats. As the state
retreats from direct involvement in development, state bureaucrats and gov-

ernment officials increase their own roles as brokers of survival. It is not uncommon to find that an implicit goal of these programs is the building of political constituencies for municipal, provincial and even national officials.

"Compensatory" policies may also be easily reoriented to manipulate social movements and to neutralize their movements' mobilizing potential. More often than not government agencies deal with poverty and marginalization from a preemptive political perspective: poverty breeds social unrest and should therefore be kept within limits. Accordingly, compensatory policies are approached as devices to prevent further threats to the social order and to keep volatile segments of the population under control.

Support for self-employment and household activities in the UIS has also been reinforced in recent years. Under the general brand of "people's economy" (*economía popular*) family shops and communal productive and social efforts are receiving financial and technical support both from government agencies and from mostly foreign NGOs. Although these programs usually have a limited scope, they may produce short-term results by moving targeted populations above the poverty line and back to the formal sector. There is little systematic information on the ability of these small productive units to advance further or to establish a stronghold in the market; media coverage usually deals with particularly successful individual cases instead of looking for a more comprehensive assessment. However, when supported over longer periods of time, or if articulated to broader development strategies, these programs may involve feasible economic alternatives, at least for early runners. The apparently successful current Chilean experience points to this particular issue.

In several aspects the Chilean case approaches some dimensions of what some years ago the United Nations Economic Commission for Latin America and the Caribbean (ECLAC) called "productive transformation with equity" (*transformación productiva con equidad*): a strategy to strengthen and prompt small, frequently family-owned shops through targeted credit, marketing, skill-development and other policies (CEPAL 1990). It is worthwhile to point out that these approaches to grassroots organization are not entirely new. Previous experiences in both Chile and Perú go back to the 1960s, such as Eduardo Frei's Democratic Christian experiment in "Promoción Popular" (1964–1970), and SINAMOS during the 1968–1975 reformist stage of the Perúvian military regime. Moreover, community development has been given support and resources through Alliance for Progress-related policies ever since the Alliance's inception in 1961. Now as then, these policy approaches may lead either to the building up or the reinforcement of clientelistic networks. In addition, it has been pointed out that these programs usually tend to rely on increased unpaid female labor, thus involving a reinforcement of traditional gender biases in development programs (Elson 1992). The ability of people directly involved in these programs to fight against these forms of gender discrimination, to defend themselves from paternalism or patronage and to keep degrees of autonomy vis-à-vis government agencies—particularly in the design of policies—strengthens the prospect for a progressive empowerment of grassroots organization.

One common trait of the above mentioned strategies—both "from below" and "from above"—is that due to their very nature they tend to fragment the people whose problems they are intended to address. As much as class reductionism conceals the specificity and relative autonomy of other dimensions of social identities—as with gender, race, nation and so on—policy and underlying conceptual aproaches stressing "the specificity of the particular" and the micro dimensions of collective allegiances tend to isolate and fragment the popular sectors as long as they deprive them of a principle of articulation that might relate them either to class, to citizenship or to both. Public policies seek a direct relation of masses to the state, substituting state bureaucracies and government agencies for political parties and unions.

The most notorious shortcomings of these strategies also derive from this segmenting and the reciprocal isolation of both "target populations"—as they are called in strategies "from above"—and most grassroots organizations. Strategies "from above" and "from below" separate poverty from the economic and political macroprocesses that contribute to its growth. Although both strategies may be, and in fact are, successful in coping with several dimensions of poverty and downgraded living conditions for specific segments of the population, they are not suited to more global, policy-related questions. The most relevant difference between attempts to deal with poverty "from below" and "from above" is that the latter are explicitly subordinated to the reproduction of current social relations. Instead, any strategy addressing social change should count on social movements' contributions and experiences.

Although the state and public policies have played a strategic role in the

current economic restructuring and in the construction of the present institutional setting, popular classes and social groups searching for socioeconomic
alternatives should look with similar emphasis for political alternatives. Social
movements, political parties and labor unions are expected to play a most
important guiding role in these searches, as far as they prove to be able to
articulate their roles to each other and to the vast popular masses pushed
toward an increasingly inorganic situation by neoliberal economics and policies. The European and Central Asian breakdown of Soviet-type political
regimes, which have never existed in Latin America—short of the Cuban
case—or of Marxist-Leninist thinking, which was much more important in
left-wing academic circles than in Latin American politics, pose no particular
questions in terms of an alleged exhaustion of critical paradigms. On the contrary, they free the creative quest for people's political and social alternatives
from the Manichean dialectics of the Cold War.

notes

This chapter was written while I was Edward Larocque Tinker Professor at the
Institute of Latin American and Iberian Studies, Columbia University. I am
indebted to Arthur MacEwan, Hobart A. Spalding and Katherine Roberts-Hite
for their most valuable comments on an earlier version. Throughout this presentation "Latin America" refers also to the Caribbean; however, Cuba is not
included due to her specificity with regard to the rest of the countries.

1. Although in recent years private international capital markets have developed a
   new interest toward several Latin American economies, sums involved are not
   comparable to those that reached Latin America in the heyday of export-led
   growth, or to the 1970s' easy lending (see Griffith-Jones et al., 1993).
2. I would like to recall, however, that one important dimension of post-Fordism,
   the retreat of mass consumption as a central concern of economic policies, dates
   back to the 1960s, as was pointed out in two seminal, timely articles by Pinto
   (1965) and Vuskoviç (1970).
3. Although I cannot fully develop this argument here, it must be said that this
   closer involvement is as much a product of specific class interests advanced by
   business elites as an ideological option of a new breed of technocrats turned into

politicans who are running a number of Latin American governments.

4. As referred to by the monthly *Latin Finance* 34 (March 1992).

5. According to Sáinz y Calcagno's estimates México's real exchange rate deteriorated by one-third between 1987 and 1991 and by slightly more than 10 percent between 1989 and 1991 (Sáinz y Calcagno 1992). Méxican private banks estimated a 11.6 percent overvaluation of the Méxican peso by mid-1993: *El Financiero,* July 28, 1993.

6. According to the pro-government Méxican Confederation of Workers (CTM), the rate of unemployment was close to 20 percent of the Economically Active Population (EAP) by mid-1993: press conference by Fidel Velázquez (CTM's top leader) on August 9, 1993.

7. As stated by José Córdoba Montoya, President Salinas de Gortari's chief of staff, at the spring 1992 meeting of the Mexican Banking Association in Acapulco.

8. In a colorful illustration of the intimate relations being forged between the Méxican government and these prominent financial groups, 29 of their top leaders convened in early March 1993 in an afterward much-publicized private meeting called by PRI's top officials, where they were invited to contribute $25 million each to the coming electoral campaign of the ruling party (see Acosta 1993b).

9. See Slater (1985) for a collection representative of the enthusiastic/romantic approach to Latin American social movements as well as Assies (1990) and Adler Hellman (1992) for more balanced perspectives.

10. See Spalding 1992: 44–46, and on the Chilean case, Schneider 1992.

references

Acosta, Carlos. 1993a. "El País puede hundirse pero los banqueros ganan bien." *Proceso* 849 (8 de febrero): 26–28.

———. 1993b. "Quiénes son y cuánto tienen los que van a financiar al PRI." *Proceso* 853 (8 de marzo). 15–19.

Adler Hellman, Judith. 1992. "The Study of New Social Movements in Latin America and the Question of Autonomy." In A. Escobar and S. Alvarez (eds.), *The Making of Social Movements in Latin America.* Boulder, Co.: Westview Press, 52–61.

Amnistía Internacional. 1990. *Guatemala: Los niños de la calle.* Madrid: EDAI.

Arriagada, Irma. 1990. "Unequal participation by Women in the Working World."

CEPAL Review 40: 83–98.

Assies, Willem. 1990. "On Structured Moves and Moving Structures. An Overview of Theoretical Perspectives on Social Movements." In W. Assies et al., *Structures of Power, Movements of Resistance: An Introduction to the Theories of Urban Movements in Latin America.* Amsterdam: CEDLA; 9–98.

Banco Mundial. 1992. *Informe sobre el desarrollo mundial.* Washington, D.C.: Banco Mundial.

Bienen, Henry, y John Waterbury. 1991. "La economía política de la privatización en los países en desarrolo." *Investigación Económica.*

Bouin, O. and Charles-Albert Michalet. 1991. *Rebalancing the Public and Private Sectors: Developing Country Experience.* Paris: OECD.

Cavarozzi, Marcelo. 1992. "Beyond Transitions to Democracy in Latin America." *Journal of Latin American Studies* 24 (3): 665–684.

Cardoso, Eliana, and Ann Helwege. 1991. "Populism, Profligacy and Redistribution." in R. Dornsbusch and S. Edwards (eds.), *The Macroeconomics of Populism in Latin America.* Chicago: Chicago University Press, 45–70.

Carton De Gramont, Ubert. 1992. "Algunas reflexiones en torno al mercado de trabajo en el campo latinoamericano." *Revista Mexicana de Sociología* 54: (1) (enero-marzo): 49–58.

CEPAL, Comisión Económica para América Latina y el Caribe. 1990. *Transformación productiva con equidad.* Santiago. CEPAL.

————. 1991. *Remesas y economía familiar en el Salvador, Guatemala y Nicaragua.* LC/Mex/R.294. Mexico City, May.

————. 1992a. *Balance preliminar de la economía de América Latina y el Caribe.* Santiago de Chile, 18 de diciembre.

————. 1992. *El perfil de la pobreza en América Latina a comienzos de los años 90.* Santiago de Chile, noviembre.

Dimeinstein, Gilbert. 1991. *Brazil: War on Children.* London: Latin American Bureau.

Dornbusch, Rudiger, y Sebastián Edwards. 1990. "La macroeconomía del populismo en la América Latina." *El Trimestre Económico* 225 (enero-marzo): 121–162.

Elson, Diane. 1992. "From Survival Strategies to Transformation Strategies: Women's Needs and Structural Adjustment," in Lourdes, Benería and Shelley Feldman (eds.), *Unequal Burden: Economic Crises, Persistent Poverty, and Women's Work.* Boulder, Co.: Westview Press, 26–48.

Giusti, Jorge. 1991. "Significado económico y social de la droga." *Revista de la CEPAL* 45 (diciembre): 145–153.

Griffith-Jones, Stephany, et al. 1993. "El retorno de capital a América Latina." *Comercio Exterior* 43 (1) (enero): 37–50.

Grinspun, Ricardo and Maxwell Cameron. 1993. "Mexico: The Wages of Trade." *NACLA report on the Americas* 26 (4) (February): 32–37.

Hobbes, Thomas. 1651. *Leviathan.* London: J. M. Dent & Sons, Ltd. [1973].

IDB, Interamerican Development Bank. 1992a. *Economic and Social Progress in Latin America.* Washington, D.C.: IDB.

————. 1992b. *Políticas de Desarrollo* 1 (4) (diciembre).

Infante, Ricardo, y Emilio Klein. 1991. "Mercado latinoamericano de trabajo en 1950–1990." *Revista de la CEPAL* 45 (diciembre): 129–141.

Kruijt, Dirk. 1992. "Monopolios de filantropía. El caso de las llamadas 'Organizaciones no gubernamentales' en América Latina." *Polémica* 16 (2ª época): 41–47.

Little, Walter. 1992. "Political Corruption in Latin America." *Corruption and Reform* 7: 41–66.

Mergier, Anne Marie. 1992. "Secuestros de niños latinoamericanos para traficar con sus órganos en Europa." *Proceso* 833 (19 de octubre).

Pinto, Anibal. 1965. "Concentración del progreso técnico y de sus frutos en el desarrollo latinoamericano." *El Trimestre Económico* 125 (enero-marzo): 3–69.

Piñero, Maité. 1992. "Secuestro de niños y tráfico de órganos." *Le Monde Diplomatique* 461 (agosto).

Pozas, Maria de los Angeles. Forthcoming: *Reestructuración industrial en México: El caso de Monterrey.*

Rodriguez Castañeda, Rafael. 1992. "La élite empresarial de Salinas." *Proceso* 819 (13 de julio): 6–7.

————. 1993. "Borrego, 29 magnates y el presidente de la República." *Proceso* 853 (8 de marzo): 6–9.

Sainz, Pedro, y Alfredo Calcagno. 1992. "En busca de otra modalidad de desarrollo." *Revista de la CEPAL* 48 (diciembre): 7–39.

Schneider, Cathy. 1992. "Radical Opposition Parties and Squatter Movements in Pinochet's Chile." In Arturo Escobar and Sonia Alvarez (eds.), *The Making of Social Movements in Latin America.* Boulder, Co.: Westview Press, 260–275.

Slater, David. 1985. (ed.). *New Social Movements and the State in Latin America.* Amsterdam: CEDLA

Smith, Adam. 1776. *An Inquiry on the Nature and Causes of the Wealth of Nations.* Chicago: The University of Chicago Press [1976].

Spalding, Hobart A. 1992. *Devastation in the Southern Cone: The Inheritance of the Neo-*

Liberal Years. Meadville, Penn.: Allegheny College.

Verbitsky, Horatio. 1991. *Robo para la corona.* Buenos Aires: Planeta.

Vilas, Carlos M. 1992. *El proceso de reordenamiento patrimonial en Nicaragua.* Managua: PNUD.

―――――. 1992–1993. "Latin American Populism: A Structural Approach." *Science & Society* 56 (Winter): 389–420.

Vuskoviç, Pedro. 1970. "Distribución del ingreso y opciones de desarrollo." *Cuadernos de la Realidad Nacional* 5 (setiembre): 41–60.

World Bank. 1981. *World Development Report.* Washington, D.C.: World Bank.

KEITH GRIFFIN and AZIZUR RAHMAN KHAN

the transition to market–guided economies

lessons for russia and eastern europe from the chinese experience

The process of economic reform in China began in 1978 and continues to this day. The process is far from over—there is much that remains to be done—but a great deal has been achieved in the last fifteen years, and much can be learned from the Chinese experience. Our purpose, however, is not to attempt a comprehensive evaluation of the economic reforms in China but to consider what lessons from the Chinese experience might be applicable to Russia and Eastern Europe as they attempt a transition from centralized quantitative planning to an economy guided by market forces. China would seem to be an obvious point of comparison for socialist countries in transition since China was and remains a socialist county which nonetheless aspires to harness market forces to serve national purposes. It would perhaps be an exaggeration to claim that China has led the way in the transition from socialism as practiced in the communist-ruled countries, since there were numerous experiments with economic reform in Russia and Eastern Europe going as far back as the 1950s, but the Chinese reforms have lasted longer, penetrated more deeply and apparently been more successful than any of the reforms introduced in other socialist countries.

The traverse from a quantitatively planned to a market-guided economy is a journey into unknown territory. There are no models to follow, no leaders to emulate, not even well-founded theories that can be used as a guide. Much is known about how market economies function, although periodic malfunctioning demonstrates how much remains to be learned. Less is known about the efficient management of a planned socialist system, although our ignorance is not as great as has sometimes been claimed, nor are the accomplishments of socialism as meager. Still less is known about how to move from one system to another, and we find ourselves groping in the dark searching for a match and candle to light our way.

One potential source of enlightenment is the experience of Western Europe in the years after World War II. The wartime economies of Europe were essentially planned economies, and the methods used to allocate resources were not very different from those used in socialist countries. The reconversion of European economies to market-guided economies was a slow and painful process, assisted after 1947 by generous quantities of foreign aid. There were several false starts, controls were removed gradually and sometimes hesitatingly, and progress was punctuated periodically by crises of various sorts. Food rationing did not end in Britain until 1951, six years after hostilities ceased. Yet the reconversion of Western Europe to a market-guided economy arguably was less difficult than the transition being attempted today by Russia and Eastern Europe. Western Europe, after all, possessed the institutions needed by a capitalist economy—secure property rights, legal codes and a court system to enforce laws of contract, a well-developed capital market with specialized financial enterprises and a dense network of markets capable of transmitting information quickly and cheaply. In the case of Western Europe, the preconditions for success already existed. In the case of Russia and Eastern Europe, however, the foundations are missing, and this lack inevitably makes the transition more difficult.

A second possible source of enlightenment is the experience of some developing countries. Particularly during the 1980s, a number of developing countries had to cope with problems that, at least on the surface, appear to be similar to those faced by Russia and Eastern Europe today: severe balance of payments difficulties, heavy foreign indebtedness, rapid inflation occasionally accelerating into hyperinflation, slow and even negative rates of growth, rising unemployment and poverty and in some sectors a collapse of production. No doubt there are lessons to be learned from Bolivia and Ghana, from Mexico and South Korea about stabilization, adjustment and restructuring, and it would be foolish to turn one's back on whatever wisdom can be gleaned from history, but the fact remains that the circumstances in the developing countries in the 1980s were very different from the circumstances in Russia and Eastern Europe in the 1990s. Above all, stabilization and restructuring in developing countries occurred within an established economic system. However prominent in economic affairs the state might have been, the economies of the developing countries were mixed capitalist economies in which resources for the most part were allocated via the market mechanism and not through quantitative controls. Stabilization and restructuring, in other words, were not accompanied by systemic change.

The problem confronting the developing countries in the 1980s, difficult but ultimately not intractable, was how to improve their existing market-guided economies in order to absorb external shocks and overcome internally generated disequilibria. The problem confronting Russia and Eastern Europe in the 1990s is how to effect a transition to a market-guided economy while simultaneously absorbing massive shocks such as the reconfiguration of national boundaries, severe disruption of long-established trading relationships, loss of export markets and curtailment of vital supplies of imported raw materials and energy. The combination of systemic change, multiple shocks and serious macroeconomic disequilibria in a large number of countries at the same time is unprecedented, and one should be cautious about drawing analogies with developing countries a decade ago.

Of course one should also be careful about drawing analogies from China, particularly since China officially remains committed to some form of socialism, whereas Russia and Eastern Europe do not. Our argument, however, is not that China is the sole or even the best source of relevant experience but that China is one source of relevant experience, one, moreover, that has been neglected in the discussions of economic reform in Russia and Eastern

Europe. In what follows we shall concentrate on four topics where China may be able to shed some light. We begin with a discussion of macroeconomic financial stability during the reform process. This discussion is followed by an analysis of the pace of growth and the level of investment during the period since the reforms. We then turn our attention to property relations and the reform of state economic enterprises. Lastly, we discuss changes in the distribution of income that have accompanied the reforms.

China has its own way of doing things, and this unique style is reflected in several features that are characteristic of the reform process. Perhaps paradoxically for a centrally planned economy,[1] the economic reforms in China were not planned at the center and imposed from the top down in conformity with a predetermined grand scheme. On the contrary, the reform process has been highly pragmatic, experimental and sequential. Reform has proceeded by trial and error on a step-by-step basis. Policies have been flexible, amendments have been frequent, enforcement has been far from uniform and reverses have occurred. An outside observer of this process might bemusedly regard the Chinese as marching to an uncertain drummer, but we believe the methods used by the Chinese reformmongers[2] account for much of their success. Indeed, one of the lessons to be learned from China is the advantage of proceeding in a flexible and incrementalist way.

Economic reforms began in agriculture, and only when their success had been demonstrated were they extended to the industrial sector. Within agriculture, numerous experiments with alternative arrangements to the commune system were conducted.[3] These experiments initially were confined to a single county and then spread to an entire province, or to several counties within a province; hence, during this experimental period several different approaches to agricultural reform were being tested simultaneously. The eventual national model—the household responsibility system—was not adopted until the various local experiments had been evaluated at the center, but once a national model was selected, it was introduced throughout the country very swiftly, albeit with considerable local variation.

The process of reform in agriculture set the pattern for reforms in other sectors. The process was characterized by (1) an experimental approach to policy making, (2) a tolerance for diversity, (3) a willingness of policymakers at the center to learn from the experience at the grassroots and (4) a tendency of reformmongers to concentrate their efforts where rapid and substantial gains from reform could be anticipated.

The pattern was repeated when the industrial reforms began. Rather than confront the difficult problem of the state economic enterprises head-on, the reforms were launched initially in the countryside by transforming the township and village enterprises into cooperatives, and private and individual enterprises. Space was created for the private sector to expand—at first only in the rural areas but later also in the cities—without altering property relations in the large, economically dominant, state-owned urban industrial sector. Privatization of state enterprises, in other words, was avoided, but the weight of the state sector in industrial output was rapidly reduced by allowing small-scale private enterprise to emerge.

The pattern was repeated yet again with the reform of foreign trade policy. China did not open up all at once by reducing tariffs, eliminating quotas, welcoming foreign capital, dismantling exchange controls and declaring its currency convertible. Indeed, by these criteria China still is far from being an open economy. Instead it moved cautiously, gradually liberalizing trade, encouraging a few joint ventures in selected industries and slowly adjusting the exchange rate. Radical experiments with a semifree trade regime were conducted in four Special Economic Zones located in two eastern coastal provinces, of which the most famous is Shenzhen, adjacent to Hong Kong. When these experiments proved to be successful, fourteen important coastal cities were allowed to engage directly in foreign trade and investment without being required to go through the center. Foreign economic policy thus became rather patchy, with considerable regional variation. The lack of uniformity, abhorrent to a Western-trained economist, had positive advantages during a period of transition: it enabled policymakers to avoid the political confrontations that would have been created by an attempt to impose a uniform national policy from the beginning, it provided valuable experience and information that could be used to fine-tune policies and it gave policymakers time to build political support on the basis of demonstrated achievements. Russia and Eastern Europe could do worse than emulate the methods of the Chinese reform-mongers.

MACROECONOMIC FINANCIAL STABILITY

The transition from an economy where resources are allocated by quantitative controls to one where resources are allocated by price is likely to be disruptive even in the best of circumstances. Prices, by design, will become much more important, and relative prices are likely to change dramatically. This change will harm some consumers and producers and benefit others. The losers almost certainly will oppose reforms, while the gainers are likely to support them. Society will thus be divided, and if the reforms are introduced in a brusque manner, intense social conflict may emerge. This scenario suggests that the transition is likely to proceed more smoothly, politically and economically, if reforms are introduced gradually and if producers and consumers are given time to adjust.

Macroeconomic financial stability in particular will provide a favorable environment for reform. Above all, high rates of inflation should be avoided. Rapid increases in the average level of prices will magnify perceptions of gains and losses and accentuate social conflict. Moreover, rapid and especially accelerating inflation almost always is accompanied by sharp and unpredictable changes in relative prices—complete indexation is neither possible nor desirable—and this change will lead to changes in the distribution of income that could undermine public support for the reform process as a whole. Inflation often is accompanied by erratic changes in relative prices, which harm consumers while making sensible production and investment plans difficult for producers. As a result, rapid inflation could well lead to a fall in the level of output and a decline in the rate of growth. If average living standards fall precipitously, the transition to a market-guided economy could be aborted. Thus, the stakes are high.

China, unlike Russia and most of Eastern Europe, has been quite successful in maintaining macroeconomic financial stability. Prior to the economic reforms, during the era of comprehensive central planning and quantitative controls, inflation was repressed, prices on average were highly stable and the prices of individual commodities often remained fixed for many years. During the period from 1965 to 1980, for example, the annual rate of inflation in China was minus 0.3 percent per annum. During the next 11 years, 1981–1991, the average rate of inflation was much higher, namely 7.2 percent a year, but in six of the 11 years the rate was 3 percent or less (see Table 1). In only three years did inflation achieve double digits, and in only one brief period, 1988–1989, did inflation threaten to get out of control.

In 1988 the economy became overheated as a result of an investment boom. The authorities reacted quickly, and in late 1988 a stabilization program was

Table 1

The Annual Rate of Inflation in China, 1981–1991

(percentage change in the GDP deflator)

1981	2.6	1987	8.8
1982	2.0	1988	20.7
1983	1.9	1989	16.3
1984	2.8	1990	2.2
1985	11.9	1991	3.0
1986	7.0	—	—

Source: United Nations, *World Economic Survey 1992*, Annex Table A.14, New York, 1992, p. 197

introduced. Government current expenditure was cut, state-financed investment was reduced sharply and the supply of bank credit was restricted. Tight monetary and fiscal policies were maintained until 1991, by which time the rate of inflation had been brought under control again and financial stability restored. It would appear, at least on the surface, that even during a lengthy transition period the authorities have been able to maintain a firm grip on the aggregate level of spending.

Beneath the surface, however, there are signs that the grip is less firm than it at first appears. All the banks are owned by the state, and banks are by far the most important source of credit. The financial system in China is poorly developed: the bond market is small and stock markets are embryonic. Hence, in principle the government should have little difficulty maintaining an orderly financial environment. In practice, however, the control of the central government over the volume of bank credit and its allocation is weak. In times of impending crisis the government can impose austerity measures, but in other, more normal times its ability to control the volume of credit is rather tenuous. Actual bank lending usually exceeds authorized lending because local bank managers are more responsive to the demands of local and provincial officials than to control figures issued by the center. Financial stability in China thus tends to be rather fragile, and the danger of overheating from excessive investment demand is ever present.

The money supply increased 25.4 percent a year between 1980 and 1990. In a fully monetized market economy this increase would have resulted in per-

sistent rapid inflation. China, however, does not have a fully monetized economy, and a significant proportion of the increase in the money supply was
held as money balances rather than spent on goods and services. This proportion is reflected in changes in the ratio of the stock of money to national
income, which rose from 33.6 percent in 1980 to 74.7 percent in 1990. The
money/income ratio now falls within the range characteristic of fully monetized economies, and it is therefore likely that if the money supply continues to
grow by 25 percent a year, China will encounter severe inflationary pressures.

The authorities seem to have recognized the danger, and emphasis within
the monetary system has shifted away from money creation to greater reliance
on the flotation of government bonds and foreign borrowing. At present the
bond market is not a major source of finance for long-term investment,
although it can be expected to grow rapidly in the future. Foreign borrowing
increased from almost nothing at the beginning of the reform process to a
small but significant source of finance today. Between 1980 and 1990, for
instance, external debt increased from 1.5 percent of gross national product to
14.4 percent, and the debt service ratio rose from 4.4 percent of total exports
to 10.3 percent. China, evidently, has been prudent about foreign borrowing;
it now needs to become more prudent about domestic money creation.

China's financial stability may be a little fragile, but it compares very favor-
ably with the instability in Russia and much of Eastern Europe. Of course the
extent of repressed inflation in prereform Russia and Eastern Europe was
higher than in China, but the fact remains that the Chinese managed their
financial affairs rather well and the Russians and Eastern Europeans did not.
The collapse of communism beginning in 1989 was followed almost everywhere by an explosive increase in inflation (see Table 2). In Poland the rate of
inflation increased from 59 percent a year in 1988 to 259.5 percent in 1989;
between 1990 and 1991 inflation rose in Czechoslovakia (since divided into
two countries) from 9.9 percent to 57.9 percent; in Bulgaria from 19.3 to 249.8
percent; and in Romania from 5.7 to 305.5 percent. Among the East European
countries in the table, only in Hungary was an explosion avoided, and even
there inflation accelerated steadily, reaching an annual rate of 35.2 percent
in 1991, far higher than even the worst year in China.

In the then Soviet Union the price explosion occurred in 1991, when the
rate of inflation reached 196 percent a year. Prices were liberalized in Russia at
the beginning of the following year, and matters went from bad to worse. By

Table 2

**Rates of Inflation in Eastern Europe and the Soviet Union, 1981–1991
(per cent annum)**

	Bulgaria[1]	Czechoslovakia[2]	Hungary	Poland[3]	Romania[1]	Soviet Union[1]
1981	0.4	0.9	4.6	24.4	1.9	1.4
1982	0.3	4.7	6.9	101.5	16.9	3.4
1983	1.4	1.1	7.3	23.0	5.3	0.7
1984	0.7	0.9	8.3	15.8	1.1	-1.3
1985	1.7	1.3	7.0	14.4	0.4	0.8
1986	2.7	0.4	5.3	17.3	0.3	1.9
1987	2.7	0.1	8.6	25.5	0.4	1.9
1988	2.4	0.2	15.5	59.0	1.7	2.3
1989	6.2	1.5	18.8	259.5	0.9	1.9
1990	19.3	9.9	28.9	584.7	5.7	5.3
1991	249.8	57.9	35.2	70.3	305.5	196.0

1. Retail prices in the state sector

2. Cost of living index for workers and employees

3. Cost of living index for workers and employees in the socialist sector

Source: United Nations, *World Economic Survey 1992*, Annex Table A-11, New York, 1992, p. 194

the final quarter of 1992 the average rate of inflation in Russia was 25 percent a month. The target for inflation in 1993, announced on January 20, was a rate of no more than 5 percent a month by the end of the year.[4] It will not be easy to achieve the target because price indexation is spreading rapidly—to the working capital of enterprises, to minimum pensions and to wages. Unless the government is able to establish macroeconomic financial stability quickly, rapid inflation may become institutionalized in the Russian economy, and the transition to a market-guided economy will become much more difficult. Rigidities will be built into the economy, allocative inefficiency will increase and, if hyperinflation should occur, barter transactions will replace market transactions. Output, employment and incomes might then begin a downward spiral. Support for economic reform probably would collapse, with unforeseeable consequences.

The Chinese experience suggests that financial stability can contribute to the reform process by creating an environment in which changes in relative prices are undisturbed by rapid movements in the general level of prices. In such an environment price signals are strong and clear, their effects on incentives are powerful and consequently both producers and consumers are likely to respond quickly. This relationship, in turn, implies that the economy will be more flexible, more responsive to profit opportunities and hence more likely to sustain high levels of output and investment. If investment can be sustained, production and incomes will rise, possibly at an accelerating rate if the economic reforms result in a greater efficiency of investment, that is, in a rise in the incremental output/capital ratio. Sustained and possibly accelerating growth will result in increased support for the reform process, thereby creating a virtuous circle of reforms leading to growth and growth leading to more reforms.

The connections between financial stability, systemic reform and economic growth are thus crucial to the transition to a market-guided economy. The Chinese reformmongers seem to have understood the importance of these connections, and their experience is highly relevant to Russian and East European policymakers as they struggle to transform their own economies.

GROWTH AND INVESTMENT

Despite all the inefficiencies of the central planning system, Russia and Eastern Europe continued to achieve a moderate rate of growth of gross domestic product (GDP) throughout the prereform period. Thus in the former Soviet Union the average annual rate of growth was 3.5 percent during the seven-year period ending in 1988. In Eastern Europe during the same period the average growth rate was close to 3 percent. Negative rates of growth did not occur until these countries attempted to convert to a market-guided economy.

As can be seen in Table 3, the introduction of reforms was accompanied by a sharp deterioration in economic performance. Indeed, in all six countries included in the table, growth rates became highly negative almost immediately. Hungary suffered the least—output declined by 8 percent in 1991—while Bulgaria suffered the most—output declined by 23 percent in the same year. Only in Poland are there signs of recovery, with a positive growth of output of 3 percent in 1992. Moreover, the decline in investment often was even more severe than the decline in output. In the worst years, investment fell 30 percent in the then Czechoslovakia (1991), 38.3 percent in Romania (1990) and 50 percent in Bulgaria (1991). The former Soviet Union, so far, escaped rather lightly, but the worst is yet to come. The so-called big bang or shock therapy seems to have destroyed inefficient but functioning economies with little sign so far that they have effected a traverse to a more productive system.

Table 3

The Growth of Output and Investment in Russia and Eastern Europe (percent per annum)

	Gross Domestic Product					Investment			
	1988	1989	1990	1991	1992	1988	1989	1990	1991
Former USSR	5.3	3.3	-2.1	-17.0	-15.0	6.2	4.7	0.6	-7.0
Bulgaria	2.6	-1.4	-11.8	-23.0	-9.7	4.5	-10.1	-12.0	-50.0
Former Czechoslovakia	2.6	1.3	-4.7	-16.0	-5.3	4.1	1.6	7.7	-30.0
Hungary	2.7	3.8	-4.0	-8.0	—	-9.1	5.6	-8.7	-11.0
Poland	4.4	0.2	-12.0	-9.3	3.0	5.4	-2.4	-10.1	-8.0
Romania	-0.5	-5.8	-8.2	-13.0	-9.6	-2.2	-1.5	-38.3	-16.8

Source: United Nations, *World Economic Survey 1992*, New York, 1993

The Chinese experience has been very different. Economic reforms in China, far from lowering the growth of output and investment, led to a slow but unmistakable acceleration. This is a remarkable achievement, particularly given the good performance in the period prior to the reforms. In fact China's growth rate during the prereform period already was very high by international standards, namely, 5.8 percent a year during the decade ending in 1978 and 6.8 percent a year during the period 1965–79/80. As can be seen in Table 4, the rate of growth of GDP accelerated to an average of more than 9 percent a year in the ten years after the introduction of the reforms. Moreover, in no year did output actually fall: the least good performance was in 1989, the year of stabilization, when GDP increased only 3.2 percent.

There was a strong tendency in China during the transition for investment to grow more rapidly than output, and consequently the ratio of investment to GDP tended to rise, reaching a peak of more than 39 percent in 1986 and 1987. The transition to a market-guided economy in China stimulated an investment boom, and policymakers often were concerned with the problem of "overinvestment"; the collapse of output commonly associated with the implementation of shock therapy elsewhere never arose in China. Domestic savings increased as rapidly as investment, and hence, except for 1985 and 1986, China relied very little on external capital to finance investment. That is, domestic rather than foreign savings financed capital formation, and high rates of investment—possibly accompanied by increases in the efficiency of investment—led to accelerated growth.

Table 4

Growth, Investment and Saving in China

	Growth Rate of GDP (%)	Gross Investment as percentage of GDP	Gross Domestic Saving as percentage of GDP
1975	8.3	30.3	30.6
1976	-5.4	28.4	29.0
1977	7.9	29.0	29.5
1978	12.5	33.4	33.2
1979	7.0	34.9	34.6
1980	6.4	32.2	32.2
1981	4.9	29.2	30.0
1982	8.3	29.7	31.6
1983	9.8	30.4	31.5
1984	13.3	32.4	32.8
1985	12.5	38.7	34.5
1986	7.9	39.3	36.1
1987	10.1	39.2	39.1
1988	9.9	38.9	38.0
1989	3.2	36.4	35.7
1990	5.2	39.0	42.5
1991	7.0	n.a.	—

Source: 1975–1989: World Bank, World Tables 1991, Washington, D.C., 1992; 1990–1991: United Nations, *World Economic Survey 1992*, New York, 1993

The difference in performance as regards growth and investment between China on the one hand and Russia and Eastern Europe on the other tells us much about the approach to reform and the transition to a market-guided economy in the two cases. In China emphasis was placed on growing out of systemic inefficiencies and on using a high rate of investment to reallocate resources and increase microeconomic efficiency. In Russia and Eastern Europe, in contrast, policymakers seem to have been unduly preoccupied with systemic reform and static allocative efficiency at the cost of stifled growth.

It is misleading to characterize the Chinese approach to reform as "gradualism" and the Russian and East European approach as the big bang. The boldness of reform and the rapidity of change in China have far exceeded what has been attempted in other economies seeking to move from a centrally planned to a market-guided system. The Chinese reform of the rural economy is an outstanding example of boldness of conception and speed of implementation. The transformation of the commune system into a system of private peasant farming was completed in a remarkably short period of three or four years. Rural institutions were totally restructured, and every aspect of the rural economy and society was affected. Yet this transformation was accomplished without disrupting production. In fact, the level of agricultural output rose and the rate of growth actually accelerated in the early years.

In order to appreciate the magnitude and significance of what was achieved, one must remember that the Chinese commune was much more than a collective farm. The communes owned and operated rural industries; they were responsible for tasks normally undertaken by local government, including the provision of basic social services; they were even responsible for the local militia. All the functions of the commune were transformed and new institutions created, and this change was done at a breathtaking pace. Agriculture was reorganized on the basis of household farming. Commune industries were reorganized as collectively managed corporations, and these reorganized enterprises spearheaded industrial growth during the period of transition. Local government institutions were created to take over services previously supplied by communes. The only comparable experience in history of such a rural upheaval is the process of collectivization in China itself a quarter of a century earlier, between 1955 and 1958.

The transformation of the commune system was not a unique achievement. China also is remarkable for the speed with which a highly dynamic, small-scale, private sector emerged after the restraints on private entrepreneurship were removed. No less noteworthy has been the speed with which export-oriented industrial zones were created and the success China has had in penetrating foreign markets. China today exports a higher fraction of its total output than does, say, India or Brazil. Even in the area of macroeconomic stabilization China has been more decisive than Russia and the East European countries. Of course, as we have seen, China never quite lost control of its macroeconomy, but when stabilization did become necessary in the late 1980s, it did not hesitate: orthodox measures were applied quickly and vigorously.

Compared to Eastern Europe, China may be said to have followed a gradualist path in two areas, namely, price reforms (including reform of the system of exchange controls) and the privatization of state enterprises. It is clear with hindsight that the Chinese policy of gradualism in these two areas was pragmatic and far more sensible than the alternative of rushing simultaneously to free all prices and privatize most public enterprises. Had the reform-mongers freed all prices at once, there would have been massive and largely unpredictable effects on the distribution of income that, in turn, would have required very large compensatory income readjustments and protective measures. Compensation on a massive scale would have been very difficult, probably would have introduced many distortions and inefficiencies, and almost certainly would have resulted in huge government deficits and loss of macroeconomic control. Similarly, a wholesale privatization of the state enterprises would have disrupted the entire industrial sector and caused an immediate reduction in output. The consequence would have been a shortage of consumer and producer goods as has occurred in Russia and Eastern Europe.

Had China not sustained macroeconomic stability and normalcy of supply of goods and services, it would have been impossible for entrepreneurship to emerge and flourish on the scale that it did outside the state sector, namely, in township and village enterprises, in the private sector and in cooperatives. Had China tolerated rapid inflation and a regime of shortage, private-sector initiatives would have been distorted and entrepreneurial talent diverted to speculative activities and rent seeking to a far greater extent than in fact occurred. Productive investment would have fallen and growth come to a halt.

There is a clear lesson to be learned from the Chinese experience. There is a conflict during the transition between maintaining control over macroeconomic variables and reducing inefficiency within the existing economic structure. The faster one attempts to remove inefficiency, the more difficult it will be to maintain macroeconomic equilibrium. The course of wisdom is to accept a slower rate of improvement in allocative efficiency in order to avoid losing control over the macro economy and adversely affecting investment and growth. A gradual reform of existing enterprises, avoiding whenever possible a fall in output, creates an opportunity for the economy to grow. Policy should concentrate on the incremental increase in output—on the marginal additions to capacity—and create incentives and institutions that channel incremental effort and resources into socially profitable activities. If growth is rapid, incremental output will be large, and if these large increments are allocated efficiently, the effect on the economy as a whole soon will be quantitatively important. The Chinese experience strongly suggests that a high rate of investment may bring about a more rapid improvement in efficiency than would a direct attempt to restructure state enterprises within a context of slow or negative growth.

PROPERTY RELATIONS AND INDUSTRIAL REFORMS

There are over 86,000 state industrial enterprises in China. At the beginning of the reform process state enterprises accounted for nearly 79 percent of industrial output, whereas today they probably account for about half. The rapid expansion of the collective, cooperative, private and individual enterprise sectors and the relative decline of the state sector occurred not as a result of a transfer of ownership from the state to the private sector but as a consequence of the explosive growth of output within the nonstate sectors themselves. Privatization of state enterprise, in other words, has played almost no role in China's transition to a market-guided economy. The state sector has continued to expand at a rapid rate throughout the transition, but the nonstate sector has expanded even faster, and as a result a mixed economy has been created in which the weight of the nonstate sector has steadily increased.

This mixed economy is in marked contrast with Russia and Eastern Europe, where great emphasis has been placed on transforming property relations by privatizing state industrial enterprises. A large number of schemes have been devised, including the sale of state enterprises by auction, the transformation of state enterprises into joint stock companies, the distribution to the entire adult population of vouchers or "rights" to acquire shares in a portfolio of state enterprises, the distribution of some shares to those who work in state enterprises, and so on. The implicit assumption seems to be that privatization is a precondition for a successful transition to a market-guided economy. The Chinese experience contradicts this assumption and suggests that the opposite may be closer to the truth, namely, that an attempt in the early stages to privatize state enterprises may slow down the transition rather than accelerate it. Why might this idea be so?

The state enterprise in China approximates what sociologists call a "total institution." It is of course an institution that produces industrial goods. In addition, it is an instrument used by the state to implement physical output targets, a vehicle for state investment and a major source of government revenue from the taxation of profits. The state enterprises also are providers of social services. They provide pensions for their retired workers, housing for their employees, guaranteed employment for the urban work force in the absence of unemployment insurance and even child care and holiday facilities. Some state enterprises also are responsible for the operation of health and educational facilities. Services that in other countries are provided by the state are provided by state enterprises in China. Hence privatization of state enterprises would entail not only a change in property relations but a complete overhaul of employment policy and the introduction of state-financed unemployment compensation, a reform of the system for allocating housing and the creation of a housing market and the design and implementation of a state-funded pension scheme for the elderly. The health and education services also would have to be reorganized.

Many of the state enterprises are regional or national monopolies. Hence privatization would have to be accompanied by a well-conceived and implemented competition policy, including a liberal import policy, in order to prevent the newly privatized firms from exercising market power and engaging in uncompetitive behavior. In the absence of antimonopoly measures, privatization could actually result in greater inefficiency in the allocation of resources.

Moreover, it is not obvious how the government could efficiently transfer state enterprises to the private sector when relative prices are subject to very large change; which will almost always be the case during a period of transition to a market-guided economy. There are two problems here: a revenue problem and a valuation problem. First, privatization would lead to a fall in government revenues from state enterprises precisely at a time when, as we have seen, it is important to maintain macroeconomic stability and contain inflationary pressures. Prior to the reforms, taxes on the profits of state enterprises accounted for about 60 percent of government revenue.[5] The proportion is much lower today, partly because the top marginal tax rate has been reduced from 100 percent to 55 percent and partly because the changes in relative prices that have already occurred have increased the number of state enterprises in deficit. Given this situation, it would appear to be unwise to aggravate the government's fiscal problems by transferring sources of revenue to the private sector, even if those sources are of diminishing significance. In time, of course, tax reforms can be designed and implemented to raise offsetting revenues from the private sector, but until such reforms are in place, privatization would lead to a fall in government revenue.

Privatization, furthermore, as we have seen, would generate a need for higher government expenditure. If industrial enterprises are relieved of the responsibility for providing pensions, housing, child care facilities, guaranteed employment and other social services, the state will have to step in and provide these services itself. This change will be, inevitably, costly. Prudence suggests that privatization should be postponed until reforms of the social services and taxation have been completed.

Second, let us turn to the problem of valuing state enterprises prior to privatization. If state industrial enterprises are given away or sold at bargain-basement prices, the government will relinquish an opportunity to obtain revenue from the sale of assets (as well as the revenue from profits taxes) and, depending on how the privatized assets are distributed among the entire population, probably will create inequalities in the distribution of wealth and income. Assuming the government wants to avoid these consequences, state enterprises should be sold at their full market value. The question then becomes how to estimate full market value. Given the distorted prices during the transition period, it is virtually impossible to know which state enterprises are likely to be socially profitable at the end of the transition and which are likely to operate at a loss and hence should be allowed to become bankrupt. In theory it might be possible to calculate shadow prices and estimate social profitability using those prices, but in practice this calculation is likely to prove impracticable, given that China has over 86,000 state enterprises. The only realistic way to determine which enterprises are socially profitable is to remove all or at least the most important price distortions, which indeed is one of the main objectives of the reform process. But as long as actual prices are highly distorted and do not reflect social costs and benefits, it will be impossible to estimate accurately the true value of state enterprises. This problem suggests, again, that privatization should be postponed until price reforms have been completed.

For all these reasons the Chinese have neither privatized state enterprises nor allowed loss-making state enterprises to go bankrupt. The arguments for delaying privatization are even stronger in countries that have adopted a strategy of shock therapy and experienced a sharp fall in outputs and incomes. An attempt to dispose of state assets through sale in such countries is almost certain to lead to disappointment. If buyers are restricted to citizens of the country, the sale prices are likely to be depressed because of lack of purchasing power; if foreigners are allowed to bid for the assets, valuations are likely to be higher, but the most profitable state enterprises are likely to end up in foreign hands. Neither outcome is attractive unless, for ideological or other reasons, privatization is desired at almost any price.

The Chinese reformmongers took the view that changing property relations was less important during the transition than (1) increasing the efficiency of state enterprises by lowering costs of production, increasing the quality of output and improving the marketing and servicing of products and (2) gradually subjecting state enterprises to market forces and heightened competition, both domestic and foreign. In 1984 a number of reforms were introduced that had the effect of giving state enterprises greater autonomy over their production, marketing and financial affairs.[6] Managers were given freedom to produce more than the planned quota, to market above-quota output as they wished and to sell above-quota output at negotiated or free market prices. This last provision created a dual pricing system in industry, to which we will return. Managers also were given more freedom to reorganize their enterprises; to acquire inputs from outside the state marketing system; to introduce bonus schemes and modify the wage structure; and, after paying a profits tax that ranged from 7 to 55 percent on the largest enterprises, to retain profits and use them as they wished.

Decisionmaking was devolved to the managers of state enterprises, but property relations were not altered. The state enterprises continued to be responsible for providing a wide range of social services while the reform-mongers began to explore ways to divest firms of these responsibilities and devise alternative ways to provide housing, social services and unemployment compensation to the urban population. Because of the incremental and gradual nature of the reform process, the reforms were inconsistent and incomplete and numerous anomalies arose. We shall mention some of the most important ones.

First, enterprise reform, and particularly reform of the payments system, proceeded more rapidly than price reform. Managers of profitable state industrial enterprises distributed some of the profits to the workers by introducing generous bonus schemes. The profits, however, often reflected not superior technical performance or greater than average effort by the labor force but rather an arbitrarily high quota price for the firm's output. Firms with losses or low profits could not afford to offer generous bonuses to their workers even when the losses were due to irrationally low quota prices rather than the failures of management or workers. The distribution of workers' incomes across state enterprises, while remaining relatively equal, became somewhat arbitrary and served no incentive or allocative function. The solution to the problem is not to terminate the wage reforms and bonus schemes but to complete price reform.

Second, under the reforms, state enterprises were allowed to retain all their profits after payment of taxes, but those firms that operated at a loss were not allowed to go bankrupt. The state thus found itself in something approaching a no-win situation. It was fully responsible for the losses of state enterprises but was entitled to only a portion (usually about half) of the profits of state enterprises. A primary justification for this policy was a desire to avoid creating massive unemployment among those who worked in unprofitable state enterprises. Given that there was no centrally funded scheme to compensate the unemployed for the loss of employment, bankruptcies of state enterprises would have caused considerable hardship in the urban areas. Moreover, since workers in China did not freely choose their jobs but had been assigned to them by the state, it could be argued that there was an implicit contract under which the state had a continuing obligation to provide employment. Another justification for the policy was recognition that during a time of transition bankruptcy did not necessarily imply that a firm was socially unprofitable, especially when the costs of providing health, education and other social services are charged to the profits of state enterprises rather than financed by taxation. As long as prices failed to measure social costs and benefits, reported profits and losses could not be relied on in allocating resources. Again, this is an argument for completing the price reform as expeditiously as possible, not for supporting loss-making state enterprises indefinitely.

Third, the asymmetric treatment of the profits and losses of state enterprises has created serious financial problems for the state that threaten to undermine macroeconomic stability. Decentralized management of enterprises combined with partial price liberalization has changed relative prices and greatly increased the number of state enterprises operating at a loss. Indeed, at present, about a third of all state industrial enterprises fail to make a profit. As a result, an increasing proportion of government expenditure has had to be used to cover the deficits of state enterprises at a time when the reduction in profits taxation has greatly reduced the ratio of tax revenues to national income. The losses of state enterprises have been covered in part by direct subsidies from central government and in part by government-ordered low-interest loans from the banking system. Whatever the technique used—subsidies or loans—the deficits of state enterprises, partly a consequence of the reforms, have created financial difficulties for the government and hamper the continuation of the reform process.

Let us consider, finally, the dual pricing system. Dual prices were an integral part of the agricultural reforms of the late 1970s, when quota prices were supplemented by free or negotiated prices for above-quota output sold on free markets or to the state, respectively. The low quota prices formed the basis for the urban food rationing system under which grain, cooking oil, and a few other products were supplied in fixed quantities at subsidized prices. During the 1980s agricultural procurement prices were raised repeatedly while the prices paid by urban households were held steady. The cost of the food rationing system thus increased continuously, which contributed to a growing government deficit. Important steps toward the resolution of the problem were taken in 1991 and 1992 when urban food prices were sharply increased to bring them closer to procurement and free market prices. At the same time the effect of higher food prices on urban living standards was tempered by a rise in wage rates.

Dual pricing in industry began in 1984 when the government allowed the state enterprises to sell above-quota output at above-plan prices. This change provided strong incentives on the margin to increase total output and to alter the composition of output in favor of goods that enjoyed strong market demand. Moreover, market prices for industrial goods could be used by planners to guide the direction of adjustment of fixed, planned prices, thereby gradually unifying the price system. Thus, there were good reasons to favor a dual price system during the transition to a market-guided economy. However, dual prices for industrial products have resulted in a series of problems that are likely to persist until the price reform is completed.

First, the dual price system has encouraged managers to engage in arbitrage, that is, to obtain industrial inputs from the state at planned prices and resell them in the parallel market at above-plan prices. This activity, in turn, has undermined the state supply and marketing systems and made it more difficult to create orderly markets. Major industries have been affected—coal, steel, petroleum—and because profits from arbitrage have not been recorded, government revenue from profits taxation has been harmed. Second, dual pricing and the associated official and parallel markets have created numerous opportunities for corruption, which has in some cases undermined public support for continuation of the reform process and for greater reliance on the market mechanism. Finally, the dual pricing system has been highly profitable for the managers of some state enterprises, which has encouraged widespread rent-seeking activity within the state enterprise sector as a whole. The presence of a dual price system has created vested interests among managers in favor of its continuation, which has also weakened support for continuation of the reform process.

All of this suggests that price reform is the key to creating a market-guided economy. The Chinese reformmongers were right to leave property relations unchanged and to treat privatization as a secondary issue. Space was created for the private sector, and entrepreneurs took advantage of this opening to establish new enterprises. Most of the new enterprises are very small, but there are many of them, and they have grown rapidly. As a result the private sector now rivals the state sector in industrial output. Meanwhile, the state industrial enterprises are being subjected to market disciplines. Competitive pressures have increased from three sources: the domestic private sector, joint ventures between Chinese and foreign enterprises, and liberalized imports from abroad. Relative prices have changed, but a dual price structure remains in many industries, which has created anomalies. Continued movement toward a unified price structure is therefore important. About a third of the state enterprises fail to make a profit, but nonetheless firms are not allowed to go bankrupt. There are three reasons for this: (1) until prices come to reflect social costs one cannot be certain that a loss-making enterprise is socially unprofitable; (2) until a scheme for unemployment compensation is in place, the government, rightly, is unwilling to make large numbers of workers jobless; and (3) until a state-funded pension scheme is created and the system for allocating housing is reformed, bankruptcies in the state enterprise sector would create massive social problems in the urban areas. The solution, again, is to push ahead with price reforms and reorganize the social services.

Only when the changes are done would it make sense to consider altering property relations and privatizing the large state industrial enterprises. The time to consider this plan is thus some years away. Moreover, it is likely that when price reforms and reforms of the social services are completed, it will be discovered that many of the state enterprises are economically viable. China could then choose, if it wishes, to have a mixed economy with a large and efficient state enterprise sector.

INCOME DISTRIBUTION AND THE SOCIAL SAFETY NET

China under the old economic regime, in common with other centrally planned economies, enjoyed a relatively egalitarian distribution of income and possessed a social safety net that protected the great majority of the population. Compared to other developing countries with a comparable level of income per head, the degree of equality in prereform China was high and the incidence of poverty was low. However the policies and institutions that were responsible for creating a relatively egalitarian society also contributed to inefficiency in the allocation of resources, to defective production incentives and to a lower rate of growth than would otherwise have been possible. The sorts of policies and institutions that had these conflicting effects include (1) guaranteed employment of peasants on communes and workers in state enterprises and severe restrictions on firing workers, (2) lack of profit incentives in state enterprises and the so-called soft budget constraint[7] and (3) a payments system in state enterprises and in the collective sector that failed to reward differences in skills, effort and performance.

Some policies, moreover, not only created inefficiencies but also accentu-ated inequality. In China and many other socialist countries the terms of trade were deliberately turned against agriculture, thereby discouraging agricul-tural production and greatly widening inequalities between rural and urban areas. Within the urban areas, the system of subsidies probably included sev-eral elements of benefit disproportionately to the well-to-do. In general, however, it appears that the arbitrary controls and policies that one associ-ates with central planning resulted in distributional equality at the expense of economic efficiency.

The process of economic reform, on the one hand, has led to a gradual cor-rection of policies that create inefficiencies and, on the other, to the removal of policies and institutions that ensured a high degree of equality and an effective social safety net. The result has been a tendency for inequality to increase. To offset this increase, it will be necessary to create alternative institutions within the reform process and to devise new policies to replace those that created the inefficient egalitarianism characteristic of centrally planned regimes. If this task is neglected it is unlikely that a worsening of the distrib-ution of income and an increase in the number of those in poverty can be avoided.

Four points are relevant here. First, the rate of growth of the economy dur-ing the transition to a market-guided system is critical. If the rate of growth is high, it is far less likely that an increase in inequality will be accompanied by an increase in the proportion of the population living in poverty. In addition, rapid growth generates extra resources, some of which can be used to extend the social safety net and assist those who fail to benefit during the transition. Both a reallocation of resources and a compensatory redistribution of income are greatly facilitated by rapid growth in overall output and incomes.

Second, it is important to pay attention to the distribution of assets during the transition and to equitable access to productive resources. In the Chinese case the distribution of land, the allocation of credit and the composition of expenditure on human capital have been central issues. There is always a dan-ger that during the reform process the ownership of assets will become heavily concentrated and that the market-guided economy that emerges at the end of the transition will be characterized by a polarization of wealth. This prob-lem can be avoided by ensuring (1) that equality of access to land is preserved if and when collective agriculture is replaced by private farming, (2) private sector enterprises (including especially the small firms) are treated in the same way as state enterprises when it comes to the allocation of credit and material inputs and (3) that price and distribution reforms are introduced in such a way that rent-seeking activities are minimized and such rents as are created during the transition are not systematically appropriated by those who have power and influence.

Third, high priority should be given to reforming policies and institutions that contribute both to inefficiency and to inequality in the distribution of income. The number of such cases may be relatively small, but they are obvious candidates for attention during the early stages of reform. Examples of what we have in mind are improvements in the terms of trade for agriculture, the abolition of payments in kind to senior officials and the elimination of subsidies that benefit higher-income groups.

Fourth, if an increase in poverty during the transition is to be prevented, a new social safety net will have to be created and those who are most vulnerable carefully targeted. Under the old system many social services such as health and education were provided in large part by the collective sector, that is, by the collective farms or communes in the rural areas and by the state enterprises in urban areas. During the transition to a market-guided economy many of these services are likely to disappear, particularly if the reform process includes changes in the structure of ownership and an increase in the degree of autonomy enjoyed by managers of state enterprises. Moreover, as the composition of output changes in response to a new set of incentives, there may be a large, even if temporary, increase in the level of unemployment. Hence, it will be necessary to reorganize the social services and the social safety net and change the basis of their financing while placing responsibility on state and local government institutions for the efficient delivery of services.

The question that arises is how well China performed under each of these headings during the early years of its transition. The country clearly deserves high marks for accelerating its rate of growth. The average annual rate of growth of per capita income has been approximately 8 percent since the beginning of the reform process. This exceptionally rapid growth has made it possible for China to absorb an increase in inequality in the distribution of income without experiencing an increase in the incidence of poverty. There is indeed no evidence that the proportion of the population falling below the poverty line has risen, except possibly in small localities or for short periods of time. The contrast with Russia and Eastern Europe is vivid. In both regions there have been sharp reductions in the level of per capita income—growth rates actually have been negative—and it has consequently been impossible to avoid an increase in the incidence of poverty. This increase would have occurred even if the distribution of income had remained unchanged, whereas in fact inequality seems to have increased quite markedly.

China also appears to have done well regarding the distribution of assets and access to productive resources. After the dismantling of the commune system there was an orderly transition to an egalitarian peasant farming system. Landlessness is virtually unknown and all households within a locality have approximately equal access to land. Inequalities in the distribution of land in the country as a whole are due in large part to differences across regions (and in types of terrain) in per capita land endowments.[8]

Less is known about access to productive resources outside the agricultural sector, although there are indications that credit and material inputs have been made widely available to township and village enterprises and to small entrepreneurs in both rural and urban areas. This availability reflects in part the policy of increasing the share of non-state enterprises by creating opportunities for entry into a range of activities rather than by privatizing existing state enterprises. Since the new private enterprises tend to be small and labor intensive, while the existing state enterprises almost always are large, the policy has resulted in a relatively equal distribution of assets.

The comparison of the Chinese experience with Russia and Eastern Europe is instructive. The ex-Soviet bloc countries are committed in principle to abolishing collective ownership, but they have yet to find a way to transform their systems of collective agriculture into egalitarian peasant farming systems. Moreover, in Poland, where private farming predominates, the distribution of landownership is relatively unequal. In the nonagricultural sectors, Russia and Eastern Europe have concentrated on privatizing existing state enterprises and although success so far has been meager, there is a danger that this policy will result in a concentration of ownership of private assets. Polarization is likely to be further accentuated because of the acute market disequilibria and greater scarcity of goods and services in Russia and Eastern Europe, compared to China, and consequently the higher scarcity premia or rents that can be appropriated by private entrepreneurs who acquire state-owned assets. Even without privatization, the existence of very large rents would enable those who appropriate them to create their own private enterprises, which would in turn lead to a concentration of wealth and income.

China has had only limited success in removing distortions that simultaneously produce inefficiency and inequality. Here an opportunity has been missed. Two major sources of income inequality in postreform China are the large gap between rural and urban incomes and the high level of subsidies in the urban areas. Let us consider each of these in turn.

The per capita income of urban households in China is 2.42 times the per capita income of rural households. This income differential is much larger than one typically finds in other developing countries in Asia. Moreover, research has shown that an increase in any component of rural income, be it an agricultural or nonagricultural source of income, would reduce overall income inequality in China as measured by the Gini coefficient, a common measure of income inequality.[9] The only exception is rural wage income, but wages account for only 9 percent of total income in rural areas.

The distribution of urban subsidies has a moderately disequalizing effect on the distribution of income in urban areas, but it has a hugely disequalizing effect on the distribution of income in China as a whole. Urban subsidies constitute 39 percent of urban household incomes on average, and these subsidies account for 41 percent of the inequality observed in urban areas. In China as a whole, urban subsidies represent less than 17 percent of total household income but they account for more than 32 percent of overall inequality in the distribution of income.[10] A reduction in urban subsidies thus would improve the distribution of income both in China as a whole and within the urban areas. At the same time, a reduction in urban subsidies would make it possible to increase the efficiency of the labor market by making resources available to raise the average level of wages and increase wage differentials.[11]

Given the large gap between the cities and the countryside, any reasonable scheme for the reduction of inequality between the urban and rural areas will reduce overall inequality in the distribution of income for China as a whole. One of the most effective ways to reduce the rural-urban gap would be to improve agriculture's terms of trade. Indeed, this improvement was made during the initial phase of the reform process. In 1979 there was a sharp increase in agricultural procurement prices, which resulted in a 15 percent rise in the terms of trade of the agricultural sector.[12] The initial improvement, however, was not maintained, and agriculture's terms of trade apparently began to erode in the early 1980s. We say apparently because the system of reporting prices changed in 1984, and after that date it is no longer possible to measure the terms of trade on a comparable basis. While quantification of changes in agriculture's terms of trade during recent years is much more difficult, available reports suggest that purchases of agricultural products by the state have been on increasingly unfavorable terms. In some cases payments to farmers by the state have been delayed for a considerable time, which inevitably has damaged incentives.

There is a direct link between the two policies on which we have focused, urban subsidies and agriculture's terms of trade. Indeed, they represent competing claims for public expenditure. A principal reason why state purchase prices for agricultural products were not raised in line with increases in prices of goods purchased by farmers is that higher agricultural prices would have increased the government's budget deficit. Had it been possible to reduce urban subsidies, however, the budgetary constraint would have eased and more resources been available to raise farm prices.

Let us turn now to the last of the four issues we have raised, namely, the provision of a social safety net. In rural China the social safety net and much of the preexisting structure of public services disappeared when the communes were dismantled. Responsibility for social services and for providing a safety net was transferred to the newly created organs of local government. This transfer often occurred relatively smoothly, but there is some evidence that the new network of services is less extensive and less effective than that which existed under the old communes. This difference is particularly true of basic health services: the number of barefoot doctors, medical workers and midwives declined sharply after the economic reforms were introduced (see Table 5). In addition, the number of hospitals, hospital beds and medical personnel in the townships declined 14 percent, 4 percent and 6 percent, respectively, between 1978 and 1985.[13] Although comparable information for Russia and Eastern Europe is impossible to obtain, reports by well-informed observers suggest that the deterioration of services there has been far greater than in China.

Further evidence of China's performance during the transition to a market-guided economy is presented in Table 6. This table contains Gini coefficients for the distribution of income in both rural and urban areas, the

Table 5

Medical Workers in Rural Areas (million persons)

Year	Barefoot doctors	Medical workers	Midwives
1977	1.76	—	—
1979	1.58	—	—
1980	1.46	2.36	0.64
1981	1.40	2.01	0.59
1982	1.35	1.65	0.55
1983	1.28	1.39	0.54
1984	1.25	1.16	0.52

Source: Athar Hussein and Nicholas Stern, "On the Recent Increase in Death Rates in China," Suntory-Toyota Center for Economics and Related Disciplines, London School of Economics, Research Programme on the Chinese Economy, CP8, September, 1990

figures for crude death rates and the infant mortality rate. The period covered, with many gaps in the data, is 1976 to 1988.

In the rural areas the distribution of income actually improved during the early years of the reforms: the Gini coefficient declined from approximately 0.32 in 1978 to about 0.22 in 1982. One reason is that the reforms began in the relatively poorer regions and proved to be highly successful. As a result, average incomes in the economically more backward rural areas increased substantially, thereby reducing intrarural income inequality. The reduction in inequality among regions offset a tendency for inequality to increase within each region, and hence overall inequality diminished.[14] This effect ceased to operate, however, when the rural reforms were extended to the already more prosperous regions. Once that extension occurred, policies intended to counter what has been called "arbitrary egalitarianism" at the local level tended to increase inequalities both at the local level and in the rural areas as a whole. As a result, the Gini coefficient began to rise steadily after 1982, and by 1988 rural inequality in China, as measured by the Gini coefficient, was comparable to that in India.

It is less easy to be certain about trends in the distribution of income in urban areas because there are only two observations. Between 1980 and 1988,

Table 6

Gini Coefficients, Death Rates and Infant Mortality Rates in China

Year	Rural Gini coefficient	Urban Gini coefficient	Crude Death Rate (0/00)	Infant MortalityRate (per 1,000 live births)
1976	—	—	7.8	44.9
1977	—	—	7.7	41.0
1978	0.32	—	7.5	37.2
1979	0.28	—	7.6	39.4
1980	0.26	0.16	7.7	41.6
1981	0.23	—	7.7	43.7
1982	0.22	—	7.9	45.9
1983	0.25	—	8.0	48.0
1984	0.27	—	8.0	50.1
1985	0.30	—	—	—
1986	0.31	—	—	—
1988	0.34	0.23	—	—

Note: — = data not available
Source: Gini coefficients: Azizur Rahman Khan, Keith Griffin, Carl Riskin and Zhao Renwei, "Household Income and Its Distribution in China," *China Quarterly*, no. 132 (December 1992); death rates and infant mortality rates: J. Banister, *China's Changing Population*, Stanford: Stanford University Press, 1987

however, there was a significant increase in the Gini coefficient in urban areas, suggesting that inequality in the distribution income must have increased. Nonetheless, the low value of the Gini coefficient in 1988 (0.23) suggests that the degree of inequality in the distribution of income in urban China is still remarkably low. Indeed, urban inequality in China appears to be much lower than in all other developing countries for which evidence is available.

In China as a whole the Gini coefficient for 1988 was 0.38. This number is higher than the coefficient in either the urban or rural areas. Unfortunately there are no comparable estimates of the overall degree of inequality for earlier years, and hence one cannot be certain about trends during the transition period. There is, however, evidence that differences in income between rural and urban areas have widened, at least since 1985.[15] It is therefore likely that in

China as a whole the Gini coefficient has increased rather rapidly, again, at least since 1985.

The data in the last two columns of Table 6 show that by some measures the well-being of certain groups declined even though there was no increase in poverty. Because of the deterioration of health services the infant mortality rate increased dramatically between 1978 and 1984. This increase is but one symptom of a general rise in age-specific mortality rates. Indeed, the crude death rate rose from 7.5 per thousand in 1978 to 8.0 per thousand in 1983 and 1984, and this rise cannot be fully explained by changes in the age distribution of the population. The rise appears to have been greater in the countryside than in the cities. Thus, the available evidence suggests that China has been only moderately successful during the transition period in providing a social safety net and preventing an unacceptable increase in equality.

The egalitarianism of the prereform era rested in large part on policies and institutions the abolition of which was a precondition for increased economic efficiency. It was almost inevitable therefore that the reform process would unleash economic forces that would result in greater inequality. Attempts were made by policymakers to counteract the tendencies accentuating inequality by ensuring equality of access to productive resources (especially in agriculture) and by constructing a new safety net. Some of the distortions that combined inefficiency and inequality, however, have yet to be eliminated. More important, the social safety net that existed prior to the reforms has not been replaced by a new safety net that is equally effective. As a result, there has been some increase in equality and some deterioriation in the social services targeted on specific vulnerable groups such as infants and young children.

The economic reforms were very successful, however, in promoting a high rate of growth, which provided a cushion of rising incomes and prevented poverty from increasing. There is no reliable time series evidence on the incidence of poverty in China, although it has been suggested by some analysts that poverty did increase during certain, relatively short, time periods.[16] It is unlikely, however, that the number of persons living in poverty in the nation as a whole, or the proportion of the population below the poverty line, has increased during the 15 years since the transition to a market-guided economy began. Indeed, it is unlikely that poverty increased during any significant subperiod of that 15-year period. In this respect the Chinese experience differs sharply from the experience of Russia and Eastern Europe.

What, then, can Russia and Eastern Europe learn from China about managing inequality and poverty during the transition? First, it must be recognized that in shifting from a centrally planned to a market-guided economy, it is highly likely that the distribution of income will become more unequal. The reason is that under a centrally planned regime the same policies and institutions that provide economic security and a relatively high degree of equality are also responsible for a high level of inefficiency in the allocation of resources. Hence, reforms intended to encourage greater efficiency are likely at the same time to reduce economic security and the degree of equality. In order to avoid a polarization of incomes, economic reforms should be supplemented by measures designed to protect the poor and the vulnerable from a deterioration in their standard of living.

Second, it is important that during the transition the rate of growth of output and of average income per capita should be high. A stagnant economy is a difficult environment in which to introduce reforms of the economic and social structure. Rapid growth acts as a cushion and prevents an increase in inequality from being translated into an increase in poverty. Rapid growth also provides additional resources, which can be used to finance policies that compensate the losers during the reform process. The faster the rate of growth, the more resources are generated that can in principle be used for compensation. And of course, to complete the circle, the faster the rate of growth, the less likely the need for compensation.

Third, the package of policies intended to compensate losses must be designed with care. The Chinese experience in this area contains both positive and negative lessons. The policy package should concentrate initially on removing policy-induced distortions that result simultaneously in inefficiency and inequality. Examples include untargeted subsidies that are appropriated largely by the nonpoor and price controls that reduce the earnings of the poor. The Chinese reformmongers have missed several opportunities in this general area.

When replacing old institutions with new ones that are more compatible with a market-guided economy, there should be a strong emphasis on equality of access to productive resources and a wide distribution of human capital. To ensure that this access occurs, reforms of the system of ownership should concentrate on creating new, small-scale, competitive enterprises rather than privatizing large state enterprises. In agriculture the Chinese were particularly successful in creating a system of egalitarian peasant farming to replace collective farming under the commune system. This experience may be difficult to replicate in Russia and Eastern Europe, where agriculture is far more mechanized and where there is greater scope for economies of scale, but even there it might be useful to experiment with greatly enlarged private plots on the collective and state farms. Elsewhere, for example in the newly independent Central Asian republics, the Chinese experience may be more directly applicable. Certainly the general approach of the Chinese to property rights and the structure of ownership deserves careful consideration.

The Chinese experience is also instructive about the difficulties of creating a new social safety net. Indeed, the Chinese are just beginning to address this issue in the urban areas, and in the countryside, where the reforms began, they have not yet succeeded fully in replacing the collective institutions that in the past provided a high level of economic and social security. If the Chinese have achieved only modest success despite firm political control and exceptionally rapid growth, the likelihood of quick success in Russia and Eastern Europe must be very low. The Chinese experience suggests that if the collective economy is abolished, society is likely to lose much of its control over the economic surplus, and this lack of control will severely limit the ability of the state to organize and deliver basic services and protect those who are vulnerable. In Russia and Eastern Europe, where growth rates have been negative, it is hardly surprising that it has been extremely difficult to put in place an effective social safety net.

CONCLUSION

The transition to a market-guided economy in Russia and Eastern Europe roughly coincided with the reform of the political system: "openness" (glasnost) and "restructuring" (perestroika) were initiated more or less simultaneously. Political reform, however, led to a loss of political control, which, in turn, had an adverse effect on economic reform. In China economic reforms were introduced first, and political reforms followed after a long lag. Indeed, one might say that serious political reforms have yet to get underway. Throughout the process of economic reform the Chinese authorities have maintained firm control over political change, at the cost of denying political democracy.

Does the sequence matter? Looking back, it appears that it does. The Russian model has so far been a huge failure. Countries following this model have in general achieved neither politic stability nor economic success. In Russia itself there is continuous political turmoil (even a threat of national disintegration) and a rapidly deteriorating real economy (combined with a threat of hyperinflation). The situation in Eastern Europe is not as bad, but nowhere in Eastern Europe is it good. China, in contrast, has enjoyed a prospering economy, albeit within a political framework that remains highly authoritarian.[17] The Chinese model has some similarities to the approach adopted in an earlier stage of development in South Korea, Taiwan and Singapore. One must be careful not to push historical parallels too far, but the Chinese experience does suggest that maintaining firm political control during a period of systemic change in the economy has enormous advantages. This point is especially true if the style of reform is experimental, flexible and incremental—as it was in China—so that the reformmongers receive a steady flow of information that enables them to monitor progress during the transition.

Another lesson from the Chinese experience is the importance of maintaining macroeconomic stability during the shift from central planning to reliance on the market mechanism. Rapid inflation should be avoided: it weakens the incentive effects of changes in relative prices, it leads to unpredictable and arbitrary changes in the distribution of income and because of the resulting high uncertainty, it makes it difficult for enterprises to plan production and investment efficiently. The Chinese seem to have understood the close connections that exist between financial stability, economic growth and systemic reform.

Indeed, sustained growth is central to a successful transition. Policymakers in Russia and Eastern Europe have behaved as if they believed that a successful transition would result in sustained growth. The Chinese have reversed the direction of causality: sustained growth permits a successful transition, while falling output and incomes greatly hamper it. This reversal is yet another important lesson from the Chinese experience. In fact, the economic reforms in China have led to an investment boom and an acceleration in the rate of growth of output. Incomes have risen rapidly, which has made it easier to continue the reform process.

The Chinese, in effect, decided to grow out of systemic inefficiencies, whereas the Russians and East Europeans have tried to reduce inefficiency by reallocating a given volume of resources within the existing production structure. The Russians, in other words, have tried to convert swords into ploughshares, whereas the Chinese have used the increments from growth to channel new investment not only into ploughshares but into a wide range of consumer goods industries. The Russian approach has been unsuccessful; the Chinese approach has been very successful. The Russians today have fewer swords and ploughshares than they had five years ago, while the Chinese have more of both, particularly the latter, and much else besides.

One can also learn much about privatization and the reform of property relations from the Chinese experience. The Chinese concentrated their efforts on creating space for the private sector to expand. No overt attempt was made to reduce the absolute size of the state sector by privatizing state industrial enterprises. (The transformation of communes into a small peasant farming system is another story.) In Russia and Eastern Europe, in contrast, enormous efforts have been made to transform state enterprises into private ones, so far with little beneficial effect.

The key to creating a market-guided economy is price reform. Privatization is a secondary matter and, in fact, premature privatization may slow down the transition rather than accelerate it. In the Chinese context, and probably elsewhere too, privatization would weaken macroeconomic stability by simultaneously reducing government revenues (from profits of state enterprises) and creating pressures for increased government expenditure (on social services and unemployment compensation). This weakening would make it more difficult to sustain high levels of investment and almost certainly would cause the rate of growth to fall. In addition, privatization, if hastily implemented, almost certainly would result in greater inequality in the distribution of wealth and income.

Privatization is thus a low-priority reform. It should follow price reform, tax reform, housing reform and reform of the social services. Meanwhile, Chinese experience indicates that if obstacles to private enterprise are removed, the private sector will expand spontaneously and very rapidly, and the relative importance of the state sector will decline steadily. It is not necessary to destroy the state enterprise sector to create a dynamic and strong private sector.

Finally, one can learn a lot from the Chinese experience about poverty and inequality during the transition to a market-guided economy. Once again, growth is critical, because the reforms are likely to result in an increase in inequality in the distribution of income. If growth is rapid, however, greater inequality need not be accompanied by an increase in the number of people living in poverty. Moreover, if poverty does increase, growth ensures that resources will be available to create a new social safety net or extend the existing one.

Much depends on the distribution of productive assets and on whether there is equality of access to credit. The Chinese reforms began in the countryside, and care was taken when the communes were dismantled to ensure that land and other agricultural assets were widely distributed among the rural population. The transition thus began with an egalitarian distribution of private wealth in the sector where the majority of the people lived and worked. In addition, when the restraints on the growth of the private sector were removed, care was taken to ensure that private entrepreneurs had ready access to bank credit to finance investment. This access enabled large numbers of very small, labor-intensive enterprises to be created quickly and helped to prevent private nonfarm capital from becoming heavily concentrated. Hence, although accelerated growth in China was accompanied by greater inequality, the increase in inequality was only moderate, and the distribution of income in China is still relatively equal compared to other developing countries.

The Chinese also understood the need to set up a new network of social services in place of the one that began to crumble, particularly in the rural areas after the abolition of the commune system. Nonetheless, some people did fall through the safety net. Real incomes rose, and there was no significant increase in poverty, but the well-being of some declined because of a deterioration in the provision of social services. This decline is most evident in the case of health services: both infant mortality rates and crude death rates rose. Thus, despite an equitable distribution of assets and rapid growth of incomes, human development suffered a setback, at least in some dimensions. Thus, the Chinese experience underlines the necessity to create an effective social safety net to protect those who are harmed during the transition to a market-guided economy.

notes

1. The degree of centralization in China is often exaggerated. See Carl Riskin, *China's Political Economy: The Quest for Development Since 1949,* Oxford: Oxford University Press, 1987.

2. The word was first used by Albert O. Hirschman, *Journeys Toward Progress: Studies of Economic Policy-Making in Latin America,* New York: Twentieth Century Fund, 1963.

3. Some of the experiments are described in Keith Griffin, ed., *Institutional Reform and Economic Development in the Chinese Countryside,* London: Macmillan, 1984.

4. "Russia's Road to Ruin," The Economist, February 6, 1993, p. 51.

5. See Athar Hussain and Nicholas Stern, "Economic Reforms and Public Finance in China," Suntory-Toyota International Centre for Economics and Related Disciplines, London School of Economics, Research Programme on the Chinese Economy, CP23, June 1992.

6. The early phase of the industrial reforms is analyzed in Keith Griffin, *World Hunger and the World Economy,* London: Macmillan, 1987, ch. 5.

7. The soft budget constraint in effect ensured that state enterprises could never become bankrupt and would always have a claim on resources regardless of how inefficient they might be. See János Kornai, *Economics of Shortage,* New York: North-Holland, 1980.

8. Terry McKinley and Keith Griffin, "The Distribution of Land in Rural China," Department of Economics, University of California—Riverside, Working Paper 93-6, 1993.

9. The data on income distribution in China in this paragraph and those that follow refer to 1988. For details, see Azizur Rahman Khan, Keith Griffin, Carl Riskin and Zhao Renwei, "Household Income and Its Distribution in China," *China Quarterly,* No. 132 (December 1992).

10. The contribution of a component of income to overall income inequality (as measured by the Gini coefficient) is equal to the product of the share of the component in total income and its "concentration ratio." The concentration ratio, in turn, is estimated from the "concentration curve" in exactly the same way as the Gini coefficient is estimated from the Lorenz curve. The concentration curve represents the proportion of income from the given source received by the lowest x proportion of *income* recipients (not the lowest x proportion of the recipients of *income from the given source*).

11. The concentration ratio of urban wages (0.18) is so much lower than the con-

centration ratio of urban subsidies (0.31 for housing, 0.13 for ration coupons and 0.21 for other subsidies) that a reallocation of public expenditure from subsidies to wages would make it possible to increase wage differentials substantially without increasing inequality in the urban areas.

12. The term of trade that we use for agriculture is the ratio of the index of farm product purchase prices to the index of rural retail prices of producer and consumer goods.

13. State Statistical Bureau, *Yearbook of Rural Social and Economic Statistics of China 1986*, Beijing, 1987.

14. This is the explanation given by the World Bank in *China: Long-term Issues and Options*, Baltimore: Johns Hopkins University Press, 1985, pp. 29–30.

15. The household surveys carried out by the State Statistical Bureau (SSB) show that the ratio of per capita urban household income to per capita rural household income increased steadily from 1.88 in 1985 to 2.31 in 1989. See SSB, *China Statistical Yearbook 1990*, Beijing, 1991. Note that these SSB ratios of urban/rural inequality are not comparable with the 1988 estimate (2.42) cited above, which is based on a different and more comprehensive system of accounting. See Khan et al., "*Household Income*," for evidence that the SSB estimates understate the urban/rural income differential.

16. The World Bank, for example, claims in *The World Development Report 1990* that the incidence of rural poverty increased from 10 percent of the rural population in 1985 to 14 percent in 1988.

17. Whether political control can be combined with democratization is an issue worth investigating. If they cannot be combined, there is a possible trade-off between political democracy and successful economic reform. We merely note this possible conflict here without expressing our own preferences about the trade-off.

ASHOT GALOIAN

marxism, the nationality question and soviet leadership

a comparative discussion
of western views and political reality

The nationality question had a greater impact on the Soviet leadership during the course of the twentieth century than any other single issue. Moreover, there were important similarities concerning this issue between the Tsarist and Soviet political systems. For instance, nationalism was the greatest force to stimulate both revolutionary struggle in the Russian Empire in the late nineteenth and early twentieth centuries and vast democratic movements in the multiethnic Soviet Union in the late 1980s.

According to John Breuilly, nationalism has an explicitly political dimension. In his words, "It appeals to people in terms of their rights and their own identities rather than in terms of their shared beliefs. These identities are already abstract from social distinctions. All this makes nationalism more immediately political and appropriate to mobilizing and organizing a variety of territorially defined groups. For all these reasons nationalist opposition has usually been much more effective politically than religious movements."[1]

At the beginning of this century Tsarist Russia was a multinational state with a total population of about 170 million, of which people of the Great Russian nationality numbered approximately 70 million. The outskirts of the empire were heavily populated by non-Russians, who comprised 57 percent of the total number. Of these, 27.5 percent were Slavs of non-Great Russian ethnic stock, namely Poles, Ukrainians and Belorussians. The rest were Estonians, Latvians, Lithuanians, Finns, Jews, Georgians, Armenians and Turkic people of the Caucasus and Central Asia.

The basic policy of Tsarist Russia toward its non-Russian peoples, was one of toleration until the assassination of Emperor Alexander II. But his assassination significantly altered the Tsarist nationality policy. The new emperor, Alexander III, embarked on a serious "Russification" campaign that was continued by his successor. All non-Russian peoples, whether Poles, Georgians, Armenians or Finns, whether Catholics, Muslims or Jews, were subject to the government policy founded on the three principles of autocracy, orthodoxy and nationality (nationalism).

This policy was proposed by Count Sergei Uvarov in an official report in 1832. To quote Benedict Anderson, "'official nationalism' can best be understood as a means for combining naturalization with retention of dynastic power, in particular over the huge polyglot domains accumulated since the Middle Ages, or, to put it another way, for stretching the short, tight skin of the nation over the gigantic body of the empire." Furthermore, "The key to the situation of 'official nationalisms'—willed merger of national and dynastic empire—is to remember that it developed after, and in reaction to, the popular national movements proliferating in Europe since the 1820s."[2]

Thus, by the end of the nineteenth century, the Russian Empire was dominated by a single nation whose people believed in its "historical" right to such dominances based on the ideas of "leading race" and "civilizing mission." By the mid-twentieth century, among each of the national minorities within the Russian borders "were those who concluded that the only way out for them was the establishment of their own countries, and the appropriate vehicle for achieving that objective was revolution."[3]

Of course, for national minorities within the empire independence from

Russia seemed to be the best solution to their problems. However, Marxism, one of the most powerful revolutionary teachings in Russia at the beginning of the twentieth century, took a different position. According to the *Communist Manifesto*, "the proletarians have no fatherland." The founders of Marxism contended that the establishment of the proletariat could end national conflicts of peoples. Karl Marx and Friedrich Engels wrote: "In proportion as the exploitation of one individual by another is ended, is the exploitation of one nation by another ended too."[4] Moreover, by ending such conflicts the proletariat could create true internationalism. As noted in the "Manifesto of the Communist Party," with the end of the class war within a nation the hostile attitude of nations to one another disappears."[5] It is clear that Marxist theorists did not expect nationalism to survive the end of capitalism and viewed each national movement on its own merits in the light of the international struggle of the working class.[6] Dan Jacobs and Therese Hill noted that according to Marxism, "nationalism was not a liberating force, but rather an integral part of capitalist machinery, for enslavement of the working masses," but the phenomenon of nationalisms "enabled the bourgeoisie to focus the hostility of the proletariat on foreign workers rather than on the bosses at home, who, Marx maintained, were the true enemies."[7]

Vladimir Lenin's attitude toward the nationality question was influenced primarily by the ideas of Marx and Engels. Nevertheless, he was a practical politician and was therefore prepared to make use of loyalty to nation to further the socialist revolution in Russia. No doubt in order to maintain his long-range political goals, Lenin proposed the theory of "self-determination," which was based on Marxism. According to Lenin, a revolutionary party had to define its tactics in relation not only to classes but also to nationalities. He noted that, at the same time, the proletariat of Russia faced

> a two-sided task: to combat nationalism of every kind, above all, Great-Russian nationalism; to recognize, not only fully equal rights for all nations in general, but also equality of rights regarding policy, i.e., the right of nationals to self-determination, to secession. And, at the same time, it is their task, in the interests of successful struggle against all and every kind of nationalism among all nations, to preserve the unity of the proletarian struggle and the proletarian organization amalgamating these organizations into a class-knit international association despite bourgeois striving for national exclusiveness.[8]

Thus at the moment of revolution, a national group on the periphery of Russia could declare its independence and establish its own state.

According to Lenin, the principle of national self-determination could be reserved only for a nation's working class or proletariat. At the same time, only the Bolshevik party, the working-class vanguard, could speak on the workers' behalf. This theory therefore provided "few guidelines for the practical problems of governing the multiethnic Soviet State" and "did help the Bolsheviks to legitimize Soviet control over Moscow's far-flung empire."[9] To quote Domenic Lieven: "The ability of Marxist-Leninist ideology to combat and compete with nationalist doctrines for the hearts and minds of the Soviet population has always been and remains very important for the rulers of the USSR."[10]

The October revolution of 1917 succeeded largely because the Bolsheviks were able to harness national movements to the cause of social revolution. Nevertheless, the radical nationalists did not join the Bolsheviks (Russian Communist party) strictly because they were dedicated to Marxism. For example, Tatar communists (radical Muslim nationalists) believed that Bolshevism was a lesser evil than the ideology of the counterrevolutionary Whites, "and they did not have the slightest illusion as to the possibility of long-lasting cooperation with the new masters of Russia."[11]

While the "Bolshevik revolution" was taking place, the disintegration of the Russian Empire in the aftermath of World War I played no small part in helping it along. During the Civil War of 1918–1920, the Bolsheviks reconquered most of the Russian Empire, and the Ukrainian, Georgian, Armenian and other nationalities that in 1918 had declared independence were exposed to forcible sovietization. Some Western scholars have interpreted the Civil War in Russia as a war of Russians against national minorities, the center against the provinces or periphery, while others have seen it as a struggle among classes.[12]

The Soviet federal structure was created in 1922 as a concession in response to the nationalism of the ethnic minorities. Moreover, the new masters of Russia, and first and foremost Joseph Stalin (the commissar for nationality affairs), managed to retain the great bulk of the former empire for the new Soviet multinational state. Despite the rhetoric of internationalism and federalism, the new Soviet state that was established was an inequitable, hierarchical and imperial one. The republics lost their real state sovereignty.

However, the policy of "nativization" (*korenizatsiia*), as encouraged by Lenin, was sincerely carried out in the 1920s, with spectacular results. Each nationality maintained its own republic or autonomous district, the ethnic republics became demographically and culturally more ethnic, the national language was to be encouraged, and so on.[13]

However, the Russian nationalist feeling that was aroused in a section of the party during the Civil War years was, in the words of Robert Tucker, the revolution-born spirit of "Red Russian patriotism," "an element in the culture that could predispose a Bolshevik to perceive certain patterns out of the heritage of old Russia as relevant to the circumstances of the present."[14] Stalin was in fact one of those Bolsheviks most infected by "Red Russian patriotism."

Lenin, at the end of his life, became very disturbed by the Russian domination of the Soviet Union and was unhappy with the structure of the Soviet federal state. His harsh criticism of Stalin and his favoring of "autonomization" was clearly expressed: "Obviously the whole business of 'autonomization' was radically wrong and badly timed.... It is quite natural that such circumstances as the 'freedom to secede from the union' by which we justify ourselves will be a mere scrap of paper, unable to defend the nonRussian from the onslaught of that true Russian man, Great-Russian chauvinist, in substance a true brute and scoundrel, such as a typical Russian bureaucrat is."[15]

Without question this criticism of Stalin was intended as a part of the substantiation of Lenin's plan to request the forthcoming Twelfth Party Congress to remove Stalin from the post of general secretary of the party's Central Committee.

Bolshevik leaders, according to Domenic Lieven, "made no bones about the fact that the Soviet Union's ruling party was a monolithic, centralized organization, governed by the rules of 'democratic centralism' which required absolute obedience to Moscow's commands from its members in the republics and regions."[16] After Lenin's death the Communist party's republican, regional, and local committees grew rapidly in power, "providing the institutional base for the rise of Stalin, as Party General Secretary, to supreme power."[17]

The basic components of Stalin's national policy were the primacy of Great Russian interest as interpreted by Stalin, the predominance of the Russian language and Great Russian culture and the expulsion of groups categorized as being in conflict with Stalinist ideals,[18] According to Stalin, national culture under the dictatorship of the proletariat "is culture that is socialist in content and national in form, having the object of educating the masses in the spirit of socialism and internationalism."[19]

Western analysts characterized Stalin's view of the ideal political organization of society as totalitarian, denoting the idea of a terroristic government seeking total control of the population by massive use of indoctrination, police and ideological brainwashing and monopoly of information and exercise of power as well as direct control over the economy. As Erik Hoffmann pointed out: "In the fully developed Stalinist system that emerged after the Great Purges, the party was reduced to more or less equal status with the other major bureaucracies—the secret police, army, and state apparatus. ... In 1937 Stalin had replaced the previous oligarchic dictatorship of the party with a personal dictatorship."[20]

World War II increased Stalin's policy of mass terror against nonRussian peoples. It is a well-known fact that he accused Crimean Tatars, Volge Germans, Chechens, Ingushes, Kalmyks, Karachai and other ethnic minorities of collaboration with the Nazis, then uprooted and dispatched them to Siberia and Central Asia. However, terror was not the only element in Stalin's repression of non-Russians. As Domenic Lieven wrote: "Centralization, which inevitably meant russianisation, was imposed in the cultural and linguistic spheres, while non-Russians were forced to learn crudely distorted versions of their peoples' histories, and were in some cases cut off from direct access to their cultural heritages and pushed into the Russian cultural orbit by the imposition of Cyrillic alphabets, etc."[21]

Nevertheless, under Stalin's leadership one of the largest and most complex multinational political units in the world was created. It was divided into 15 union republics, 20 autonomous republics, 8 autonomous provinces and 10 national districts, all organized on the basis of nationality, comprising some 100 nations and nationalities, 22 of which numbered over 1 million people each. After World War II, Stalin's policy toward national minorities did not change. In the words of Robert Tucker, World War II "gave a powerful further impetus to the Great Russian nationalism which had become evident in Stalin's personal political makeup by the beginning of the 1920's and a prominent motif in Stalinist thought and politics in the 1930's."[22] However, despite the numerous facts of political repression, the minority nationalities in the Soviet Union were not destroyed or assimilated.

In the post-Stalin period, his successor, Nikita Khrushchev, tried to develop various reform programs. He gradually put together a "great design"—"a coordinated set of new domestic and international goals and policies that included peaceful coexistence with the West; serious efforts to uprate agriculture, light industry, and consumer goods; systematic application of scientific discoveries and technological innovations to production problems and national defense; and social and economic egalitarianism."[23] To quote Erik Hoffmann: "Khrushchev made an enormous contribution to Soviet politics by forswearing terror as a means of resolving political disputes."[24]

It is a well-known fact that Khrushchev did not attain his major political goals. However, at the Twenty-Second Party Congress in 1961, Khrushchev asserted that "the party has solved one of the most complex problems which has plagued mankind for ages and remains acute in the world of capitalism today—the problem of relations between nations."[25] Moreover, Khrushchev's talk of attaining full communism by 1980 promoted the idea of the diffusion of the national, for it was possible that by 1980 the Soviet Union would be one gigantic melting pot in which, through "fusion," the new Soviet citizen was to be formed. From an ethnic Russian perspective the process of fusion (*sliyanie* in Russian), according to Peter Duncan, "might entail a corruption of Russian values whereby a denationalized 1980s Soviet person would emerge. National-conscious non-Russians might regard the fusion of Soviet peoples as a threat to their distinctiveness, who must fear that their nationality will be absorbed by the Russians, imposing their will even more than they already do."[26]

Communist party authorities (nomenklatura) never forgave Khrushchev for his attempt to shake the foundation of the Soviet political system. His ouster in October 1966 was the result of his autocratic ideas power and Party leadership, his unpredictable political style and his inclination for unrealistic projects and idealistic goals. After he was ousted, the bureaucrats felt as if they were the real masters of the country. Party authorities, ministers and national satraps sat back in their armchairs, seemingly forever.

Khrushchev's immediate successors—the Brezhnev administration officials, during their initial mood (primarily between 1964–1969)—devoted important efforts to creating stable and clearly defined institutional relationships in the Soviet Union. "The content of Leonid Brezhnev's grand design included détente with the United States; the rapid enhancement of strategic defense capabilities; the use of advanced Western technology to spur Soviet

economic development; a strong commitment to improve agricultural production; and wage increases for the lowest paid workers."[27] These ideas were
similar to Khrushchev's objectives. Again, there was no mention of the nationality problem, which party authorities considered solved forever.

In the beginning Brezhnev was more pragmatic than Khrushchev. He hoped
that "procedural adjustments would generate political and technical support
from the officials and specialists, whose contributions were essential in formulating as well as implementing a realistic and farsighted national
program."[28] He recognized the significance of uncontested and regularized
methods of governing. As Erik Hoffmann pointed out, "The power to set pri-
orities and assess results was exercised by collective leadership composed of
representatives of all the key party and state bodies. Initiative and responsibility were diffused among many individuals and organizations."[29]

It was a period of paradoxes in the development of the Soviet Union. On
the one hand, the 1977 Soviet Constitution maintained the federal system.
There was sloganistic talk of the coming together of nationalities. The country made advances in industrial development and living standards for all of
the regions and republics. Societies were established to restore historical monuments, for example, allowing the Armenians to build a memorial to the
Armenian genocide of 1915.[30] With the establishment of the All-Russian
Society for the Preservation of Historical and Cultural Monuments, which
essentially focused on religious matters, Russian nationalism, in the words of
Peter Duncan, had its "first official voice."[31]

On the other hand, the expectations of the Soviet nationalities grew at a
faster rate than the Soviet political system could handle. For instance, the
indigenous elites consolidated their power in the non-Russian republics, and
national minorities protested that the central government was exploiting the
national resources of their republics. Furthermore, in a large demonstration
that took place in Tbilisi in April 1978 thousands of citizens marched on the
party Central Committee building after Edvard Shevardnadze tried to remove
a clause in the constitution that established Georgian as the official state language.

These conditions were fertile ground for the growth of nationalism in the
Soviet Union. At the end of the 1970s it was more obvious than ever that the
nationalities issue would become increasingly significant for future Soviet
leaders. Nevertheless, in the preceding decades the Soviet Union had reached

a new stage in its development. It had become predominantly urban, although national and regional traditions still weighed heavily in many ways.

In the 1980s and 1990s, the Soviet leadership was confronted by many problems directly related to national policy. In December 1982, new party leader Yuri Andropov delivered a major address on national relations in which he reminded his audience that "Soviet successes in solving the nationalities question certainly do not mean that all the problems engendered by the very fact of the life and work of numerous nations and nationalities in the framework of a single state has disappeared. This is hardly possible as long as nations exist."[32]

From the days of his appointment as general secretary of the Communist Party of the Soviet Union (CPSU) in March 1985, Mikhail Gorbachev attracted much attention with his radical ideas of perestroika and glasnost and very limited attention to the "issue of balancing interest and aspirations among nationalities."[33] Referring to the "fruit of Lenin's national policy," the Soviet leader, as Peter Dostal pointed out, "obviously has not been able, or willing to present a well-delineated policy regarding the complex issue of balancing delicate political relations among the numerous Soviet nationalities."[34]

Evidently Gorbachev's national problem was at once different and more serious than those faced by his predecessors. It was different because of the enormous social, economic and political changes that have transformed the role of nationality in Soviet life since the death of Stalin. Perestroika and glasnost were a perfect medium for awakening national consciousness. And it was more serious due to Gorbachev himself, his immediate political needs and his long-term policy goals, which were a kind of challenge to the status of Soviet ethnic communities.

According to John Stuart Mill, "The strongest cause for the feeling of nationality...is identity of political antecedents; the possession of national history, and consequent community of recollections; collective pride and humiliation, pleasure and regret, connected with the same incidents in the past."[35] Nationalist unrest emerged in 1988 as the greatest threat to democratic reform in the Soviet Union. Its impact was serious because it undermined Gorbachev's fundamental thesis that there was sufficient consensus among the Soviet peoples for Soviet society to successfully realize reform. However, the political interest of the non-Russians, to quote Ronald Suny, "could no longer be sacrificed on the altar of economic development.... At times,

Kremlin leaders appear to hope wistfully that their policies of economic stim-ulation, if blessed by the fruits of prosperity, will dampen the order of the nationalists. While that certainly might help, the prolonged failure to solve fundamental economic problems promises a great danger of material and psy-chological discontents being expressed in ethnic struggles."[36] Gorbachev repeatedly defended greater diversity of opinion by arguing that diversity of views does not mean the basic political framework of the country is being questioned or contested; individual liberty is compatible with a stable gov-ernment.

In February of 1988, the Nagorno-Karabakh issue exploded. This conflict was the first major threat and an early fatal blow to glasnost and perestroika. Escalating violence in the southern republics of Armenia and Azerbaijan throughout 1988 seemingly proved Gorbachev wrong. The question of Nagorno-Karabakh has its roots in the depths of history. The land has been occupied by Armenians since the first century AD, a time when one of the oldest peoples of the Caucasus—Caucasian Albanians—were in their last throes of existence. A large portion of Albania, the lands extending from Lake Sevan to the Caspian Sea, was conquered by the forces of the Armenian king-dom. The Armenian national, cultural and religious influence remained in full force in this area, despite the fact that after the fourth century mountain-ous (Nagorno) Karabakh exchanged hands many times. In the course of over one thousand years, the Mongols, the Arabs, the Turkmen, the Turks and many others, one after the other, conquered this land. Finally, in the seven-teenth century, Karabakh passed into the hands of the Persians, but the permanent population of the region continued to be basically Armenian. In the religious life of Karabakh, Christianity was dominant despite numerous attempts at Islamization.

It was the Armenian Church that initiated the establishment of ties with Russia. As early as 1701 the first Armenian delegation was sent to Peter I to ask for his protection. However, by 1813, the Khanate of Karabakh was ceded to Russia through the Treaty of Guliston following a series of Russo-Persian wars.

After the Bolsheviks came into power in 1917, civil unrest and wars among Caucasian nations continued in full force. In the early 1920s, following the establishment of Soviet power in Transcaucasia, the national wars came to an end.

Despite the fact that 90 percent of the population of mountainous Karabakh comprised Armenians, in the 1920s, Stalin, as commissar of nationalities, arbitrarily decided to establish the autonomous region of Nagorno-Karabakh within the domain of Azerbaijan. This decision was judged by all Armenians, within as well as outside the Karabakh region, as unjust and irrational. Following the sovietization of the area, persecution of the Karabakh Armenians occurred through the obstruction of economic and cultural ties with Armenia, the shutting down of schools and churches, and so forth. These activities increased in the days of the future member of the Politburo and first secretary of the Central Committee of Azerbaijan—Haydar Aliev.

The Armenians were the first nation to experience, in the twentieth century, what is known today as "man's inhumanity to man." In the period 1915–1923, 1.5 million Armenians perished through murder and disease as a consequence of genocidal acts perpetrated by the Ottoman Turkish government. This number comprised half the population of a people that had lived on lands they called their own for over two thousand years.

Based on numerous examples of national persecution, and feeling with good reason that it was their Russian cousins who had saved them from extermination at the hands of Turks, the Armenians of Nagorno-Karabakh appealed to Moscow in February of 1988, asking the Central Committee of the CPSU to cede this region of Karabakh to Armenia. In this instance, CPSU officials acted as arbiter between Armenia and Azerbaijan until this complex and contentious matter was resolved. The Karabakh problem, emanating from the historical past, demanded a just and rational solution from the new Soviet leadership.

Hundreds of thousands of Armenians repeatedly organized demonstrations and went on strike to support the Armenians in Karabakh. This movement, based on specific national feelings and anxieties, turned into a national front with a generally socialdemocratic content. The members of the Armenian national front, the Karabakh Committee, became the Armenian people's favorite leaders. From the beginning, Gorbachev turned against the Armenian national movement instead of establishing a dialogue with the Karabakh Committee.

Sporadic incidents of violence culminated in the massacre of Armenians in the Azerbaijani town of Sumgait. Soviet authorities never expressed condolences to the Armenians. Moreover, during the trial, the killers were tried not for murder but for "hooliganism." By mid-January 1989, more than three hundred thousand refugees had taken to the roads fearing a recurrence of the killings. However, the cecession request of the Karabakh Armenians was rejected. In December 1989, the Kremlin made a decision to return Nagorno-Karabakh to Azerbaijan. This decision intensified the radicalization of the Armenian national movement and gave rise to the bloody war that continues to this day.

The demand for historical truth sparked powerful national movements in Latvia, Lithuania and Estonia. The events in Transcaucasia and the Baltic republics set an important precedent for other nationalities in the multiethnic Soviet state. Gorbachev himself saw the serious implications of the ethnic conflict in the Caucasus. At a special Supreme Soviet Presidium meeting devoted to the national problem, he said that perestroika requires extremely great cohesion among the people, but "what is offered is strife and national distrust."[37] In the words of Gail Lapidus, "the increasing intensity of eth-nonationalism among Russians and non-Russians alike, sometimes taking extreme and chauvinistic forms, has not only provoked increasing alarm among Soviet citizens and leaders, it has also precipitated a sharp controversy over Soviet policy toward the 'nationalities question' and over the nature and future of the Soviet federal system itself."[38]

Thus, nationalist unrest emerged as the most potent threat to Gorbachev's leadership and to the future of his reforms. This threat was frequently misunderstood in official circles in Moscow. Patrick Cockburn, a former Moscow bureau chief for *Financial Times*, has noted that this misunderstanding is "rooted in the diversity" of the USSR's "ethnic mosaic," which "provides some evidence for every theory about its nationality problem." Moreover, Cockburn said "often Western commentators interpret ethnic conflicts as insoluble crises in the making and underestimate the effect of government countermeasures."[39]

Nationalist unrest broke up the Soviet Union; constituent republics and nationalities began to form independent states. In short, perestroika failed. The non-Russian republics were the first in which Gorbachev's reforms found a mass response, which shows that ethnic minorities found a natural way of solving a most important historical task—that of creating independent states with the further development of democracy. Perestroika and glasnost were a perfect medium for awakening national consciousness.

The logical follow-up to this political process was Boris Yeltsin's attempts to create a principally new community of independent states. The extent of the interest each member of this community has in securing a collective future will determine whether or not it will become more truly vital and able to replace the former federation, known as the USSR, in the twenty first century.

notes

1. John Breuilly, *Nationalism and the State*, Manchester, UK: Manchester University Press, 1981, pp. 49–50.

2. Benedict Anderson, *Imagined Communities: Reflections of the Origin and Spread of Nationalism*. London: Verso, 1990, p. 86.

3. Dan N. Jacobs and Therese M. Hill, "Soviet Ethnic Policy in the 1980's: Theoretical Consistency and Political Reality," *Soviet Politics: Russia After Breshnev*, ed. Joseph L. Nogee, New York: Praeger, 1985, p. 155.

4. Karl Marx and Friedrich Engels, "Manifesto of the Communist Party," in *Marx and Engels: Basic Writing on Politics and Philosophy*, ed. Lewis S. Feuer, New York: Anchor Books, 1959, p. 11.

5. Marx and Engels, "Manifesto," p. 26.

6. *K. Marx and F. Engels*, vol. V, (Berlin: Diztz, 1956–1968, p. 80.

7. Jacobs and Hill, "*Soviet Ethnic Policy*," p. 155.

8. "Lenin: The Right of Nations to Self-Determination," *The Lenin Anthology*, ed. Robert Tucker, New York: 1975, pp. 179–180.

9. Domenic Lieven, "Gorbachev and the Nationalities," *The Center for Security and Conflict Studies*, London, November 1988, p. 1.

10. Lieven, "Gorbachev and the Nationalities," p. 1.

11. Alexander Bennigsen, "Marxism or Pan-Islamism: Russian Bolsheviks and Tatar National Communists at the Beginning of the Civil War, July 1918," *Central Asian Survey*, vol. 6, no. 2, (1987), p. 62.

12. See, for example, Firus Kazemzadeh, *The Struggle for Transcaucasia (1917–1921)*, New York: Philosophical Library, 1941; Richard Pipes, *The Formation of the Soviet Union: Communism and Nationalism, 1917–1918*, Cambridge, Mass.: Harvard University Press, 1957; Ronald Suny, "Nationalism and Social Class in the Russian Revolution: The Cases of Baku and Tiflis," *Transcaucasia, Nationalism, and Social Change: Essays in the History of Armenia, Azerbaijan, and Georgia*, ed.

Ronald Grigor Suny, Ann Arbor, Mich.: University of Michigan Press, 1983.

13. Ronald G. Suny, "State, Civil Society and Ethnic Cultural Consolidation in the USSR: Roots of the National Question," *The Soviet System in Crisis: A Reader of Western and Soviet Views*, eds. Alexander Dallin and Gail W. Lapidus, Boulder Colo.: Westview Press, 1991, p. 419.

14. Robert C. Tucker, "Stalinism as Revolution from Above," *Stalinism: Essays in Historical Interpretation*, ed. Robert C. Tucker, New York: Norton, 1977, p. 103.

15. "Lenin: The Question of Nationalities, or 'Autonomization,'" *The Lenin Anthology*, p. 720.

16. Lieven, "Gorbachev and the Nationalities," p. 3.

17. Lieven, "Gorbachev and the Nationalities," p. 3.

18. Jacobs and Hill, "Soviet Ethnic Policy," pp. 164–165.

19. Joseph Stalin, *Marxism and the National-Colonial Question*, San Francisco: Proletarian Publishers, 1975, p. 391.

20. Erik P. Hoffmann, "The Evolution of the Soviet Political System," *The Soviet Union in the 1980s*, ed. Erik P. Hoffmann, New York: Academy of Political Science, p. 4.

21. Lieven, "Gorbachev and the Nationalities," p. 4.

22. Tucker, *Stalinism as Revolution from Above*, p. 105.

23. Hoffmann, "The Evolution of the Soviet Political System," p. 6–7.

24. Hoffmann, "The Evolution of the Soviet Political System," p. 7.

25. *Pravda*, no. 292 (15782), October 18, 1961, pp. 8–9; and no. 293 (15783), October 19, 1961, p. 7.

26. Peter Duncan, "The Phenomenon of Russian Nationalism Today," *Nationalism in the USSR (Problems of Nationalities)*, ed. Alexander Bon and Robert Van Varen, Amsterdam: Second World Center, 1989, p. 53.

27. Hoffmann, "The Evolution of the Soviet Politican System," p. 8.

28. Hoffmann, "The Evolution of the Soviet Politican System," p. 9.

29. Hoffmann, "The Evolution of the Soviet Politican System," p. 9.

30. Beginning April 24, 1965, Armenians would march on that date year after year to commemorate the genocide of 1915.

31. Duncan, "The Phenomenon of Russian Nationalism," p. 53.

32. *Pravda*, no. 356 (23517), December 22, 1982, p. 2.

33. Peter Dostal, "Regional Interest and the National Question Under Gorbachev," *Nationalism in the USSR, (Problems of Nationalities)*, Amsterdam: Second World Center, 1989, p. 28.

34. Dostal, "Regional Interest," pp. 28–29.

35. Alfred Zimmern, *Modern Political Doctrines,* London: Oxford University Press, 1939, p. 206.

36. Ronald G. Suny, "Nationalities and Nationalism," *Chronicle of a Revolution*, ed. Abraham Brumberg, New York: Pantheon Books, 1990, p. 125.

37. *Pravda*, no. 202 (2554), July 20, 1988, p. 2.

38. Gail W. Lapidus, "Gorbachev's National Problem," *The Soviet System in Crisis: A Reader of Western and Soviet Views,*" Boulder, Colo.: Westview Press, 1991, p. 430.

39. Patrick Cockburn, "Dateline USSR: Ethnic Tremors," *Foreign Policy*, 76, (Spring 1989), p. 182.

STEPHEN RESNICK and RICHARD WOLFF

lessons from the USSR

taking marxian theory the next step

CAPITALISM AND MARXISM

Marxism has long been a dialectical "other" of capitalism. As a set of theories, it has been continuously generated and regenerated by, while being simultaneously denounced as the antithesis of, capitalism. The transformations of capitalism have profoundly influenced Marxism, and vice versa. The same dialectic applies to the set of social movements that called themselves Marxist. The varieties and contradictions of the different kinds of actually historical capitalism have their counterparts in the complex diversity of Marxisms. Crises of capitalism have reflected as well as provoked crises of Marxism. Such interdependence is once again the case, we shall argue, today.

Capitalism's contradictions have recurringly provoked anticapitalist upsurges. Although these reactions have so far been repressed, the repressions themselves have served as lessons for antitcapitalists. Slowly, increasingly systematic insights into and revolutionary responses to those contradictions have been developed. In Europe, the 1848 revolutions, the Paris Commune, the rise of German social democracy, and the Russian revolutions of 1905 and 1917 were major moments of anticapitalist upsurge, repression, and learning. Parallel moments have occurred in all other continents. Not only did Marxism—or rather, Marxisms—emerge from this process, so too did the awareness that anticapitalist revolutionaries could transform repression, defeat, and defeatism into lessons for the next assault by means of a rigorous process of criticism.

The criticism aimed not only at better understandings of the dynamism, varieties, and weaknesses of existing capitalisms. At its best, it also included revolutionary self-criticism, which entailed intense inquiry into whether, how, and why various anticapitalist theories, strategies, and tactics had contributed to the failure to supersede capitalism. It also meant choosing which among alternative, contesting revolutionary tendencies should, with appropriate modifications and adjustments, inform future strategies and tactics.

Thus, Karl Marx's work was deeply committed first to sorting out why the revolutionary hopes of 1848 had been frustrated and later why the Paris Commune was defeated. Likewise, Vladimir Lenin returned to Marx's analysis of the Paris Commune to understand the defeat in 1905. Antonio Gramsci never lost sight of the need to learn the lessons of the frustrated general strike in Torino. Mao Tse-tung returned repeatedly to the lessons of 1927 and Louis Althusser to those of 1968. Moreover, from their criticisms each of these writers drew conclusions as to which existing or new tendencies within the Marxian tradition needed to displace those that had proven inadequate to the revolutionary tasks.

The USSR from 1917 to 1990 represents the longest and most sustained anticapitalist upsurge in modern history. Now that it has been so bitterly defeated, anticapitalists in general and Marxists in particular need urgently to undertake the sort of criticism and self-criticism that can once again yield the "other" of defeatism, namely, lessons for more successful wars of position against capitalism.

One lesson to be learned is that capitalism must no longer be analyzed as uniform. Its dynamic ability to alter its forms to cope with shifting social con-

ditions must take a central place in Marxist understanding, strategy, and tactics. A second, related lesson is that Marxist theorists must recognize that
Marxism is a tradition encompassing basically different strategies built around
basically different concepts of class, one of its central concerns. The defeat
of the 1917 anticapitalist upsurge in Russia imposes the need now to identify
and choose among the different concepts and theories of class and the different revolutionary strategies they imply.

DIFFERENT MARXIAN THEORIES

The USSR has always presented analysts interested in class with a challenge:
what exactly was its class structure? Most Marxists and non-Marxists responded that it was no longer capitalist, not (or not yet) communist, and thus
something in between and variously defined as "socialist." Dissenters from
this majority have argued that either the capitalist or the communist label
was the more applicable, or that no label applied.

However, no analysis of Soviet class structure that we could find based its
arguments on the particular Marxian concept and theory of class we will use
here. That is, none focused its inquiry and thus its conclusions on the precise
ways in which surplus labor was produced, appropriated, and distributed in
the USSR.[1] Rather, both Marxists and non-Marxists used other, very different
concepts of class—concepts centered on power rather than on surplus labor
—and so theorized differently and reached very different conclusions.

If class is defined as a matter of power—who wields it over whom versus
who does not—then it follows that the USSR after 1917 profoundly altered its
class structure in that sense. Power was drastically redistributed and reorganized. The power to control access to resources and products—that kind of
power usually called property—was taken from its former wielders (private
owners) and transferred to the state. The power to distribute resources and
products was transferred from independent private agents dealing in markets
(often abolished) to state planning bureaucrats. At the same time, the power to
control the state was shifted from an alliance of the czar, landlords, and the
Russian bourgeoisie to the Communist party. Power in industrial and agricultural production sites was also redistributed from its former wielders to
new groups of politically organized peasants, factory committees, trade
unions, party groups, etc. If the newly established distributions of power after
1917 are understood as new *class* structures, then indeed new labels such as

socialist or communist might be in order to designate the achieved class transformations.

However, we do not define class in terms of power (Resnick and Wolff
1986), and our Marxian theory is different from the others within the tradition
(Resnick and Wolff 1992). We are persuaded by our reading of Marx that revolutionary social analyses focused on power and property—which have been
popular at least since the time of ancient Greece—*miss* a dimension of social
life, namely, the way in which the production and distribution of surplus labor
are organized. We believe that the neglect of this dimension has undermined
revolutionary projects. Hence, we share and seek to develop further Marx's
commitment to contributing a systematic analysis of surplus labor so that
future revolutionary upsurges against capitalism will be more likely to succeed.

Different Marxian theories define and use concepts of class in different
ways and reach different conclusions. When a Marxian analysis such as ours
focuses on class understood as the social organization of surplus labor, the
post-1917 USSR displays a striking continuity in the capitalist class structure
of its industries. In other words, while the distribution of power changed dramatically after 1917, the organization of surplus labor did not. As we shall
show, private capitalist class structures were replaced by *state capitalism.*[2]

Capitalist class processes entail exploitation defined strictly as a situation in
which the fruits of surplus labor do not accrue to the performers of that
labor—they are not theirs to consume or distribute. That is, in capitalist class
structures, the laborers who perform surplus labor are exploited.[3] In contrast,
Marx stressed that communist class processes are not exploitative: the laborers collectively produce and dispose of their surpluses.[4]

The Marxian theory we use begins with this difference between capitalism and communism as exploitative versus nonexploitative class structures,
a difference with profound social consequences. Exploitation tends to foster
the alienation of workers from their products, from their work activity (and
hence self-development), from solidarity with other workers, from the natural environment, and thus from their own potential as members of
communities. Capitalist exploitation fosters economic inequality (in wealth
and income) and economic conflict by inducing costly, continuous competition and struggle over the size and distribution of the fruits of surplus labor.
Finally, we believe that exploitation, alienation, and economic inequality help

to undermine most current projects for political and cultural equality. The capitalist class difference between producers and appropriators of surplus labor often intertwines with the nonclass differences among individuals to yield an antagonistically stratified population. Access to economic, political, cultural, medical, and natural resources becomes systematically skewed toward capitalist appropriators and their favored dependents and away from the productive workers, and often even further away from those without any place within the capitalist class structure.

The persistence of a capitalist class structure inside the USSR contributed to the reproduction of many of these characteristics there. That we can justifiably point to positive social developments across the history of the USSR does not undermine a Marxian criticism of the capitalist exploitation retained there and its consequences. Marx and Marxists have recognized all kinds of social achievements within private capitalisms while focusing on the injustices and social costs of retaining capitalist class structures. Our position here in regard to state capitalism is quite parallel.

PRIVATE VERSUS STATE CAPITALISM

Marx constructed a theory of capitalism appropriate to the particular historical conjuncture in which he wrote. Hence, the opening sentences of *Capital*:

> The wealth of those societies in which the capitalist mode of production prevails, presents itself as "an immense accumulation of commodities," its unit being a single commodity. Our investigation must therefore begin with the analysis of a commodity. (1967a, 35)

Marx is not arguing that the capitalist mode of production can only or must always exist with commodity exchange, that is, individual private owners transacting in markets, money, and so on. In terms of our argument here, he never claimed that such a mode of production must always be *private* as opposed to *state* capitalism. On the contrary, he acknowledged other possibilities, other social conditions within which capitalist class processes could exist. In *Capital*, Volume 2, for example, he wrote about "state capital, so far as governments employ productive wage-labour in mines, railways, etc., perform the function of industrial capitalists" (1967b, 97).

Capitalism is simply not uniform. It has existed and exists today in the form of industry organized as individual, competitive enterprises, but also in

the forms of joint stock and monopolistic corporations. It has variously coexisted with unregulated, individual labor markets; with collective bargaining;
with state-mandated minimum wages; and with full state allocation of labor
supplies and state determination of wages. Capitalist class structures can be
national or transnational in form, open or closed in terms of their economic,
political, and cultural relations with the world economy. They may be inter-
twined with democratic and parliamentary political systems or with absolute
monarchies or dictatorships. Workers in capitalist enterprises may have their
every moment supervised and controlled by an army of managers other than
themselves, or they may engage in total self-management of both their necessary and their surplus labor.[5]

The question we pose is, then: Can we theorize a state form of capitalism,
and does it pertain to the USSR after 1917? Two definitive features demar-
cate the state from the private form of capitalist class structure: the *location* of
surplus appropriating enterprises and the *connection* of individuals therein to
the state. In private capitalism, individuals with no necessary connection to
the state establish enterprises that exist outside the state. In state capitalism,
individuals *with* a necessary connection to the state exploit labor in enterprises that occupy integral positions *within* the state apparatus. Although this
manifestation of these two features certainly alters the particular social form
of capitalist exploitation, such exploitation is not thereby eliminated.

State capitalism means that persons within a state apparatus exploit labor in
state institutions. State capitalism also has its varieties. For example, centralized or decentralized state legislative bodies may establish state industrial
capitalist enterprises. These enterprises may have boards of directors—sur-
plus-labor-appropriating capitalists—appointed or elected by the legislative
body. They may purchase raw materials, means of production, and labor
power from private owners in their respective markets or acquire them from
the state by means of nonmarket, planned allocations. State capitalist enterprises may sell their products as commodities, thereby realizing surplus value
and then distributing it so as to secure their continued existence; or their
products may be administratively distributed with administered prices
attached to them. State capitalist enterprises may exist within a predomi-
nately private capitalist system. A small minority of state capitalist enterprises
may then have to compete with private enterprises in all markets.
Alternatively, private capitalist enterprises may be marginalized or delegiti-

mated altogether, leaving most or all production to occur through state capitalist enterprises.[6]

Consider the particular variant of state capitalism in which (1) administrative (command) allocation replaces markets in the distribution of both the inputs and the outputs of industry, and (2) collective (state) replaces private ownership of industries' means of production. To show how this remains a state *capitalism* is especially necessary in view of the determinant importance given to the command-versus-market and collective-versus-private ownership dichotomies that are central to other, different conceptualizations of the USSR's economy, conceptualizations focused on power rather than surplus labor concepts of class.

In these different conceptualizations, the class structure is called capitalist *because* (1) all resources and products are privately owned and traded in markets, (2) workers lack productive property and so must sell their labor power, and (3) capitalists who own means of production must buy labor power to secure the surplus value they need for their reproduction as capitalists. It follows then that capitalism vanishes if the workers seize the state and their state both expropriates the capitalists' property and abolishes markets in favor of state-planned allocations of all resources and products.

By contrast, the Marxian theory we use focuses not on property and markets but rather on the specific form of the production, appropriation, and distribution of surplus labor. We believe that collectivizing property and abolishing markets do not by themselves abolish the capitalist form of surplus labor production, appropriation, and distribution. The question to ask is: How do collective property and nonmarket state allocations of resources and products affect the organization and distribution of surplus labor and its fruits? If state enterprises replicate private enterprises in this regard, then state capitalism has replaced private capitalism. Capitalism has changed its form; it has not been overthrown. Communist class processes have not been established, though that may have been the goal of the state and of the anticapitalists who seized the state in a revolutionary upsurge. That goal may motivate state capitalist enterprises to devote their surpluses to all sorts of public purposes and to grant their workers all sorts of managerial powers. Some will assert that an intermediary, transitional class structure—socialism—is therefore in place, but a state capitalist class structure is what actually exists.[7]

Capitalist exploitation is multiform. It can appear as private enterprises, privately owned means of production, and market exchanges of industrial inputs and outputs. Alternatively, it can be organized as state enterprises, collective ownership of means of production, and administered prices, profit rates, and allocations of inputs and outputs. Indeed, every possible mix and match of portions of both of the above alternatives can occur, and many combinations have actually existed.

Of course, capitalist exploitation will differ quantitatively and qualitatively depending on the extent of private versus state enterprises, private versus state ownership, and markets versus administered commands. Our argument is not that such differences do not matter. They do. Every dimension of the quality of life for all citizens living in capitalist economies depends in part on the particular kind of capitalist class structure that emerges from any one of the possibilities sketched above.

Our point is rather that the differences *among* kinds of capitalist class structure should not be confused with the differences *between* capitalist and communist class structures. To avoid such confusion requires that analysis separate the differences between private and state enterprises, between private and collective ownership, and between market and nonmarket exchanges from the dichotomy between capitalist and communist organizations of the production and distribution of surplus labor. That analysis requires the particular kind of Marxian theory that defines class in terms of surplus labor. Because that analysis of the USSR has not yet been undertaken, the insights it could yield have not yet been published and debated.

STATE AND PRIVATE CAPITALISMS: A HISTORY OF OSCILLATION

State capitalist class structures have repeatedly displaced and been displaced by their private counterparts.[8] For example, in regions where private capitalism was the first form of capitalism to develop out of precapitalist class structures, the interaction of its economic contradictions with their social context eventually reaches a "crisis" point, provoking a greater or lesser shift to state capitalism. In other words, private capitalist enterprises (some, many, or most) are changed into state capitalist enterprises.[9] At some later point, when the interaction of state capitalism's economic contradictions with their social context reaches proportions comparably interpreted as a social crisis, a greater or lesser shift back to private capitalism occurs, and so on.[10]

Typically, each form has its champions. They argue that their preferred form will lead society out of a perceived social crisis and create some version of "the greatest good for the greatest number." The debates between successive generations of such champions have accumulated a vast economic literature. Its arguments swirl around the virtues and vices of private markets versus state planning, state ownership versus private ownership, competition versus cooperation, state regulation versus "free" enterprise, and so on. Often these dichotomies are interpreted as the contest between socialism or communism and capitalism. Beyond economics, these same debates have been generalized and integrated into grand contestations of democracy versus bureaucracy, state versus citizen, initiative versus sloth, and freedom versus slavery. And once again, many have interpreted these oscillations between kinds of capitalism as great contests between socialism or communism and capitalism.

Some brief historical examples may illustrate these oscillations. The 1929–1933 depression in the United States drove Franklin D. Roosevelt's government to pass the National Industrial Recovery Act (NIRA). The government sponsored, organized, and enforced cartels of and codes for private industry, amounting to a program of such extensive and intensive regulation that it approached outright state capitalism (achieved in the case of the Tennessee Valley Authority) as an antidote to the collapse of private capitalism. Culminating in the Reagan-Bush era, post-World War II economic development in the United States has been a long retreat (with deregulation, competition, and efficiency as its watchwords) back toward private capitalism and away from all that the NIRA represented and suggested. Today, in the Clinton era, we hear once again calls to move back from deregulated capitalism toward a more state-regulated capitalism so as to revive or save the economy or nation. Once again, not a few commentators welcome or denounce these oscillations in terms of socialism versus capitalism.

Other countries also illustrate the private to state to private oscillations. In Great Britain's nineteenth-century, private capitalism faded away in the face of the Great Depression, John Maynard Keynes, and postwar Labour nationalizations. Margaret Thatcher's regime represents the swing-back-to-privatization reaction. François Mitterrand's party, during its recent reign, managed the same sort of oscillation in a much shorter span, as had happened before in twentieth-century France[11]. Germany moved far more drastically from private to state capitalist forms under the rule of Adolf Hitler, but Konrad Adenauer and Ludwig Erhard rolled Western Germany back after

World War II. After 1868, state capitalist enterprises led the rapid economic development of Japanese capitalism; later, the lead passed to private capitalist enterprises, although always in close cooperation with the state. In country after country of the Third World, state capitalist industry and state-directed private capitalism led the way in the three decades after World War II. Dissatisfaction with the results produced a broad shift to private capitalism over the past twenty years. Lastly, in the USSR, as we will argue in some detail, the twentieth century has seen broad shifts, from private capitalism to state capitalism after the 1917 revolution and then the reverse movement under Mikhail Gorbachev and Boris Yeltsin.[12] In these examples, too, the poles of the oscillations were often characterized as socialism or communism versus capitalism.

Among the critics of private capitalism, an extreme Right position sometimes gained ascendancy. It aimed to regenerate an organic hierarchical community in place of private capitalism's individualism and democracy, its resulting social divisions and antagonisms, and its loss of the religious or national purity that was thought to have existed before capitalism. Various fascisms tended to merge private and state capitalist enterprises as an integral step toward recovering national unity and preeminence. Fascism never got much beyond that step.

On the other end of the political spectrum, there were Left critics of private capitalism, especially those inspired by Marxian literature. Their objectives often went far beyond replacing private with state capitalism toward extending political into full economic democracy as well. Their goal was a radical break with capitalism. By this they meant varying combinations of strictly collective and egalitarian distributions of wealth and power (especially the distribution of products according to need) and nonexploitative organizations of production (i.e., what we have designated as communist class structures). Lenin, for example, viewed state capitalism as, at best, a temporarily necessary step toward the transition from capitalism to communism, after which the state as well as its capitalist class structure should and would wither away.[13] While those on the Left never got much beyond that step, many consoled themselves by designating the step itself a socialism or even a communism that had vanquished capitalism.

The debates between proponents of state and private capitalism continue unabated. So, too, do the tendencies—both Marxist and non-Marxist—that insist upon calling some or all state capitalisms "socialism" or even "communism." Our goal is to change the terrain of the debates, to win at least understanding and at best acceptance for the proposition that the history of anticapitalist struggles has not yet produced a sustained experiment in communism. Instead, it has produced oscillations between state and private capitalisms. We follow Marx in believing that to commence such an experiment in communism presupposes, among other requirements, a Marxian theory that is able systematically to differentiate the multiple forms of capitalist class structures from the communist alternative. It also presupposes a criticism, based on such a Marxian theory, of the epochal Soviet period, one that can learn from its successes, failures, and defeats and transform them into weapons for the next upsurge. In the remainder of this chapter, we sketch such a criticism.

THE CAPITALIST CLASS NATURE OF SOVIET SOCIETY

We begin by asking the questions about the class structure of the USSR that are invoked by a Marxian theory whose entry point into social analysis is the production and distribution of surplus labor. Who performed that surplus labor? Who first received the fruits of that surplus labor? And, finally, to whom did these receivers then distribute this surplus: in what portions, for what purposes, and with what consequences?

Our reading of factory and farm reports, histories, and management studies persuades us that from the Bolshevik revolution to today, individuals other than the workers in state enterprises were always the first receivers of the surpluses produced by those workers.[14] This difference between those who produced and those who received the surplus stands in stark contrast to the identification of the two as the same that stands as the class *definition* of communism.[15] Hence we conclude that no communist form of surplus labor production and distribution existed in the USSR's state enterprises, despite collective property ownership and state planning.

Nor are we persuaded, on the basis of our empirical research to date, that other noncommunist class structures, such as the feudal or slave, existed in state enterprises. We find little evidence that state officials received surpluses in the feudal form of corvée labor or rents or in the slave form of direct labor services. Additionally, we find little evidence of the particular kinds of political, cultural, and economic institutions that would serve to secure either the feudal or slave class structures. Soviet workers, for example, were not the property of surplus labor receivers or others, as in slavery, nor were they tied to the property owned by receivers through personal obligations, as in feudalism. We have thus concluded that throughout its history the particular class structure of Soviet *state* enterprises—factories and farms—did not resemble the communist, feudal, or slave forms. The evidence persuades us that it did resemble a form of capitalism.

Still other labels—"bureaucratic regime," "state-commanded economy" and so on—have been widely used to describe the USSR's class structure (Sweezy and Bettelheim 1971; Resnick and Wolff 1993). However, our focus on surplus labor rather than the power focus of most other approaches suggests capitalism rather than the other labels that stress political considerations. Moreover, a class analysis in terms of surplus labor has been notably lacking in the literature on the USSR. Thus, we believe that the USSR displays a capitalist class structure, which, like all capitalisms, has its particularities. These details include a relation to the state that differentiates this structure markedly from the private capitalisms that are more familiar to historians and theorists.

Soviet state ministers, in particular the Council of Ministers (COM), strike us as the individuals who were in the (class) position to be the first collective receivers of the surplus produced by the workers in state enterprises. The COM was thus also the first distributor of the surplus. Its distributions were chiefly to (1) capital accumulation in heavy industry; (2) salaries and budgets for the rest of the state bureaucracy, the Communist Party, and the military and police establishments; and (3) subsidies of the provision of public goods for collective consumption by all Soviet citizens (including those who produced this surplus). These public goods passed to Soviet citizens largely *without* going through market exchanges: "free" goods provided by "socialism," in the popular idiom.

The COM thus both received the surplus produced by state workers in industry and agriculture and distributed it. The goals of its distributions were to secure specific social conditions—political, cultural, and economic—that helped to constitute the COM as receiver and distributor of the surplus. As is recognized in other texts, these state ministers functioned in ways analogous to corporate boards of directors in countries where private capitalism was the norm.[16]

In our analysis, the COM's state capitalist "function" was defined, as per Marxian theory, by its acquisition and consumption of workers' labor power. By "consumption" of labor power we mean setting workers to work on raw materials with tools and equipment. Part of the resulting product (the part Marx called "necessary" labor) returned to these workers as their remuneration and part was reserved to replace the raw materials, tools, and equipment used. What remained, defined as the surplus product (the fruit of surplus labor), accrued immediately and automatically to the COM.

In the Soviet context, this surplus product took the form of surplus value. However, Soviet surplus value was distinctive. It was shaped not by market transactions, as in private capitalism, but rather by state determination of the values of labor power, resources, and most products. Thus Soviet surplus value depended not only on technology, resource availability, length and intensity of the working day, and the other usual determinants but also on the state's procedures for assigning values. By contrast, surplus value in private capitalism depends on the usual determinants plus the particular conditions of the market that assigns values.

In sum, then, the Soviet COM, as the first receiver of the surplus value produced by state workers, occupied the position of capitalist in relation to them. It exploited them in a manner closely analogous to that of private capitalists. The COM appropriated the surplus value generated in the productive enterprises of the state, both industrial and agricultural. Across Soviet history, first the "commanding heights" and then most of the rest of productive activity were reserved for state enterprises that functioned in this way: hence our designation of the USSR as state capitalist.

Now, the COM sought to secure a politics—a distribution of power and an establishment of political processes—that would keep it in the class position of first receiver of surplus value. The COM developed structures of election or appointment of individuals to positions in the COM. It also supported a system of state and party politics that empowered the COM to set input and output values in such a way that surplus value accrued to the COM. The COM worked for laws to be enacted—and interpreted, enforced, and adjudicated—to secure the COM as the legal personification of state enterprises (comparable to boards of directors as such in private capitalisms). It supported laws charging the COM with responsibility as the economic arm of the state, including its effective use of the allocated labor power and collectively owned means of production. The COM also developed a system of command and discipline in every industrial and farm state enterprise to push workers to perform surplus labor.

To promote these diverse political processes—legislative, administrative, and judicial—the COM distributed portions of appropriated surplus as salaries and operating budgets to a vast array of bureaucratic agencies, from its own subagencies and their various managerial levels (including managers of specific state factories) to the planning apparatus of Gosplan (the state planning agency), the officials of the Communist Party, and the state legislative and judicial institutions. Reproducing this bureaucracy helped in turn to reproduce the COM as, in Marxian terms, the personification of capital, of the self-expansion of value.

Among the economic conditions of existence for the COM to function as state capitalists was the operation of a system or "law" of value. This law of value was, of course, specific to the particular configuration of social processes in the USSR. The latter excluded price-determining market transactions and included the activities of Gosplan in calculating and assigning values to inputs and outputs according to what the agency determined to be the amounts of direct and indirect labor required for their production.[18] Thus, in terms of value, different forms of produced wealth existed in a state-administered rather than a market-administered relationship to one another.

Other parts of the state bureaucracy established other key variables composing the USSR's system of value. They set, for example, the length of the work day and the production technologies to be used in conjunction with party, trade union, and factory organizations. These variables yielded the bases for Gosplan's accounting of the value of raw materials and machinery and the value added by living labor in production. Finally, various state bureaucracies, together with party and workers' organizations, decided how many hours' worth of output would be returned to the workers as wages and salaries to reproduce themselves (the necessary labor).

The COM's appropriated surplus value thus represented the difference between state-administered values placed on produced outputs and those placed on all inputs. The ratio of that surplus value to the sum of the values of means of production and labor power measured state capitalism's rate of profit. Such rates of profit, calculated in this way across different state industries, could be used to shape how resources were allocated and how capital was accumulated (along with whatever other criteria the COM established, including minimizing ethnic and national conflicts, securing military needs, achieving socialist aims, etc.[19]

To secure these different economic processes—distributing inputs and outputs, making and disseminating value calculations, accumulating capital—the COM distributed portions of the surplus as salaries and budgets to the appropriate state agencies. By the same token, the receipt of surplus value by the COM depended in part on the existence and reproduction of these specific economic processes.

The COM's capitalist class position also depended on a specific set of cultural processes that established and disseminated certain particular ideas and meanings. The COM's existence was the product, in part, of an ideology that suppressed the concept of state capitalism in favor of affirming a definition of the USSR as socialist or communist. Soviet socialism or communism was portrayed as the absence of class exploitation, the supersession of class society, and thus the first historical achievement of real (as opposed to merely formal) democracy. Such interpretations helped to push workers to perform surplus labor for a collective other than themselves (the COM) because those workers came to believe, at least in part, what the official culture affirmed. In that sense, the Soviet worker came to resemble the U.S. worker. Notwithstanding their differences, the two cultures nonetheless produced a common result: few of either country's class of productive laborers believed that they participated in any form of class exploitation. This factor became a powerful means, in both places, of enabling and perpetuating such exploitation.

Thus the COM distributed another portion of the surplus as operating budgets and salaries to Communist Party officials, educators, mass media organizations, and so forth to produce and disseminate these structures of meaning in publications, schools, speeches, films, and museums. This distribution of surplus value for "cultural purposes" was added to the aforementioned distributions to secure various political and economic processes. All together, these distributions permitted the state, party, and others to provide many of the conditions needed for the COM to reproduce its capitalist class position.

In the USSR, the reiterated self-image of a "culture of socialism marching toward communism" meant that nearly everyone identified the successes of what was actually state capitalism with such "socialism." This image entailed the risk, if and when failures occurred, that state capitalism would escape all blame. Thus, when failures did occur in the 1970s and exploded in the 1980s, the blame fell on socialism and communism. Therefore, the solution seemed necessarily to be a shift to the "other" of socialism and communism, namely capitalism. What is actually a transition from state to private capitalism thus continues to be discussed and debated by most of its supporters and detractors alike as if it were a transition from socialism to capitalism.

A BRIEF CLASS HISTORY OF SOVIET STATE CAPITALISM

Soviet state capitalism, like its private capitalist counterparts, has had an uneven history. On the one hand, it produced some spectacular successes. By mobilizing economic resources despite the devastation of World War I, the new USSR overwhelmed the White Army and its foreign allies in the Civil War that followed the revolution. Recovery and growth in the 1920s was sufficiently fast and extensive, despite the trauma and losses of collectivization, that the USSR could contribute significantly to the defeat of German fascism. The USSR again recovered quickly from the devastation of a second world war only to enter a costly new (cold) war with the United States, the most powerful private capitalist industrial nation in the world. Nonetheless, by the late 1950s, only forty years after Lenin launched state capitalism, the USSR had achieved superpower status.

On the one hand, this rise to power was accomplished without free markets in much of the economy; without private property in the means of production; and with some significant power in workers' hands inside factories as well as with significant social spending on education, health, transport, housing, parks, sports, and cultural facilities.

On the other hand, this record of achievement correlated with a lack of many personal and political freedoms for the great mass of the population. Stalinism's intolerance suppressed argument and debate about the nature of Marxism and the class nature of Soviet society. Widespread microinefficiencies haunted and constrained state capitalist production and distribution of wealth. Macroeconomic planning, while it eliminated some of the economic wastes of private capitalist competition, also introduced a complex structure of costly and wasteful competition among enterprises, industries, and ministries for favorable decisions by central planners and the party apparatus.

The successes and failures of Soviet state capitalism occurred in the context of a society that included several different class structures. The complex, contradictory interaction of these different class structures helped to shape the uneven development of Soviet state capitalism. We borrow Marx's term "ancient" to designate an important class structure that existed *outside* state enterprises, especially in rural areas, throughout Soviet history. "Ancients" refers to relatively small, independent farmers or craft producers who individually appropriated the surplus labor that they themselves produced as individuals.[20]

This ancient class structure, widespread before 1917, expanded in the 1920s under Lenin's New Economic Policy (NEP), in industry and especially agriculture. Indeed, the NEP's market and property reforms directly encouraged this development of ancient producers. Their individually appropriated surpluses had been heavily taxed by the new state capitalist bureaucracy under the "War Communism" of 1918–1919. Those tax revenues helped to finance state capitalism and its eventual victory over the White Army. Ancient reactions to such heavy taxes had, in turn, provoked the resulting food crisis that threatened state capitalism's further development.

What emerged in the early 1920s followed Lenin's development strategy: encourage ancient class structure of production in agriculture to generate a food surplus to feed the growth of a state capitalist class structure in industry. In this way, Lenin hoped, ancients would voluntarily secure certain economic conditions of existence of state capitalism (as they had done involuntarily under War Communism). However, even as Lenin's strategy succeeded, the ancients' growing wealth and power tended to threaten and undermine state capitalism because of the class's different and often contending economic, political, and cultural agendas.[21]

The ancient class structure, responding positively to market and private property reforms, posed a fundamental challenge to the aims of the Soviet state. Ancient farmers could and sometimes did refuse to play the economic roles assigned to them by a state capitalism focused on industry. Indeed, one of the more interesting aspects of this challenge took the form of a private capitalism emerging transitionally out of the success of some ancient producers who hired those who had failed. The social formation changed as the class structural balance began to shift to the increasing development of private appropriation (whether ancient or small capitalist) and its associated institutions: private markets and property. Only some dozen years after the launching of state capitalism, its future was thought to be problematic.[22] The great paradox was that a communist class structure would suddenly be imposed upon agriculture to save state capitalism in industry.

Starting in the 1930s, Joseph Stalin transformed the relationship between state capitalism in industry and the ancient and private capitalist class structures in agriculture. The goal was to break the resistance of rural ancients and capitalists to Stalinist industrial policies. As is well known, the regime directly eliminated the richest ancients and the private capitalists in agriculture. Most importantly, it created, in the form of collective farms, an entirely new, decentralized *communist* class structure within the social formation. This class's communist nature rested on the fact that the producers of the surplus seem to have been identical to those who collectively appropriated it.[23] The mass of Soviet rural laborers moved to these farms (although widely retaining the ancient class structure in the "private plots" that coexisted within collective and state farms).

Shortly after collectivization, Stalin first limited the further development of communist class structures in the collective farms and then transformed their class structures yet again. First, state-administered prices of agricultural and industrial products were turned against the collective farms. The prices for industrial goods sent to rural areas were raised relative to the agricultural goods for which they were exchanged. This policy effectively squeezed resources out of agricultural communism and made them available to support and expand state capitalist industries. Similarly, the state established machine tractor stations (MTS's) that charged high fees to the collective farms for the use of the increasingly necessary tractors. The additional revenues from these pricing and tractor policies enabled state capitalist industry to develop more quickly than state capitalist industrial surpluses alone would have allowed.

However, to ensure such resource transfers, state policy soon shifted against continued dealings with the sometimes recalcitrant, decentralized communist class structure. Instead, state officials decided to reorganize the collective farms as agricultural analogues of state capitalist industry. They were to become more like (or merge into) the already existing huge state capitalist farms and thus more amenable to central controls. Thus, state industrial capitalism engendered a transition from communism to state capitalism in agriculture.

In summary, the social formation in the USSR exhibited shifting and contending class structures. A large-scale *state capitalism* predominated in industry after 1917 and came to agriculture shortly after collectivization. The numbers and social influence of *ancient* producers and *private capitalists* rose (1920s) and fell (1930s), depending on the particular historical circumstances. A *communism* in agriculture arose and vanished. The post-World War II Soviet social formation comprised a dominant state capitalism in both industry and agriculture in a complex coexistence with an ancient class structure in rural areas.[24]

The development of this social formation generated a crisis in the 1980s. Today's proposed solutions resemble those proposed for the crisis of 1921. Where the latter yielded the NEP—market and property reforms encouraging the rise of private capitalism and ancients—the current crisis moves in the same direction.

THE LATEST CRISIS OF SOVIET STATE CAPITALISM

We may analyze this crisis by focusing on the surplus value accruing to the COM from all state capitalist enterprises over recent decades. As noted, the COM distributed the surpluses with the aim of securing various economic, political, and cultural conditions required for the existence of Soviet state capitalism. Its successes and failures depended in part on the relation between the different distributions of surplus and the conditions they aimed to secure.

Remarkable economic growth can be traced to distributions for rapid capital accumulation in heavy industry.[25] On the other hand, this capital accumulation policy also constrained real wages through its bias of expanding heavy industry at the expense of consumer goods production. The contradictions that develop in such a situation may confront the state not only with the pent-up demands of frustrated consumers but also with limited or decreased surpluses that those same consumers may be willing to produce in their capacity as laborers.

The achievement of superpower status after World War II was made possible partly by distributions of the surplus to create a vast military complex. On the other hand, this complex also helped to produce a détente with the West and thus an end to the continuous sense of siege that had motivated work and sacrifice. It became increasingly difficult for the state to argue for continued real wage sacrifices and to maintain a climate of suppression of personal freedoms.

In claiming that the state had created a successful "socialism," Soviet spokespersons pointed to the extensive provision of "free" collective consumption: education, medical care, and so on. It was "free," of course, only because the state distributed a share of the surplus for such purposes. This distribution supplemented the relatively low real wages received by these workers; it expanded their collective ("public") consumption at the same time that their individual ("private") consumption was being constrained.[26] The contradiction looming in this arrangement concerned the very identification of socialism with the provision of such collective consumption. When other urgent demands on the surplus pressured the COM to consider reduced distributions for collective consumption, that reduction proved very difficult because it would appear as a reversal or betrayal of the commitment to socialism. Finally, the USSR's economic record and superpower status depended in part on vast party and state bureaucracies sustained by the COM's distribution of surplus to them. Yet this distribution also helped create a swollen officialdom that bred economic inefficiencies, corruption, and widespread resentment of official powers and privileges.

Thus, while the COM's surplus distributions financed the successes of Soviet state capitalism, they also contributed to the contradictions, the escalating problems, that describe the crisis of the 1980s. Demands on the surplus grew from immensely costly pressures of Cold War competition with the United States, notwithstanding détente, as well as from costly new industrial technologies. An increasingly restive population demanded the growth in consumption that had been promised but too long deferred.[27] More pressures on state and party bureaucracies to manage a rapidly growing and changing economic and political system with a population making new demands likewise called for more of the COM's surplus to pay for more bureaucrats deploying more costly management systems. The crisis exploded as the diverse demands on the surplus exceeded the surplus that workers were able and willing to produce. The COM, the state, and the party faced the dilemma of an insufficiency of surplus to sustain the continued existence of state capitalism. They had either to find new sources of surplus or else preside over the demise of their state capitalism (understood, of course, as socialism).

One conceivable solution was to extract more surplus from workers in state capitalist enterprises by lowering their wages while requiring the same work and/or by drawing more workers (especially women and rural people generally) into industry. However, the first alternative threatened to unleash anger and resistance that were as problematical as the insufficiency of the surplus, while the latter possibility had already been exhausted. Similarly, accelerating exhortations to Soviet workers to greater effort yielded meager results.

Nor was it possible to cut distributions of surplus to some recipients in favor of others. Capital accumulation, military production, bureaucracy, and collective consumption had sedimented into virtually unmovable institutions. The system had hit gridlock. It could not extract more surplus, yet its surplus no longer sufficed to secure its conditions of existence. Across the 1970s and 1980s, the erosion of those conditions undermined the quantity of surplus produced. This decrease, in turn, deepened the insufficiency of the surplus, which further undercut the conditions of existence. The downward spiral proved beyond the control of the leaders. A general crisis seemed at hand.

It was and is deemed to be a general crisis of socialism rather than state capitalism. Gorbachev and Yeltsin moved to solve the crisis by a transition to "the" alternative, to their socialism, namely private capitalism. Here, then, the historically familiar oscillation between private and state capitalisms displays yet another particular incarnation disguised as a swing from socialism to capitalism. And, of course, the enthusiasts of this particular oscillation celebrate its virtues once again in the standard hyperbole of how it will ensure greater democracy and prosperity.

The Marxist issue, however, remains on the agenda now as it did in 1917. When, where, how, and why will a crisis of either state or private capitalism result not in a transition from one to the other but rather in a revolution to communism?

notes

1. In Marxian theory as we understand and use it, surplus labor is defined in relation to necessary labor. The latter is the amount of labor needed to produce the goods and services that make up the historically determined standard of living of the laborer. Surplus labor is the amount of labor performed in excess of necessary labor. The fruits of surplus labor may accrue to the laborers or to others

who may consume and/or distribute them. The social organization of who produces, receives, distributes, and finally obtains the fruits of surplus labor is what is meant by a society's class structure. This structure can take various forms: slave, feudal, capitalist, ancient, and communist are among the forms that Marx distinguished.

2. The basic differences between our notion of state capitalism and the power-based concepts of other commentators who have used the term is presented in Resnick and Wolff (1993).

3. For Marx, "The rate of surplus value is therefore an exact expression for the degree of exploitation" (1967a, 218). Exploitation refers *not to* the power or domination relations between capitalists and productive laborers but rather to the *class relations*, the relations of production and appropriation of the laborer's surplus labor. Power relations are among the causes and effects of exploitation (as are, say, cultural relations), but they are distinct from the class relations.

4. This surplus-labor approach to class leaves open the question of how power over the size and distribution of the surplus is distributed. In all class structures, different social groups have varying and often contested powers of that sort. However, power over the size and distribution of surplus is a different matter from the specific social organization (who produces it, to whom does it accrue, by whom is it distributed, etc.) of surplus production and distribution per se. In short, power and surplus labor condition one another—in different ways depending on the particulars of how both are organized and their social contexts—but that is no warrant for collapsing them into one identity.

5. A large literature conceptualizes worker self-management as the antithesis of capitalism (for examples, see Sirianni 1982, who identifies this as socialism, and Vanek 1975, 11–36, who does not). This concept strikes us as another conflation of power analysis with surplus labor analysis. Who manages the labor process is, for us, a different matter from how surplus labor is produced and distributed. Whether workers manage their own labor is a separate issue from whether they collectively receive and distribute the fruits of their own surplus labor. Worker self-management is the antithesis of management by others; it is not the antithesis of workers producing surplus for others.

6. Space limitations prevent us from considering here such related possibilities as (1) state-owned productive properties being distributed by plan or by market to private capitalist enterprises and (2) various patterns of competition arising among and between state and private capitalist enterprises, state and private

owners of productive property, and state planning agencies and state enterprises. A systematic analysis of state capitalism would have to investigate these and other variations.

7. It is possible that the state or the workers or both will establish enterprises in which the producers of surplus will themselves receive and distribute that surplus. Such actions would replace capitalist with communist class structures. However, that is neither a necessary consequence of anticapitalist upsurges nor a necessary evolution of state capitalism. Whether the establishment of communist class structures is an outcome or even a goal of revolutionaries depends on the social context of their activities, including which variant of Marxist theory, if any, they embrace.

8. John Hicks (1969, 2, 9–24, 160–167) presents a parallel notion of oscillations between market and state. He admits the influence of Marx upon his argument and tangentially uses a concept of surplus labor, although not as we do.

9. Depending on historical conditions, state capitalist enterprises may be allowed greater or lesser autonomy from central planning and control authorities, greater or lesser freedom to compete with one another. We do *not* make the degrees of such autonomy or competitiveness or the extent of markets the indices of capitalism versus socialism, as do others: see Sweezy as against Bettelheim (Sweezy and Bettelheim 1971, 34ff.) and Hilferding (1950).

10. Such oscillations can and often have occurred at the level of an industry, rather than an entire economy. Moreover, since each phase of such oscillations is affected by the phases that preceded it, the oscillations occur between continuously changing state and private forms.

11. Carole Biewener uses a class analytical approach to discuss (1987, 1990) how "power relations" and Keynesian economic management rather than class came to define French socialism.

12. There have also been shorter-lived shifts within these broader movements: for example, Lenin's 1921 New Economic Policy. Similar reverse shifts may lie in the future of East European countries as their experiments in private capitalism encounter all manner of obstacles, difficulties, and reactions. Finally, there is evidence of comparable shifts in China, too (Hinton 1990).

13. Thus Lenin in 1921: "We must first set to work in this small-peasant country to build solid gangways to socialism by way of state capitalism. Otherwise we shall never get to communism." (1961, p. 696).

14. Valuable research assistance in regard to who in the USSR were appropriators

and distributors of surplus labor was provided by Allan MacNeill. Particularly helpful among the various materials consulted were Gregory (1990), Lane (l985a, 1985b), Hough and Fainsod (1979), Millar (1981, 1990), Conyngham (1973), Granick (1954, 1960), Spulber (1969), Berliner (1957, 1976), Gorlin (1985), Bettelheim (1976, 1978), Davis and Scase (1985), and Richman (1965). Of course, as in all social formations, different class structures coexisted. In the text, we will briefly comment on important noncapitalist class structures inside the USSR that significantly influenced the history of its state capitalism.

15. For further elaboration of what is a communist society from a surplus labor perspective, see our "Communism: Between Class and Classless" (1988).

16. For example, in reference to the role of Soviet politics in economics, Nove (1989, viii) claims,"Being for most of the period in command of the major part of economic life, the politicians were, for most of their waking hours, the board of directors of the great firm U.S.S.R. Ltd." In discussing the Soviet economic bureaucracy, Gregory (1990, 52) writes, "The Soviet economic bureaucracy is headed by the Council of Ministers of the USSR, which serves as the board of directors of the bureaucracy."

17. "The USSR Council of Ministers (Soviet Ministrov SSSR) is the highest oversight and executive committee of the Soviet economic bureaucracy. It is responsible for the enactment of the economic policies of the Communist Party by the state bureaucracy" (Gregory 1990, 25). Also see Kerblay (1983, chaps. 7, 10) and Hough and Fainsod (1979, chaps. 10 and 11).

18. Political processes overdetermine socially necessary labor time in a private capitalism operating with markets as well. The power wielded by board members in private capitalist enterprises helps to constitute the matrix of input-output coefficients operating there. However, a difference does exist between the effectivity of politics operating in these two different kinds of capitalisms. In a private capitalism with markets, the process of private exchange exists in conjunction with the politics of board members, while it is absent in the state capitalism discussed. Hence the absence of markets (the presence of state planning) in the USSR helps to bestow a particular kind of effectivity on political processes there that is different from that operating in a capitalism in which private markets operate.

19. Parallel to all social entities, value, surplus value, and profit rate in Soviet state capitalism reflected the specific configuration of processes existing in that society. They reflected, for example, the COM's understanding of the diverse tech-

nologies available at any moment to produce wealth as well as the complex pressures on them to choose among such technologies. Some of these pressures emanated from various state agencies that pushed the COM to adopt a strategy more conducive to a full employment ethic than one of minimizing costs; other pressures pushed it to secure the needs of a particular ethnic region, even if that strategy meant more rather than less labor was used to produce wealth; still other pressures pushed it to prolong the work day so as to increase the surplus to finance an expanded capital accumulation. Whatever the involved agencies and their respective aims, the point is that they produced a complex, shifting interaction among politics, culture, and economics that together overdetermined what we refer to as the administered value of a commodity.

20. In the case of the USSR, these "ancients" often have been referred to as independent or individual peasants (Chayanov 1966). In economic history literature generally, the terms "independent production" or "petty mode of production" are more common. For a systematic treatment of the Marxian notion of ancients, see Gabriel (1990).

21. One difference between the two class structures was underscored by the market and property reforms initiated in and by the NEP. Whereas ancients produced wealth for a market and owned their own means of production, state capitalists did not. Another difference was represented by the individualistic ideology of the ancient versus the claimed socialist ideology of what was in fact state capitalism.

22. The well-known Soviet industrialization debate in the 1920s was over what to do in regard to these contending class structures: whether state capitalism ("industry") or private ancients/small capitalists ("agriculture") should be encouraged or whether a balance should be struck between them.

23. Our notion of the collective as communist is very much influenced by our interpretation of Davies (1980), particularly our understanding of who were the first receivers and distributors of the surplus produced in collective farms. Although the collective seemed to appropriate the surplus that it produced, the state used its considerable power to direct members in how that appropriated surplus was to be distributed, i.e., how much of it was to go to taxes, accumulation, rents for equipment, various funds, and so forth. This political issue of who wielded power over the distribution of the surplus, however, is different from the class issue of who were the first appropriators and distributors of it.

24. Inside Soviet households, class structures of production (of cooked meals, clean-

ing services, clothing, etc.) functioned as well. Surpluses were produced and distributed. Complex and contradictory relationships between household and enterprise class structures (these were sometimes identical) played their role in shaping Soviet state capitalism. In a forthcoming work, we include a detailed analysis of household class structures; space limitations prevent that here.

25. Extensive surplus growth, capital/accumulation may be characterized by an expansion in the mass of surplus value accomplished by an expansion of productive labor. Our guess is that the capitalist rate of exploitation also increased because of attempts to increase the intensity of labor and prolong the work day in Soviet factories, especially in the 1930s and 1940s, and because of a rise in agricultural productivity—first in ancient, then in communist, and finally in state capitalist farms—that likely resulted in a net fall in the value of labor power, despite some increase in the food wage.

26. Such a strategy in the state capitalism of the USSR was the opposite of what took place in the private capitalisms of Western Europe and particularly of the United States. There, higher private consumption out of higher real wages was offset by smaller public consumption. In the 1980s this higher private consumption achieved by Western private capitalist nations—promoted by the Western media and state alike as a major index of the success of capitalism over socialism—became an issue of contention for Russian workers. Often lost in the controversy was the collective consumption received by such workers, i.e., it was overlooked until such times as its continuation became threatened.

27. Détente also introduced Soviet citizens to the much higher levels of private consumption in the West, often via advertising that implicitly valued private over collective consumption.

references

Berliner, Joseph. 1957. *Factory and Manager in the USSR*. Cambridge: Harvard University Press.

————. 1976. *The Innovation Decision in Soviet Industry*. Cambridge: MIT Press.

Bettelheim, Charles. 1976. *Class Struggles in the USSR First Period: 1917–1923*. New York and London: Monthly Review Press.

————. 1978. *Class Struggles in the USSR Second Period: 1923–1930*. New York and London: Monthly Review Press.

Biewener, Carole. 1987. "Class and Socialist Politics in France." *Review of Radical Political Economics* 19, 2 (June), 61–76.

––––––. 1990. "Loss of a Socialist Vision in France." *Rethinking Marxism* 3, 3&4 (September), 12–26.

Chayanov, A. V. 1966. *The Theory of Peasant Economy.* Homewood, Illinois: Richard D. Irwin, Inc.

Conyngham, William. 1973. *Industrial Management in the Soviet Union.* Stanford: Hoover University Press.

Davies, R. W. 1980. *The Soviet Collective Farm, 1929–1930.* Cambridge, MA: Harvard University Press.

Davis, Howard, and Richard Scase. 1985. *Western Capitalism and State Socialism.* Oxford and New York: Basil Blackwell.

Gabriel, Satya. 1990. "Ancients: A Marxian Theory of Self-Exploitation." *Rethinking Marxism* 3, 1 (Spring), 85–106.

Gorlin, Alice. 1985. "The Power of Soviet Industrial Ministers." *Soviet Studies* 37, 3, 353–370.

Granick, David. 1954. *Management of the Industrial Firm in the USSR.* New York: Columbia University Press.

––––––. 1960. *The Red Executive.* Garden City, N.Y.: Doubleday and Co., Inc.

Gregory, Paul. 1990. *Restructuring the Soviet Economic Bureaucracy.* Cambridge: Cambridge University Press.

Hicks, John. 1969. *A Theory of Economic History.* London: Oxford University Press.

Hilferding, Rudolf. 1950. "State Capitalism or Totalitarian State Economy." In Julian Sternberg, ed. *Verdict of Three Decades.* New York: Duell, Sloane and Pierce, pp. 446–453.

Hinton, William. 1990. *The Great Reversal: The Privatization of China, 1978–1989.* New York: Monthly Review Press.

Hough, Jerry, and Merle Fainsod. 1979. *How the Soviet Union Is Governed.* Cambridge, MA: Harvard University Press.

Kerblay, Basile. 1983. *Modern Soviet Society.* New York: Pantheon Books.

Lane, David. 1985a. *Soviet Economy and Society.* Oxford: Basil Blackwell.

––––––. 1985b. *State and Politics in USSR.* New York: New York University Press.

Lenin, V. I. 1961. *Selected Works,* Volume 3. Moscow: Foreign Languages Publishing House.

Marx, Karl. 1967a. *Capital,* Volume 1. New York: International Publishers.

––––––. 1967b. *Capital,* Volume 2. New York: International Publishers.

Millar, James. 1981. *The ABCs of Soviet Socialism.* Urbana and Chicago: University of Illinois Press.

———. 1990. *The Soviet Economic Experiment.* Urbana and Chicago: University of Illinois Press.

Nove, Alec. 1989. *An Economic History of the U.S.S.R.* Harmondsworth and New York: Penguin Books.

Resnick, Stephen, and Richard Wolff. 1986. "What Are Class Analyses?" In Paul Zarembka, ed. *Research in Political Economy,* Volume 9. Greenwich and London: JAI Press, pp. 1–32.

———. 1988. "Communism;: Between Class and Classless." *Rethinking Marxism* 1, 1 (Spring), 14–42.

———. 1992. "Radical Economics: A Tradition of Theoretical Differences." In Bruce Roberts and Susan Feiner, eds., *Radical Economics.* Boston: Kluwer Academic Publishers.

———. 1993. "State Capitalism in the USSR: A High Stakes Debate." *Rethinking Marxism* 6, 2 (Summer), 46–68.

Richman, Barry. 1965. *Soviet Management.* Englewood Cliffs, N.J.: Prentice-Hall.

Sirianni, Carmen J. 1982. *Workers Control and Socialist Democracy: The Soviet Experience.* London: Verso.

Spulber, Nicolas. 1969. *The Soviet Economy.* New York: W.W. Norton and Co., Inc.

Sweezy, Paul M., and Charles Bettelheim. 1971. *On the Transition to Socialism.* New York: Monthly Review Press.

Vanek, Jaroslav, ed. 1975. *Self-Management: Economic Liberation of Man.* Harmondsworth and Baltimore : Penguin.

SU SHAOZHI

rethinking marxism in the light of chinese reforms

In the spring of 1989 the democracy movement in mainland China was crushed by the Chinese authorities. Later, a series of communist regimes in East European countries and the former Soviet Union collapsed. These events are used as proof by the pundits and the press of "the end of Marxism."[1] Some hold that the peoples in the former socialist countries identified Stalinism with Marxism and discarded both.[2] Others insist that "Marx not be held responsible for the bad applications of his theories (e.g., for Stalinism).[3] Regardless of one's attitude toward Marxism, it cannot be denied that Marxism has received a heavy blow. The vitality of Marxism has not ended, but nowhere does Marxism retain the status as the master discourse that it once enjoyed.[4] Yet Marx's reputation as a great thinker has continued to grow, and his historical influence cannot be neglected. It is therefore still possible to assess Marxism with new insight. Through critical analysis, we can still find some useful ideas in Marxist political and academic theories. Marxism still deserves to be probed seriously. The reforms in China since late 1978 furnish a practical backdrop for a critical analysis of Marxism.

MARXIST MATERIAL INTERPRETATION OF HISTORY
HAS NOT BEEN FALSIFIED BY THE CHINESE REFORMS

Friedrich Engels remarked that the material interpretation of history and the concept of surplus value are two of the great discoveries of Karl Marx.[5] The material interpretation of history is the core of the basic principles put forth by Marx.[6] To confirm or negate a material interpretation of history is to confirm or negate the basic problems of Marxism. Analyses of Marxism around the world always revolve around this issue. In the preface to *A Contribution to the Critique of Political Economy*, Marx presents a classic explanation of the material interpretation of history. I need not quote it here in full because it is too long and most scholars know it quite well. There are many different annotations. According to Marx himself and Engels's additional remarks, I will try to sum them up as follows:

• Society's relations of production correspond to a definite stage of development in society's productive forces. Such relations of production will promote the development of the productive forces. Otherwise, the relations of production will impede productive forces, and the productive forces will eventually break through such a fetter. The relations of production must be changed in order to allow further development of productive forces.

• The economic structure of society, constituted by its relations of production, is the real foundation of society. It is the base upon which legal and political structures are built and to which correspond definite forms of social consciousness, the superstructure of the society. The superstructure, which corresponds to the base, will function to consolidate the base.

• The productive forces decide the relations of production, which decides the superstructure. But the factors of the relations of production and superstructure will influence the development of history, often greatly. So, among productive forces, relations of production (base) and social consciousness (superstructure) will influence one another. The development of human society is, in the final analysis, conditioned by the development of productive forces. This is what G. A. Cohen summed up as (1) the primary thesis and (2) base/superstructure thesis.[7]

According to those principles, Marx reached a scientific conclusion: "No social order ever perishes before all the productive forces for which there is room in it have developed; and new, higher relations of production never appear before the material conditions of their existence have matured in the womb of the old society itself."[8]

Although "Western Marxists" have opposed [this idea] with virtual unanimity,[9] the history of the Chinese Communist Party (CCP), seeking truth from reality, proves the validity of Marx's material interpretation of history. The successes of the CCP are based on this theory, and the failures of the CCP are a result of neglecting it.

The most successful period of the CCP was during the period of new democratic revolution (1921–1949). During that period, the CCP, under the semicolonial and semifeudal conditions of the old China, called not for socialist revolution but rather for new democratic revolution and for the implementation of new democracy during a relatively long historical period. The CCP received the support of the Chinese people and achieved the victory of the new democratic revolution.

In the early years after the founding of the People's Republic of China (PRC), the leaders of the CCP were relatively modest and prudent. They were objective, starting from reality and following a line based on Marx's material interpretation of history. They accomplished the task of land reform and the recovery of the national economy in three years. It is a pity that the good times did not last long. The accomplishments of the CCP seemed too quick and too easy. Among other problems, the CCP leaders became too arrogant and eager for the transition to socialism. They deviated from the material interpretation of history.

In September 1952, Mao Zedong put forward the "general line of the transition period of the CCP." Mao wanted to give up the new democracy and was eager for the transition to socialism, all at a time when the social force of production was still very backward and the market economy was still undeveloped. A "Leftist" line was beginning to form and becoming more severe day by day. The crux of the Leftist line was that it transcended the stages of historical development, ignoring objective laws and overestimating the role of subjective initiative. Basically, it deviated from Marx's material interpretation of history.

The CCP and Mao Zedong advanced further and further along the Leftist line. During the Cultural Revolution, Mao almost completely departed from the material interpretation of history. He held that in the relationship between politics and economics, politics was primary; in the relationship between consciousness and being, consciousness was primary; and in the relationship between the base and the superstructure, the superstructure was primary. He believed that the motive force in development was not the economy—not the productive forces—but politics, class struggle, and moral forces. He not only denounced economic interests, economic measures, and even economic laws, but he also criticized the development of productive forces as "productivism" (*wei shenchanli lun*). This departure shows that Mao had become an absolute idealist, relying on voluntarism and standing for the antithesis of Marx's material interpretation of history. The voluntarism that prevailed during the Cultural Revolution brought China to the verge of economic bankruptcy and was a great disaster for the Chinese people.

We can conclude that the history of the CCP, from its early successes to later failures, is a history of Mao's goal to replace Marx's material interpretation of history with voluntarism. However, after the death of Mao and the end of the Cultural Revolution the CCP began to implement reforms. Chinese reforms have not negated Marx's material interpretation of history. On the contrary, Chinese reforms can be explained by the material interpretation of history.

The necessity of reform in China is basically due to the fact that the relations of production have hindered the productive forces. Over the past thirty years the CCP pursued an increasingly Leftist line. It held that, with respect to the relations of production, the "higher" the better. "Higher" referred to the level and the scale of ownership, with state ownership as the primary, or highest level. State ownership is higher than collective ownership, the big collective ownership is higher than the small collective ownership, and the small collective ownership is higher than individual ownership. Following Mao's theory of continuously changing relations of production to promote the development of productive forces, CCP officials were eager for the transition to state ownership.

In fact, in the relations of production, greater public ownership is not better.

We cannot determine which ownership is lower or which is higher. We can only say which ownership corresponds to the nature and level of productive forces and which does not. Only that ownership which corresponds to the nature and level of productive forces can promote the development of the economy. Because the relations of production during Mao's time did not fit this requirement, they could not promote development but only hindered it.

The CCP under the direction of Mao's ideas of Leftist utopian socialism often neglected the role of economic laws. For example, early in 1958 Mao emphasized the abolition of bourgeois rights. He held that the eight ranks of the wage system, monetary exchange, "to each according to his work," and so on, were no different from the tenets of the old society. They all belonged to the category of bourgeois rights and deserved to be abolished. He always tried to achieve his ideal communism from the distribution and consumption sphere. In his later years, as Mao increased his criticism of productivism, China sank into serious crisis, both economic and political.

The people wanted a change. They asked for the abolition of voluntarism and for the development of the productive forces and the economy. This demand is the core reason for the reform in mainland China. Not only has the necessity of reform in China proved the validity of the material interpretation of history, but so has the experience of all of the other former socialist countries. The failure of those regimes is due to the neglect and negation of the scientific conclusion of Marx's material interpretation of history: "No social order ever perishes before all the productive forces for which there is room in it have developed, and new, higher relations of production never appear before the material conditions of their existence had matured in the womb of the old society itself."[10] In opposition to this idea, all of those regimes were based on Lenin's premature notion that capitalism was moribund and on Stalin's hasty declaration of the establishment of socialism. All of the socialist regimes needed to return to a Marxist material interpretation of history and implement reforms.

The essence of the economic reforms in those countries has been to reestablish correspondence between the relations of production and the productive forces. The relations of production should correspond to the nature and level of the productive forces, namely, to produce the prerequisites of socialized large production and a fully developed market economy; to restore what had been abolished, such as the multiple ownership of means of production—"to each according to his work"—and to learn advanced science and technology, business administration, and financial systems from the capitalist countries. In brief, the task of reform is to move from a command economy to a market economy in order to make up the missed lessons of capitalism.

The economic reforms in mainland China have been relatively successful because China recognizes this truth: the market economy provides better development and a more abundant supply of goods. But because the leaders of the older generation continue to uphold a one-party dictatorship, political reform cannot keep pace with the progress of economic reform. The stagnation and even retardation of political reform becomes an obstacle to economic reform and even reform in general. Political reform should keep pace with economic reform. This equalization is a requirement of the material interpretation of history regarding the relationship between the base and superstructure.

Erik Olin Wright, Andrew Levine, and Elliott Sober, in their book *Reconstructing Marxism*, make a very interesting point that pertains to the collapse of former socialist countries in Eastern Europe and the Soviet Union.

> It is ironic that the collapse of authoritarian state socialisms should be a stimulus for proclamations of the "end of Marxism" as a social theory by anti-Marxists, and for self-doubt by Marxists and their sympathizers. From the perspective of *classical* Marxism, the collapse of these regimes and their return to a "normal" path of capitalist development is eminently predictable. If anything, the long detour from the Bolshevik Revolution to *perestroika* was a challenging anomaly to historical materialism. The restoration of capitalist property relations in relatively underdeveloped industrial economies, on the other hand, actually corroborates the theory. If Marx was right, socialism is not achievable until the forces of production have developed massively under capitalism, and further development is fettered by capitalist property relations. The attempt to construct revolutionary socialism by an act of will in violation of this "law of history" was therefore doomed from the start.[11]

The reality of Chinese reform adds further weight to Wright, Levine, and Sober's point and proves the validity of Marx's material interpretation of history.

THE PRACTICE OF CHINESE REFORM: A CHALLENGE TO MARXISM

The reforms in China, as well as the reforms in the other communist countries, represent a redistribution of political and economic interests. Obstacles and struggles in the process of reform are unavoidable. Ideological obstacles and struggles are especially significant. The conservatives often oppose the reform in China under the banner of Marxism-Leninism and Mao Zedong Thought, much of which is based on a misunderstanding of Lenin, Stalin, and Mao. There are numerous such misunderstandings, and a book could be written on this subject alone. Of course, some such misunderstandings can be traced back to the expositions of Marx himself. Thus, it is really necessary to analyze and criticize the actual thought of Marx. I will try to examine the expositions of Marx and Engels in light of the practice of Chinese reforms. The theoretical system of Marx is too extensive to analyze in full; thus, I have only chosen those aspects that deeply influence the practice of the Chinese reforms.

Marx and Engels lived in the era of the beginning and early mature stage of capitalism. What Marx was most concerned with and studied in depth were the contradictions and the development of capitalism. Through ruthless critical analysis he explored the future of capitalism and advanced the theory of the historical task of the working class. His analysis has had a great influence on modern views of history, sociology, economics, and literary criticism. Ideas traceable to Marx's writings are reflected in current policies in the capitalist countries, such as those of social welfare, the environment, securities-law enforcement, and so on.[12]

Marx did not attempt to study a future society, nor did he intend to construct a blueprint for it. Through an analysis of the contradictions of capitalism, he expressed some tentative ideas about future society, but he did not fully prove these ideas, so his thoughts unavoidably had some utopian elements. Marx wrote very little concerning socialism and communism. If we can say that Marx established a comprehensive theory of socialist revolution, we cannot conclude that he established a comprehensive theory of socialist construction as well.[13]

Marxists after Marx ossified and dogmatized Marx's tentative ideas about socialism and communism and took them as a fixed model. They endeavored to construct socialism according to this model. Just as Norberto Bobbio has said, "They had neglected the task of constructing a feasible form of socialism, capable of empirical scrutiny, and engaged instead in a scholastic repetition and exegesis of the classic works of founding fathers—an occupation that has blinded them to the practical shortcomings of their texts."[14] The result is a contradiction between ideas and practice.

Marx's ossified theories have been used by the Chinese conservatives as a theoretical weapon to oppose the reforms. In general, the following represent the basic problems.

ON CRISIS IN SOCIALIST SOCIETY

The idea of crisis in socialist society does not represent any part of Marxist thought. Marx and Engels held that the basic contradiction of capitalism was the contradiction between the socialization of production and the private ownership of capitalism. Once ownership is transferred from private to public, the contradictions and crises of capitalism will definitely be solved. Marx and Engels assumed that future society would develop as a harmonious whole, no longer riven by class conflicts, where the "associated producers" would act collectively (and somehow spontaneously) to promote the common good.[15]

This idea is based on: (1) Marx's naively optimistic opinion of "human nature" in future society; and (2) Marx's overly optimistic appraisal of the influence of the transition from private to public ownership—the "fetish of public ownership." From these points, Marx often reached many overly optimistic and utopian positions. As Bobbio has said, "Marx sought to correct a pessimistic view of human nature with an over-optimistic account of life under communism, where a combination of altruism, abundant resources, maximum co-ordination and agreement concerning human interest would prevail."[16]

The reality has proven quite different from Marx's assessment. In mainland China, after the realization of public ownership, both before and during the process of reform, contradictions, and even openly antagonistic contradictions and crises continued. Crises are not only particular but also general; not only are they political and economic, but they are also social, moral, and ideological.[17] In 1989, after ten years of reform, a general crisis emerged, which then developed into the general democracy movement. The CCP regime repressed the movement by military force, shocking the entire world. In the communist countries of Eastern Europe and the former Soviet Union, after their socialist transformation, crises never stopped even after the collapse of the communist regimes.

ON PLANNING AND THE MARKET IN SOCIALIST SOCIETY

The overly optimistic appraisal of human nature in socialist society and the "fetish of public ownership" resulted in Marx's idea that once public ownership replaced private ownership, there would be no conflict of individual interests, and planned management would be easy to implement in socialist society. Engels made this point when he said:

> In communist society, when the interests of individuals are not opposed but identical, competition ceases.... Private appropriation, the goal of the individual to enrich himself, will disappear in the production and distribution of the necessities of life, and so will trade crises disappear by themselves. In communist society, it will be easy to know production and consumption. Since it is known how much an average individual needs, it will easily be estimated how much a certain number of individuals need, and since production will no longer be controlled by private owners, but by the community and its administration, it will be easy to *regulate production in accordance* with the requirement.[18]

Marx assumed, therefore, that socialism was incompatible with the market. In socialist society, planned production (a planned economy) will replace the anarchy of production and the market economy; that is, the economy would be controlled through planning and a centralized administration. Marx assumed that in communist society there would be no money-capital. He said, "If we conceive society as being not capitalistic, but communistic, there will be no money-capital at all in the first place, nor the disguises cloaking the transactions arising on account of it. The question then comes down to the need of society to calculate beforehand how much labor, means of production and means of subsistence it can invest."[19]

Although this idea was never tested for its feasibility, it was accepted by the leaders of all communist countries. In fact, such an idea had been tested in the "War Communism" period during the early days of Russian revolution, and it ended in a miserable failure. But the communists never learned from such lessons. The model of a highly concentrated, unified planned economy was accepted by all of the countries under communist rule as a standard model to be followed. Such a planned economy excludes commodities, markets, and competition; it negates a market economy, controls too much and is too rigid, and results in subjectivism and bureaucraticism. The entire national economy is monopolized by the state. Monopoly results in corruption, and the social economy loses its vitality. Everyone knows that in any society the relationship among production, distribution, exchange, and consumption is very complicated. The variety of commodities is in the millions and hundreds of millions. It is too great even to be manipulated by a supercomputer. Oskar Lange's idea of "computer socialism" is unrealistic. The idea that the needs of society can be calculated beforehand and that there are no disguises cloaking the economic relationship is too utopian. The result will be huge wastes, losses, scarcity of goods, and stagnation of economic progress. These are the reasons that all of the communist countries need reform, with no exception.

If a communist country wants to reform, first it should reassess the relationship between planning and the market and discard the utopian ideas discussed above. It should be understood that a market economy is an essential prerequisite for the development of a social economy. In an underdeveloped country, the full development of a market economy is especially needed. It is wrong to rely on the plan as opposed to the market. On the contrary, the plan should make use of elements from the market economy. In short, the essence of economic reform in a communist country is the transition from a planned economy (strictly speaking, a command economy) to a market economy. Due to the fetters of dogmatism, however, it is not easy to recognize the validity of such an idea, and it is even more difficult to implement it.

During the tortuous road of economic reform, the Chinese authorities have slowly recognized this idea step by step. China first developed the idea of a "planned commodity economy," then the formula "the state regulates the market and the market guides the enterprises," and now the concept of "the socialist market economy."

The success or failure, and the extent of the success or failure, of the Chinese economic reforms, as well as those in other communist countries, depends on the degree of marketization. Reform without marketization will face a dead end. Therefore, the practice of the Chinese economic reforms has disproved the Marxist idea that there is no commodity, money, or market in socialist society.

ON CLASS, STATE, AND DEMOCRACY

Many scholars have assumed that political science is a weak link in the theoretical work of Marx. Umberto Cerroni stressed the general and persistent backwardness of Marxist studies in other branches of the social sciences, and above all in political science and in legal studies.[20]

One of the reasons for the lack of political science studies is Marx's theory of the withering away of the state. Since it was understood that the state will wither away, and the new state will exist only during the transition period, one would naturally pay less attention to the organization, laws, and administration of the state. Although Marx had painstakingly probed the case of the Paris Commune, the problems of political organization on a large scale cannot be solved by depending on the experiences of the Paris Commune. As a result, some important political science problems were not studied by Marx in detail. These include the following.

On the Theory of the State

Among Marx's grave omissions, as Louis Althusser has pointed out, was the lack of a theory of the state.[21] In fact, this absence is not literally the case, but Marx's theory of the state is far too generalized. The state is defined in Marx's famous thesis as an instrument of repression that serves the dominant class. In other words, Marx emphasized the coercive role of the state. In addition, he held that all states, by virtue of being states, are such that the transition from a bourgeois state to a proletarian state would simply be a transition from one dictatorship to another.[22] Marx's definition of the state is obviously too simple. Gramsci's major contribution to Marxist thought is his exploration of the fact that the domination of the ruling class is not only achieved by coercion but is also elicited by consent.[23]

From the praxis of China's reform, Marx's theory of the state should be revised to include the following features: (1) Marx's theory that the state is a set of repressive apparatuses, such that there is a direct relationship between the state and repression, needs to be revised. The aged leaders of the CCP are deeply influenced by this theory. They have made a fetish of using force, even violent force. They are willing to use force and even a military crackdown against any dissent and opposition. Since late 1978, after the implementation of the reforms, there have been many campaigns to repress dissent. In the end, the CCP regime used military force to repress the democracy movement in the Spring of 1989. (2) Marx's definition of the state does not explain the power struggle in China's leading group. Even after the implementation of the reforms, the power struggle in the Chinese leading group has continued. Neither does this definition explain the military conflicts among the former communist countries.

On Democracy

Since the founding of the PRC, the main historical lesson to be learned from the CCP is that it did not consciously establish democratic politics. The lack of democracy is a long-standing and huge error in all communist countries and is a basic reason for the disasters that these countries have suffered. Of course, the neglect of democracy in communist countries is mainly due to the nature of the communist parties themselves. The shortcomings of Marx's theory of democracy have a grave responsibility for this.

Some scholars argue that, Marx and Engels in fact paid great attention to democracy because in their "Communist Manifesto" they wrote, "The first step in the revolution by the working class, is to raise the proletariat to the position of ruling class, to win the battle of democracy."[24] However, Marx and Engels assumed that democracy is not an end but merely a means. As Engels later wrote:

> The proletariat too needs democratic forms for the seizure of political power but to it they are, like all political forms, mere means. But if today democracy is wanted as an end one must seek support in the peasantry and petty bourgeois, i.e., in classes that are in the process of dissolution and reactionary in relation to the proletariat as soon as they try to maintain themselves artificially. Furthermore, it must not be forgotten that precisely the democratic republic is the logical form of bourgeois rule.... And yet the democratic republic always remains the last form of bourgeois rule, that is it which goes to pieces."[25] Engels even mentioned, "Democracy is quite needless to the proletariat if it is not at once used as the means to further measures directly attacking private property and securing the existence of the proletariat.[26]

What Engels said about "further measures directly attacking private property and securing the existence of the proletariat" is eventually the function of proletariat dictatorship. Indeed, communist parties usually declare that proletariat dictatorship itself is socialist democracy. Marx and Engels never explored how to implement democracy in socialist and communist society. As Steven Lukes has written, "Marx never addressed the procedural issue of what forms of collective choice or decision-making should take place under communism, whether at the lower or higher stage."[27]

In my opinion, we cannot conclude that Marx and Engels opposed democracy in socialist and communist societies. Given Marx's optimistic assessment of human nature and his "fetish of public ownership" as a starting point, we should rather say that Marx and Engels took socialist democracy for granted. Thus, Marxists hold as a commonplace the idea that socialism will necessarily implement democracy. Based on the experience of China and the other communist countries, however, such a view is unrealistic.

Socialism does not necessarily need to be democratic. In socialism, it is just as easy to implement dictatorship as democracy. In fact, it is easier to implement dictatorship. First, until now the transition to socialism (in those societies that call themselves socialist) has only taken place through internal or external violence, and the original violence has been inherited by the ensuing system of government.[28] Second, public ownership in socialist society is in fact mainly state ownership. The control of the economy by the state has formed a state monopoly. In socialist society abuse of power is likely, especially in countries ruled by a communist party where the one-party dictatorship has prevailed. The party is the pillar of state power. The party-state, or party-cracy, is an insurmountable obstacle on the road to democracy. Therefore, once socialist society has implemented dictatorship, the successful transition to democracy is difficult.

On Class Struggle

In the "Communist Manifesto," Marx and Engels wrote at the beginning, "The history of all hitherto existing society is the history of class struggle." In the 1888 English edition, Engels added a note: "Precisely speaking, the history here referred to is the recorded history."[29] Thus, one-sidedness and oversimplification were avoided.

The same famous idea that class struggle is the driving force of history has been accepted by most Marxists without serious study. However, Karl Kautsky (1927) argued that some of the class struggles mentioned in the "Communist Manifesto" were in fact conflicts between status groups, and Marx and Engels's own observation was that precapitalist societies were all characterized by a "manifold gradation of ranks."[30] Since 1989, the overthrow of communist regimes has largely been the outcome of conflict between a distinctive ruling elite and a broad democratic movement rather than specific class conflict.

Even if we recognize that this idea is correct during the period of social revolution, it does not explain and resolve all of the development problems in every society. Mao Zedong had a one-sided understanding of this idea. He put forth the theory of class struggle in socialist society, saying that during the entire historical period of socialism, there would be struggles between two classes (proletariat and bourgeois), two roads (the socialist road and the capitalist road), and the fact that the danger of capitalist restoration would always exist. He said that everyone should take class struggle as the key link and that by grasping class struggle, everything will work well (*jieji douzheng yizhua jiulin*). He believed that every event in society is the reflection of class struggle. Every problem can be solved if we firmly grasp the idea of class struggle. Of course, following this idea into all aspects of political and social life will end in negative results. Since the founding of the PRC, many campaigns based on class struggle have resulted in heavy losses for China.

After the Cultural Revolution the CCP put forth a policy of considering economic construction as its main task, and it criticized and abolished the slogan of taking class struggle as the key link. But eventually many aged leaders of the CCP again became obsessed with class struggle as the key link. After the implementation of the reforms, the communist regime launched a campaign against spiritual pollution in 1983 and against bourgeois liberalization in 1987; a military crackdown on the democracy movement in 1989; and thereafter a campaign against "peaceful evolution." Such campaigns and struggle hindered the progress of reform and development. We must abolish these ideas of class struggle and return to a material interpretation of history, stressing the development of the forces of production.

CONCLUSION

Reform in China has, on the one hand, shown that the basic core of Marxist theory—the material interpretation of history—is still valid. Of course, this is a macroanalysis observation, and it is not applicable to every concrete and detailed event. On the other hand, the progress of reform has shown that we cannot expect that the thoughts of Marx and Engels can solve all problems, especially because there were many shortcomings and omissions in their ideas. We should reassess and reach a new understanding of Marxism based on praxis and modern science. Only through persistent examination, criticism, and constant revision can Marxism exist and develop and have a bright future.

notes

1. Stanley Aronowitz, *The Crisis of Historical Materialism* (Minneapolis: University of Minnesota Press, 1990), p. viii.

2. Ernest Mandel, "Socialism and the Future," *October Review* (in Chinese) (Hong Kong) 5/6, (1992), p. 20.

3. Norberto Bobbio, *Which Socialism?* (University of Minnesota Press, 1987), p. 105.

4. Aronowitz, *The Crisis of Historical Materialism*, p. xxiv.

5. Friedrich Engels, "Speech at the Graveside of Karl Marx," *Sosial-demokrat* (Zurich), March 1883.

6. As discussed in Milos Nicolic, "Ten Years of the International Roundtable of 'Socialism in the World,'" *Socialism in the World*, 52 (1988).

7. Erik Olin Wright, Andrew Levine, and Elliott Sober, *Reconstructing Marxism*. (London: Verso, 1992), pp. 16–17.

8. Karl Marx, *A Contribution to the Critique of Political Economy*, in *Socialist Thought: A Documentary History*, edited by Albert Fried et al., (New York: Doubleday, 1964) p. 298.

9. Wright et al. *Reconstructing Marxism*, p. 14.

10. Karl Marx, *A Contribution to the Critique of Political Economy* (Moscow: Progress Publishers), p. 21.

11. Wright et al., *Reconstructing Marxism*, p. 190.

12. Henry F. Myers, "Das Kapital: His Status Falls, His Shadow Persists: Marx's Critique of Capitalism Still Influences Events," *The Wall Street Journal*, May 25, 1991.

13. Yu Guanyuan developed this idea in China in 1983 and was criticized by orthodox conservatives.

14. Bobbio, *Which Socialism?* p. 6.

15. Tom Bottomore, "Crisis in Socialist Society," *A Dictionary of Marxist Thought*, 2nd ed. (Blackwell, 1991), p. 121.

16. Bobbio, *Which Socialism?* p. 5.

17. Su Shaozhi, "Rethinking Socialism in the Light of Chinese Reform," *China Information*, 5, 4 (Spring 1991), p. 17.

18. Engels, "Zwei Reden in Elberfeld," *Marx/Engels Werke*, Bd. 2, S. 539. See K. Marx, F. Engels, V. I. Lenin, *On Scientific Communism* (Moscow: Progress Publishers, 1967), p. 43.

19. Karl Marx, *Capital*, Vol. II (Moscow: Progress Publishers, 1962), p. 93. See *On Scientific Communism*, p. 156.

20. Bobbio, *Which Socialism?* p. 31.

21. Bobbio, *Which Socialism?* p. 172.

22. Bobbio, *Which Socialism?* p. 106.

23. Ralph Milband, "The State," *A Dictionary of Marxist Thought*, 2nd ed., p. 532.

24. Karl Marx, *The Communist Manifesto*, A Norton Critical Edition, edited by Frederic L. Bender (W. W. Norton & Co., 1988), p. 74.

25. Engels to Lafargue, March 6, 1894, Karl Marx and Friedrich Engels, *Selected Correspondence* (Moscow: Foreign Publishing House, 1955).

26. Engels, "Grundsatze der Kommunismus," in Marx et al., *On Scientific Communism*, p. 253.

27. Steven Lukes, "Democracy," *A Dictionary of Marxist Thought*, 2nd ed., p. 133.

28. Bobbio, *Which Socialism?*, p. 98.

29. Marx, *The Communist Manifesto*, p. 55.

30. Marx, *The Communist Manifesto*, p. 55.

notes on contributors

Stephen Cullenberg, Department of Economics, the University of California, Riverside. Professor Cullenberg has written widely on Marxian economics and international political economy. He is the author of *The Falling Rate of Profit: Recasting the Marxian Debate*, and co-editor of *Marxism in the Postmodern Age*. He is an editor of the journal *Rethinking Marxism*. His forthcoming books include *The New Internationalism* and an edited volume entitled *Postmodernism, Economics and Knowledge*.

Ashot Galoian, Department of Political History, Yerevan State University, Republic of Armenia. Professor Galoian received his doctorate in Political History from the Yerevan State University. He is the author of numerous articles on social and political revolution in Russia, Armenia and Transcaucasia. He has also written on the "national problem" in the former Soviet Union.

Keith Griffin, Department of Economics, the University of California, Riverside. Professor Griffin was formerly President of Magdalen College, Oxford. He has served as an adviser and consultant to various governments, international agencies, and academic institutions in Asia, Africa, and Latin America. He is the author of *Alternative Strategies for Economic Development*, editor of *The Economy of Ethiopia*, and co–editor of *The Distribution of Income in China*, among other books. He is currently doing research on measures to alleviate poverty in Mongolia.

Abdul JanMohamed, Department of English, the University of California, Berkeley. Professor Jan Mohamed is the author of *Manichean Aesthetics: The Politics of Literature in Colonial Africa*, and editor (with David Lloyd) of *The Nature and Content of Minority Discourse*. He was convenor of the first collaborative research group on Minority Discourse at the University of California Humanities Research Institute.

Douglas Kellner, Department of Philosophy, the University of Texas at Austin. Professor Kellner is the author of *Herbert Marcuse and the Crisis of Marxism; Critical Theory, Marxism, and Modernity; Jean Baudrillard: From Marxism to Postmodernism and Beyond;* and with Steven Best, *Postmodern Theory; Critical Interrogations,* as well as other books and articles on social theory, culture, and politics.

Azizur Rahman Khan, Department of Economics, the University of California, Riverside. Professor Khan received his Ph.D. in economics from Cambridge University. He has written numerous articles on development economics, proverty and income distribution, and socialist development. Mr. Khan is the author of *The Strategy of Development in Bangladesh, Poverty in Rural Asia, Agrarian Policies and Institutions in China after Mao, Collective Agricultural and Rural Development in Soviet Central Asia.*

Bernd Magnus, Department of Philosophy, the University of California, Riverside, is founding director of the Center for Ideas and Society, the author of numerous articles and several books on recent European philosophy, including *Heidegger's Metahistory of Philosophy, Nietzsche's Existential Imperative,* and *Nietzsche's Case: Philosophy as/and Literature,* with S. Stewart and J-P Mileur. His *Postmodern Postures: A Philosophical Analysis and Geneaology* is in preparation for Routledge.

Andrei Marga, Universty of Cluj. He is Professor of Philosophy, Babes–Bolyai University, Romania, and recently was appointed Rector of the University of Cluj. He was a student of Habermas and has translated and published many works on neo-Marxism in Romanian. Professor Marga also has been active in civic reform movements.

Stephen Resnick, Department of Economics, the University of Massachusetts, Amherst. Professor Resnick has been instrumental in the development of Marxian economics and radical political economy in the United States. His publications (with Richard Wolff) include *Rethinking Marxism: Essays for Harry Magdoff and Paul Sweezy, Economics: Marxian vs. Neoclassical,* and *Knowledge and Class.*

Gayatri Chakravorty Spivak, Avalon Professor of Humanities, Department of English and Comparative Literature, Columbia University. Professor Spivak is the author of numerous articles and books, including *In Other Worlds: Essays in Cultural*

Politics, Selected Subaltern Studies, edited with Ranajit Guha, *Inscription,* and *The Post-Colonial Critic: Interviews, Strategies, Dialogues,* edited by Sarah Harasym, and *Outside in the Teaching Machine.*

Su Shaozhi, School of Journalism and Department of Political Science, the University of Minnesota. Former director of the Institute for the Study of Marxism–Leninism (China), Su Shaozhi is one of the important theorists who helped to formulate the ideology for the open policy of the Party in the recent decade until the breakdown of this policy in June 1989. Since then he has been in exile in the West. He is the author of *Marxism in China,* and *Democratization and Reform.*

Carlos Vilas, Centro de Investigacione Interdisciplinaria en Humanidade, National University of Mexico. His works include *Nicaragua: A Revolution Under Siege,* edited with Richard Harris, *The Sandinista Revolution: National Liberation and Social Transformation in Cental America,* and *State, Class and Ethnicity in Nicaragua: Capitalist Modernization and Revolutionary Change on the Atlantic Coast.* Mr. Vilas was an important economic adviser to the Sandinista government in Nicaragua.

Richard Wolff, Department of Economics, the University of Massachusetts, Amherst. Professor Wolff has been instrumental in the development of Marxian economics and radical political economy in the United States. His publications (with Steven Resnick) include: *Rethinking Marxism: Essays for Harry Magdoff and Paul Sweezy, Economics: Marxian vs. Neoclassical,* and *Knowledge and Class.*

Zhang Longxi, Department of Literatures and Languages, the University of California, Riverside. Zhang Longxi is the author of *The Tao and the Logos, Essays in Comparative Literature,* edited with Wen Rumin, *A Critical Introduction to Twentieth–Century Theories of Literature.* He is an important critical voice in debates concerning the representation and significance of Tiananmen Square, especially in *Critical Inquiry.*